Saving Central Park

SAVING
CENTRAL PARK

A History and a Memoir

ELIZABETH BARLOW ROGERS

Alfred A. Knopf · New York · 2018

THIS IS A BORZOI BOOK PUBLISHED BY ALFRED A. KNOPF

www.aaknopf.com

Knopf, Borzoi Books, and the colophon are registered trademarks of
Penguin Random House LLC.

Library of Congress Cataloging-in-Publication Data
Names: Rogers, Elizabeth Barlow, [date] author.
Title: Saving Central Park : a history and a memoir / by Elizabeth Barlow Rogers.
Description: First edition. | New York : Alfred A. Knopf, [2018] |
"A Borzoi book." | Includes bibliographical references.
Identifiers: LCCN 2017023487 (print) | LCCN 2017035973 (ebook) |
ISBN 9781524733551 (print) | ISBN 9781524733568 (ebook)
Subjects: LCSH: Central Park (New York, N.Y.)—History. | Rogers, Elizabeth
Barlow, [date] | Central Park Conservancy (New York, N.Y.)—History. |
Central Park Conservancy (New York, N.Y.)—Biography. |
Conservationists—New York (State)—New York—Biography. | Landscape
architects—New York (State)—New York—Biography. | Women
conservationists—New York (State)—New York—Biography. | Women landscape
architects—New York (State)—New York—Biography. | New York (N.Y.).
Department of Parks and Recreation—Officials and employees—Biography.
Classification: LCC F128.65.C3 (ebook) | LCC F128.65.C3 R642 2018 (print) |
DDC 333.78/3092 [B]—dc23
LC record available at https://lccn.loc.gov/2017023487

Jacket photograph by Annie Leibovitz / *Vanity Fair* / Trunk Archive
Jacket design by Janet Hansen

Manufactured in Malaysia
First Edition

For the men and women who built and rebuilt Central Park

CONTENTS

Introduction: Implausible Ideal · *ix*

Chapter One · NEAR DEATH · *3*

Chapter Two · EARLY ADVOCATES · *17*

Chapter Three · LOOKING BACK · *27*

Chapter Four · MOVING FORWARD · *35*

Chapter Five · DESIGN MASTERPIECE · *53*

Chapter Six · MULTIPLE LIVES · *81*

Chapter Seven · POWER PLAYER · *93*

Chapter Eight · LEARNING CURVE · *119*

Chapter Nine · CHANGING TIMES · *151*

Chapter Ten · TROUBLED WATERS · *163*

Chapter Eleven · GARDENING DAYS · *187*

Chapter Twelve · GOING ABROAD · *207*

Chapter Thirteen · DARKER SIDE · *233*

Chapter Fourteen · GROWING PAINS · *241*

Chapter Fifteen · TWO BETSYS · *247*

Chapter Sixteen · MONEY MATTERS · *253*

Chapter Seventeen · GOLDEN AGE · *265*

Chapter Eighteen · SAFFRON CELEBRATION · *275*

Acknowledgments · *287*

Bibliography · *289*

Index · *295*

INTRODUCTION

Implausible Ideal

The memoir of a financially secure author who came of age in the 1950s in an atmosphere of privilege that included parental love, a comfortable home, educational advantages, conscientious moral instruction, and bodily health is not likely to be as compelling as ones written by women and men whose autobiographical narratives grow out of less advantageous and more unconventional circumstances. Those books written by authors who have participated in war or been its victims have history as background interest. Ones by people who have fought mental or physical affliction, social injustice, or racial discrimination inspire sympathy. Explorers into the unknown and adventurous travelers to exotic locales have ready-made dramatic material at their command. Memoirs by politicians and celebrities are sure to sell.

In this light, my life story would not be particularly interesting except for one improbable fact: at a time when Central Park was on the brink of collapse, I became, through a combination of zeal and luck, the leader of the cause to save it from destruction. Because what was being saved—and still must be protected—is both a masterpiece of landscape design and a great democratic institution, what follows is as much a history of how the park itself was built and altered during successive eras as it is a chronicle of my role in its renaissance.

Becoming the torchbearer for this cause was even more improbable given my gender, generation, and class. For middle-class girls like me growing up in the years immediately following the Second World War, there was a stigma attached to being a salaried professional woman. At that time the term "career girl" was a mild pejorative, and the notion of becoming a female lawyer, doctor, or business executive was virtually unknown. "Poor Mrs. Brown," my mother told me when I was around nine years old, "she has to work"—adding that if I found myself in such a position, my options were restricted to the jobs of nurse or schoolteacher, as in Mrs. Brown's case. Like me, most of my classmates at Saint Mary's Hall, the San Antonio private girls' school I attended from fifth through twelfth grade, were expected to go east to college for two years before transferring to the University of Texas, joining a sorority, making their debut into society, finding "Mr. Right," becoming engaged, marrying, and raising a family.

My decision not to leave Wellesley College after my sophomore year, to obtain a master's degree in city planning from Yale, and to use my skills as a writer about nature, open space preservation, and the history of landscape design was my unwitting springboard to an unusual and immensely satisfying self-created career. What the reader will observe in this book, therefore, is the trajectory of a life lived on the cusp of societal change, in which I have been gratefully buoyed up by the women's movement while at the same time benefiting from some of the positive values conferred by an older ethos of middle-class womanhood without being stereotypically trapped by convention.

It is not an exaggeration to say that Wellesley changed my life by enlarging my sense of self in relation to the world around me. Since it is an all-women's institution, Wellesley implicitly accorded its students the status of honorary men in the classroom, if not in the dormitory where weekend dating was still governed by strict parietal rules. But after graduation a girl's (we twenty-one-year-olds weren't yet referred to as women) diploma did not carry with it the assumption that she was prepared for work outside the home. No matter how brainy and self-sufficient we might have felt ourselves to be with our good educations and leadership skills, very few of my classmates opted to go to graduate school and earn a PhD as opposed to an MRS. The salutation "Ms." had, of course, not come into common usage, and none of us dreamed of retaining our maiden surnames after marriage. Nevertheless, I thought it was going a bit too far when our Wellesley commencement speaker exhorted us to consider using our liberal arts educations to reanimate our minds and pursue the intellectual interests we had developed at Wellesley *after* we had raised our children and sent *them* off to college.

Here a distinction should be made between my professional life and the model for today's successful Wellesley woman, whose taken-for-granted career ambition has, if not completely shattered the proverbial glass ceiling, at least created some notable cracks. In my case, it might be more accurate to say that I wormed my way through the soil of a green rooftop. Being who I am, I'm glad my somewhat novel vocation didn't land me in a chair at the head of the table in a boardroom or on the political campaign trail. Instead, I found myself looking up at the blue sky, uncertain if the clouds would turn to rain but at least with a pilot's license that would allow me to fly.

With no aviation instructions, I still had to figure out how to get off the ground. My ascent, however, was actually made easier by the seemingly innocuous nature of my job. After all, nurturing the park was not unlike nursing a patient, and gardening, like elementary school teaching, has traditionally been considered a female activity. Moreover, because what I was doing seemed quixotic and nobody really had any idea whether my mission was plausible, gender was irrelevant and questioning my competence to do my job was simply a wait-and-see matter. That would only come later when the Central Park Conservancy had become a conspicuous institution within the life of New York City with the capability of raising "serious money." By then I knew that I had supplemented my original vision to save Central Park with sufficient leadership and management skills to make any presumption of my inability to do my job insulting.

How best can I now tell the story of the growth of what was once an implausible ideal into a common cause, and of my own transition from young matron to professional woman? Fortunately, I have a record made at the time. It consists of a series of four journals I kept between 1978 and 1991. Besides chronicling my personal life during these years, they portray Central Park during the period before, during, and after the founding of the Central Park Conservancy. However, it will become obvious to the reader that this book is more than the narrative of the origins of the Conservancy and subsequent course of its development. It is also a story of urban nature, history, and design, and of my long love affair with the park itself.

Although I stepped down from the presidency of the Central Park Conservancy on December 31, 1995, I continue to be in the park on an almost daily basis, and for me, as for so many other people, it offers spiritual sustenance as well as recreational opportunity. To see that I am not alone in my passion for this place, take a look sometime at the words and names on the plaques on more than four thousand benches. They are there as a result of the desire by people through charitable gifts to the Conservancy's endowment fund to celebrate anniversaries and other important life events, to memorialize relationships of love and friendship, to commemorate deceased family members, and to express gratitude for the simple existence of the park itself. These testimonials confirm the fact that, more than any other New York City landmark, this 840-acre landscape in the center of Manhattan is a cherished amenity, causing countless people to proclaim, "I don't know how I could live here without Central Park."

One cannot write about the existence of Central Park without recognizing it to be a palimpsest, an enduring yet ever-altering landscape recording the mores of succeeding generations. Thus, there are chapters that cover the park's conception in nineteenth-century civic weal; its design and building by Frederick Law Olmsted and Calvert Vaux; its radical alteration between 1934 and 1961, when Robert Moses reigned as New York City parks czar; and its fall into ruin through neglect, abuse, and mismanagement during what I call the anything-goes era from the mid-1960s through the mid-1970s. The park's most recent incarnation, spanning the years from the second half of the 1970s to the present, the era of my close involvement in its fortunes, is where history and memoir merge. This is therefore a book about place and time—the park's several lives as well as my own— and both history and memoir are necessarily intertwined into a single narrative.

Choosing book titles is often difficult. This one could have been *The Fortunes of Central Park* or *The Multiple Lives of Central Park,* but I selected *Saving Central Park* because it reflects the projects, plans, and politics involved in rescuing the park from its prior status as a taken-for-granted legacy with a brilliant but mostly forgotten and later perceived-as-irrelevant design that had been often compromised over the years as the park descended to its nadir through misuse and abuse. This book's implied message therefore is that Central Park's current beauty, safety, and cleanliness depend on unflagging good stewardship and the role of a citizen-led partnership with government in achieving this goal.

To summarize the book's historical content, I will discuss how the world's first purpose-built metropolitan park for the people was created, a remarkable achievement that provided the paradigm for future urban planning and park building in burgeoning cities throughout the country. That this was so is testament to its superb design—a progressive nineteenth-century engineering infrastructure overlaid with romantically picturesque scenery—and its incontrovertible social success. That Central Park is also one of the greatest expressions of American democracy is indisputable, for unlike the conversion of royal hunting preserves or princely gardens into public promenades in Paris, London, and Berlin or the original role of the New England common as communal pasturage, its creation was the result of a campaign on the part of civic idealists who wished in the first place to emulate these European pleasure grounds for the sake of the city's citizenry.

A general assumption on the part of many is that Central Park was created by the conversion of a well-vegetated scenic tract of land, comprising fifty-one street blocks and three avenue blocks, exempted from development according to New York City's 1811 grid plan, into a ready-made park needing nothing more than enclosure of the resulting long, rectangular site with a low wall punctuated with various entrances for visitor access. It is necessary, therefore, to reiterate here that Central Park is an entirely man-made artifact and tell the story of how its construction was accomplished through the sculpting of a barren landscape into a representation of picturesque nature. Readers will learn how this entailed the use of gunpowder charges to blast away numerous bedrock outcrops and the recycling of much of the resulting debris as building material. They will also discover how miry swamps were dredged and turned into lakes and ponds and how engineers created a hydrological system to furnish water for these as well as for the park's artificial streams and ornamental fountains.

Some will be surprised to learn that the park's current topography is the result of importing five hundred thousand cubic feet of topsoil in horse-drawn carts to remodel the terrain as broad, grassy meadows and gently swelling knolls, and that this newly created landscape had to be vegetated through the planting of several hundred thousand nursery-grown trees, shrubs, vines, and ground covers. The heroes of this chapter of park history are Olmsted and Vaux, the park's designers and builders, and founders of the profession of landscape architecture in America.

Central Park's most radical transformation was the repurposing of its scenic acres to serve as simply so much available open space for the construction of facilities for sports, games, and children's play during the period between 1934 and 1961 when Robert Moses was New York City parks commissioner. The chapter devoted to this alteration of the park's landscape is followed by the story of its subsequent destruction and resurrection. It is under these circumstances that I became instrumental in launching the Central Park Conservancy as a means of enlisting the citizens of New York City in an effort to reverse the park's dereliction. This civic enterprise was undertaken with the intent of honoring the park's rich historical past while preserving its contemporary recreational uses. To succeed in implementing such a challenging vision required the creation of a then-unknown type of charitable organization, the public-private park partnership, as a means for citizens to undertake projects and programs that city government was no longer able to provide.

"What do you think we should call it?" asked New York City Parks Commissioner Gordon Davis as, sitting in his office a few weeks after having accepted the newly created position of administrator of Central Park with yet-to-be defined responsibilities, I broached the idea of founding a private organization to work in concert with his administration to arrest the further decline of Central Park. "I like 'Central Park Conservancy,'" I replied. "That sounds good to me," he assented.

This was in 1979, a year after Edward I. Koch (1924–2013) had taken office as mayor of a crime-plagued city in fiscal disarray. At this time,

Edward I. Koch   *Gordon Davis*

many companies had moved their headquarters out of Manhattan and built corporate campuses in the suburbs. The white-collar middle-class exodus that had gained momentum in the late 1960s was ongoing; burned-out, abandoned buildings in the South Bronx gave this part of the city the appearance of a war zone; and drug lords ruled Harlem. In short, it would have been inconceivable to think then that today's reenergized economy, soaring new office and residential buildings, historically preserved neighborhoods, clean subways, and new and rebuilt parks would ever come into existence.

Koch, of course, cannot be solely credited with the city's renaissance, but this ebullient, born-and-bred, heart-and-soul New Yorker appeared fearlessly optimistic and brashly confident about generating the recovery of the city's vitality by arresting economic decline, curing social ills, stemming population dispersal, and reversing physical deterioration as government fought to recover from a state of fiscal crisis. To accomplish this, his policy was to choose qualified deputy mayors and appoint commissioners who were capable of reforming their dysfunctional agencies.

Gordon Davis's first challenge was to reorganize the administration of the Parks Department. Our discussion about coining the name "Central Park Conservancy" had arisen because he had become aware

of my quixotic ambition to develop a means whereby the citizens of
New York could take the initiative in overseeing what city government was then incapable of doing: saving Central Park.

Before formalizing the charter of an organization capable of undertaking this challenge, I continued to cogitate the semantics of the word
"conservancy." There was at the time no nomenclatural use broader
than that designating an organization dedicated to natural areas protection, an apt term to apply to the Nature Conservancy, whose mission
is "to conserve the lands and waters on which all life depends." However, the term had not yet been deemed applicable to a group of citizens whose efforts were focused on the stewardship of an urban park.
Although Central Park is a naturalistic landscape and haven for wildlife, its principal function is popular recreation rather than wilderness
preservation. Furthermore, unlike the Nature Conservancy, which is
an international organization that funds environmental research sci-
entists and enters into agreements with individuals, governments,
and other not-for-profit organizations, the entity we sought to create
would have a boldly broad but specifically local objective.

After consulting the *New Oxford American Dictionary,* I discovered
that one definition of the verb "conserve" is "protect from harm or
destruction," which does in fact encompass the preservation of aes-
thetically and culturally important objects and artifacts as well as natural resources, and that one meaning of the noun "conservation" is
"preservation, repair, and prevention of deterioration of archaeological, historical, and cultural sites and artifacts." Why then, I thought,
shouldn't there be something akin to the conservation department of
a museum for the purpose of restoring Central Park's lost beauty and
protecting it in the future through good custodianship?

This opinion was confirmed when a *New York Times* art critic who
had heard about what was being contemplated with regard to the park
came to interview me. "You mean you think of these trees and statues and structures as collections?" That is it exactly, I said, mentally
adding to the list the park's lakes, wooded areas, lawns, meadows, and
architectural features. Now confident that the name Davis and I had
agreed upon was the right one, we were able to have our idea endorsed
by the mayor and our nascent organization incorporated by the State

of New York as a not-for-profit corporation with the name we had chosen: Central Park Conservancy. Its mission statement was simple: "To make Central Park clean, safe, and beautiful."

Often in the future someone would take exception to the word "beautiful," uncomfortable with its relation to "pretty," a term some people associate with effeminacy. I always maintained, however, that this element of the Conservancy's triple mission was aesthetic, not cosmetic, for Central Park's landscape is nothing less than a great work of art. The *Times* art critic had it right: along with all the other reasons to restore it, the conservation of its beauty was essential to its original and continuing purpose of providing a refreshing counterpoint to the surrounding city, a peaceful haven in which to experience the changing seasons of the year along with the geological, botanical, and ecological wonders of nature. Yes, human beings are inextricably part of nature, and beauty is an essential element for their spiritual well-being.

My personal emotional response to Central Park, like that of so many others, is sensory—stretching out on a large sun-warmed rock outcrop, watching Frisbee players and picnickers on the Great Lawn, seeing a great production of *The Tempest* in the Delacorte Theater in the gloaming of a summer evening, a flash of red from the plumage of a ruby-crowned kinglet on a spring day in the Ramble, walking barefoot on the grass of the Sheep Meadow, the memory of skating on the frozen Lake on New Year's Day 1981, listening to the moody sound from a saxophone being played beneath the one of the park's reverberant stone arches . . . I could go on.

My passion for the park is also rooted in my admiration of its remarkable history, for I never cease to be astonished by the genius of its original design. I have been a member of the National Association of Olmsted Parks since its inception and enjoy my ongoing relationships with the creators of conservancies for other Olmsted parks. Indeed, I don't believe that I have entered Central Park once since 1970, when I began writing *Frederick Law Olmsted's New York,* that Olmsted's name and genius haven't come to mind.

Saving Central Park

Chapter One

NEAR DEATH

I t was obvious when Gordon Davis and I settled on the name "Conservancy" what a long way we had to go toward realizing the new
organization's mission to make Central Park clean, safe, and beautiful
once more. To get a sense of the park's dire condition when the Conservancy was formed in 1980, it is necessary to turn the clock back to
1965, when John Vliet Lindsay was elected New York City's 103rd
mayor. With the good intention of energizing his administration with
new talent, Lindsay appointed as parks commissioner Thomas Hoving,
who was then curator of medieval art at the Metropolitan Museum.
One might have thought that Hoving would approach the job with
the perspective of a historical preservationist. Instead, he chose the
path of radical showmanship.

Hoving's Happenings

Although a scion of the establishment, Hoving was eager to dethrone
the old guard. Aligning himself with the vibrant hippie era of psy-
chedelic drugs, mass rock concerts, student riots, and Vietnam War
protests, he shook things up from the day he took office. Acting as

Thomas Hoving

impresario, he led Central Park into its Events Era. With a well-developed instinct for publicity, he announced that his administration would make "an all-out attack on a kind of repetitive, conservative design associated with the Parks Department since the Depression days of the W.P.A. that critics have alternately called naive or Neanderthal." Proclaiming that "we're boiling up a creative pot," he announced that "Moses men" (employees whose employment dated to the prior regime of Parks Commissioner Robert Moses) who were not protected by their civil service status would be dismissed. In their place he assembled a staff whose ages ranged from twenty-four to thirty-four, his own age. While previously the only women employees in the Parks Department's headquarters in the Arsenal* were secretaries, now Mary Perot Nichols, an editor at *The Village Voice,* was hired by Hoving to manage press relations.

Hoving also hired Henry Stern, a thirty-year-old lawyer who would himself become parks commissioner one day, as executive director and counsel, with the mandate "to bring back the opportunity for imagination, taste, and creative design that existed in the nineteenth century." With this laudable goal in mind, he persuaded George Delacorte's Make New York Beautiful foundation to underwrite a contract with Milton Glaser's Push Pin Studios for new park signage. He invited Pratt, Columbia, and other schools of architec-

---

* Located at Fifth Avenue and Sixty-Fourth Street, the Arsenal was originally built as a munitions supply depot for New York State's National Guard. It subsequently served as a police precinct, a weather bureau, the first Museum of Natural History, and a makeshift zoo before it became the headquarters of New York City's Department of Parks and Recreation.

Easter Sunday 1971, Central Park, New York City, *photograph by Garry Winogrand*

ture and landscape architecture to engage students in studio projects involving innovations in park design. Hoving also met with community leaders in East Harlem to say that from now on there would be town-hall meetings to hear what kind of parks people wanted.

Famous as an ironfisted political czar who brooked no opposition, the recently dethroned Moses now had a brash foe who was his equal in terms of arrogance. More used to being insulting than insulted, Moses was unable to respond with a withering retort when Hoving told him to his face, "Your design is absolutely appalling and you never gave a damn for the community." Again sounding the trumpet of the angels, Hoving proclaimed, "We've got to get back to the concept that a park is a work of art." To further this perspective, he appointed an architectural historian, Henry Hope Reed (1916–2013), as curator of Central Park, an unsalaried advisory position.

Helped by citizen protest, Hoving quashed the proposed encroachment on the park by A&P heir Huntington Hartford, who sought to donate a café, a large two-story structure that was to be sited by the Pond near the Fifth Avenue and Fifty-Ninth Street entrance. When Hartford complained, "Moses suggested the location, and he is a very great man . . . He knew a hell of a lot better than anyone else," Hoving replied, "We just have to be resolute about some things. One, two, three—bang!"

Lindsay and Hoving's most significant contribution to Central Park was to introduce a ban on motorized vehicles. Announced as an experiment on March 1, 1966, this initiative set off a protracted fight with the traffic commissioner, Henry A. Barnes. In April Barnes agreed to compromise by permitting traffic closings for the sole purpose of bike races. In spite of this concession, which was enthusiastically supported in newspaper editorials, the Automobile Club of New York and the Taxi and Limousine Commission continued to wave the banner of protest. Opposing them were environmentalists arguing for the protection of vegetation from heavy doses of carbon monoxide. At last a deal was struck. For those who remember having to dodge traffic on the park drives back in those days, their closing during the weekend represented a victory for the Lindsay administration and a big boon to the park's users. Following the ongoing positive public opinion that continued to build over the years, the park has been progressively closed to automobiles for longer durations.*

Hoving's "happenings," as they were called, became a staple of his administration. Thanks to Nichols's press releases and Hoving's flair for colorful statements, these events were frequent news topics of the moment. During the same period the *Times* was supporting the traffic closings, it carried the headline "Old Central Park Will Rock 'n' Roll: Go-Go Concerts and Dancing to Discotheque Combos Planned for Summer; Hoving Thinks Attractions Will Draw Teen-Agers and Make Park Areas Safer."

Always ready to direct a jab at Moses, Hoving said, "We're going to open it up and have a little bit of—how shall we call it—Central Park à Go Go . . . No longer are we going to restrict ourselves to square dancing and ballroom dancing." He began meeting with professional

---

* Today it is completely free of motorized traffic north of the Seventy-Second Street Cross Drive, and cars are banned in the remaining southern portion, except on weekdays between 8:00 a.m. and 10:00 a.m., when the park is open to cars on the West Drive between the Central Park West and Seventy-Second Street entrance and the Central Park South and Seventh Avenue entrance, and on the East Drive between the Central Park South and Sixth Avenue entrance and the Fifth Avenue and Seventy-Second Street entrance.

pop-concert booking agents and soon announced that Central Park would host "the largest outdoor music festival in the world."

During the summer of 1966 and in subsequent years, Wollman Rink operated as the venue for rock 'n' roll, jazz, folk, pop, and ethnic music concerts sponsored by Rheingold Breweries. Overlooking the objections of his recently appointed Central Park curator, Henry Hope Reed, Hoving played on the public's justifiable fear that the park had become unsafe at night: "It's my responsibility to make it so exciting that people will come there in droves, and that also is protection." He did not foresee the extent to which his "attractions to draw teenagers" would stimulate the consumption of alcohol and the sale of drugs in the park, nor the effect this would have on the park's landscape and future safety.

Happenings could be artistic as well as musical. On May 16, 1966, the *Times* reported a Hoving happening featuring a 105-yard-long canvas set up below the Metropolitan Museum of Art for a "cartoon performance." As he doodled a caricature of himself over the slogan "Three Cheers for Fred L. Olmsted," Hoving cried, "It's marvelous. It lets people come in and smash away." At such high-profile occasions it did not seem to matter that vandals were smashing away in more destructive ways elsewhere in the park. Without Moses's control over the park police, rules were no longer enforced and muggings and more serious crimes were on the rise. Hoving's cartoon performance anticipated the avant-garde's appreciation of graffiti as a form of public art. It is not surprising, therefore, that at the same time that subway cars were becoming moving graffiti murals, all the hard surfaces in the park—walls, buildings, surfaces of rock outcrops, granite bases of statues, and carved stonework—were being systematically defaced.

When it came to further encroachments, Hoving dismissed park curator Reed's objections, but in ignoring them and the growing citizen movement to preserve the park's landscape, he learned that big dreams for big building projects in Central Park could go down in defeat. At the time—after fourteen months in office—Hoving resigned as parks commissioner in order to become the director of the Metropolitan Museum of Art, a campaign to thwart his proposal to build a $6.4 million stable for mounted police horses and polo players' thoroughbreds, complete with a three-hundred-seat arena and thousand-seat belowground amphitheater at the north end of the Great Lawn, still simmered. The task of championing its construction fell to Hoving's successor, August Heckscher (1913–1997), a former consultant to President Kennedy on the arts.

After Heckscher took office in 1967, he made the lofty prediction that the project would "capture the ceremonial significance of equestrian sports." Not surprisingly, defenders of the park as a populist institution joined the proponents of preserving its landscape in protest against turning the Great Lawn into a field for polo players. Heckscher continued to promote the construction of a belowground arena for training the horses used by the mounted police, but by 1970, with dwindling city funds available for capital projects, the proposal was dropped, and opponents were able to celebrate a victory in the fight to stem encroachments on Central Park's landscape.

In other ways Heckscher followed the course set by Hoving, and the park remained the venue of choice for mass events and bizarre happenings. One of his first initiatives in office was to discuss the possibility of an archaeological "occurrence" with the Israeli government. "The idea," he said, "is to erect a mound and fill it with several thousand shards of ancient pottery, statuary, and glass, which the Israeli government is contributing, and then let kids dig for it." This never took place, but many other events did. Ron Delsener, the impresario of the Rheingold Central Park Music Festival, staged more than sixty programs during the summer of 1967. With overflow audiences on the slopes around Wollman Rink five nights a week, erosion left only bare dirt patterned by rainwater runnels.

Heckscher disapproved of flag burning by anti–Vietnam War protestors in Central Park, but he was in favor of other kinds of events: an Easter "yippee" celebration, a kite-flying contest, and a Ringling Brothers parade to announce the circus coming to town. This anything-goes policy extended to "be-ins," mass rallies, concerts on the Sheep Meadow, and the assembly of a contingent of the Poor People's March on Washington. A 1969 New Year's Eve party for two thousand offered fireworks, rock music performed by the Mighty Mellotones, and dancing at Bethesda Fountain. There was a mass vigil on July 20, 1969, the eve of the moon landing. "I'm asking everybody to come dressed in white," Heckscher announced, "and we're working with the broadcasting companies to have live TV or huge screens, so great crowds can participate in this wonderful moment."

The Price

Because of these large-scale events and unregulated sports use, the Sheep Meadow had by this time become a dust bowl. In 1966 Restaurant Associates was given a concession permit to turn Bethesda Terrace into an al fresco café, which continued operation until 1974, when rampant drug dealing on the fast-eroding surrounding slopes caused it to close. The Terrace came to resemble a bazaar, populated by illegal vendors hawking merchandise. Its balustrade finials were knocked off, and the intricately carved stairway side panels were vandalized and slathered with graffiti. Since the park appeared so unkempt everywhere that no one seemed to think it wrong, and such rules as "do not pick the flowers" no longer were enforced, each spring when those daffodils still left in the untrampled ground came into bloom and the cherry and crabapple trees were in flower, one saw people leaving the park with large bouquets and broken-off branches. An estimated fifty thousand square feet of graffiti covered walls, statue bases, and bedrock outcrops. Unvegetated slopes eroded, exposing the roots of dying trees. The Boathouse on the Harlem Meer that Moses had built in the mid-1940s became a restaurant in 1973, but shaky finances forced it to close the following year, leaving the building prey to vandals. It soon became a charred ruin, and the adjacent Meer, which Moses had encased in concrete and rimmed with iron fencing, was a silted, algae-coated bed of mud.

Lacking Robert Moses's indomitable ability when he was parks commissioner to face down the heads of other city agencies, Heckscher was forced to allow a permit to be granted to the New York City Department of Environmental Protection in 1970 to dig a shaft and construct a valve chamber for Water Tunnel No. 3 on 1.2 acres of Cedar Hill. Hemlocks were planted to partially screen the wooden fence protecting the work site, but this did not alter the fact that the north side of the hill—a favorite sledding slope—remained off-limits to the public during the construction project, which lasted more

Vandalized Belvedere before restoration

Slope next to the park's perimeter wall at Central Park West and Seventy-Second Street

Lake edge of the Ramble before restoration

Bethesda Terrace staircase before graffiti removal

Dislodged copestones surrounding Bethesda Terrace

Harlem Meer Boathouse as a vacant, burned-out ruin

Algae-covered Harlem Meer before dredging, with floating garbage deposited from oil drums used as park litter receptacles

Eroded ball fields before resodding of Great Lawn

Eroded Sheep Meadow and Heckscher Ballfields before resodding

than twenty years. In the early 1980s the park was further penetrated belowground at Sixty-Third Street and Fifth Avenue with the boring of a fifteen-hundred-foot subway tunnel.

Budget cuts exacerbated the park's woes at this time, and the Lindsay administration began to use funds from the city's capital budget to cover the operating costs of the parks. Now rusting oil drums passed for garbage receptacles. The workforce diminished through attrition as employees retired, and their positions were left vacant. The plethora of events and the lack of a policy for rules enforcement demoralized the remaining workers. Broken benches, bridges, and lights; compacted soil incapable of supporting anything other than the hardiest weeds—all were results of the park's lapsed management system. The Sheep Meadow was a barren dirt plain, and for lack of routine park maintenance, the Great Lawn's softball outfields had also gone from grass to weeds to bare compacted soil.

With increasing cuts in the parks budget as the heavy spending of the Lindsay years was curtailed, prestige drained from the office of commissioner, and the job was handed over to a series of career civil service employees. The administration was staffed through patronage appointments dictated by City Hall, and playground attendants and trained gardeners disappeared. The Central Park police precinct abandoned its policy of enforcing park rules and regulations, there were no more foot patrols, and the only remaining visitor protection was in the form of two-man squad cars patrolling the drives. Interviewed in 1975, Richard M. Clurman (1924–1996), the former chief of correspondents of the Time-Life News Service, who had served as commissioner during the last year of the Lindsay administration, summed up the situation: "You've got to start managing people and equipment much more. Park workers have no goals. They have no targets. There is simply no management of routine work."

Quixotic Quest

Central to New York City both geographically and in name, the deteriorated park by this time had become a symbol of severe municipal decline that many people assumed was irremediable. During the mayoralty of Lindsay's successor, Abraham Beame, the city entered a protracted state of fiscal crisis. In response, New York State formed the Municipal Assistance Corporation (MAC) in order to prevent municipal government from defaulting on its bond obligations. To fall in line with MAC's mandated strictures, it was necessary for city agencies to cut their workforces. This involved the unprecedented act of firing employees, many of whom were unionized civil service personnel. In this situation, federal funds were eagerly sought as a stopgap. Within the Parks Department, this meant that monies that had been allocated through the 1973 Comprehensive Employment and Training Act (CETA) to provide jobs and skills for the long-term unemployed and low-income high school dropouts were used to hire back workers whose jobs had been terminated. Under these conditions, the vision that Central Park could be rescued and restored seemed hopelessly quixotic. What kind of Pollyanna was I to assume otherwise? And what were the chances that this starry-eyed mission could succeed?

Looking back, I realize that the birth of the Central Park Conservancy was essentially a matter of luck and timing. The current unquestioned acceptance of the concept of public-private park partnerships and the cooperative alliance between New York City government and the Conservancy today makes it hard for us to believe the degree of resistance to its creation in the first place. The proposal to form an official working partnership between city government and a group of private citizens was viewed warily and would probably not have been accepted at that time by public officials jealous of their authority and reluctant to give up the opportunities that elected office grants when political patronage is the norm. In addition, if the city had not been under duress, the municipal workers union (District Council 37) would have claimed that privately funded employees were usurping the jobs of union men. Even if this were not the case, objections would be raised by residents maintaining that they were taxpayers, ergo the care of parks was a city responsibility. Moreover, some existing not-for-profit park support organizations were questionable. "Private groups should not get in bed with the city," declared a board member of one, explaining that the role of citizens' groups was to criticize the policies and practices of public officials and to campaign for reform, not to act as a partner of government.

I discovered opposition in another quarter when I went to see Senator Daniel Patrick Moynihan, who was advocating that the National Park Service take over Central Park. After I was ushered into his office, I explained why I thought citizen support was a better alternative. It was clear that he did not take seriously my belief that a group of private citizens could rescue Central Park from its state of dire deterioration. He also made it apparent that he did not believe in home rule or the relevance of community boards. When I countered this argument, he politely hinted that I did so to protect my new job as Central Park administrator.

It was clear that he was adamant in his position that the park was in such terrible condition that only the federal government would be able to rescue it. "I really shouldn't be lecturing you," he said, proceeding to lecture me on why the park's best interests demanded the strong, centralized control that National Park Service administration would provide. "Right now you can't even walk in the park because it is so unsafe," he said. "I walk in it every day," I countered. "Well, we all know *you* are exceptional," he replied indulgently, still convinced that sane people no longer went there.

Chapter Two

EARLY ADVOCATES

Disappointed but not discouraged by the lack of support for the notion of a group of citizens forming a partnership with city government for the purpose of restoring and maintaining Central Park, I remembered that it was in fact a group of citizens who had advocated the creation of Central Park in the first place.

First Proponents

In 1844 poet and newspaper editor William Cullen Bryant encouraged the establishment of the kind of park that would satisfy the ambitions of civic-minded New Yorkers who wished their burgeoning metropolis to emulate great European cities in this regard. Yet, unlike the Old World parks, which had their origins as the domains of kings and princes, and in spite of the fact that some proponents were initially uneasy over the proposed admission of the hoi polloi, the New York park was intended to be a people's park open to all classes of society. In promoting this democratic objective, Bryant suggested that the forested area known as Jones Wood, a 154-acre parcel bounded by Sixty-Sixth and Seventy-Fifth Streets between Third Avenue and the East

William Cullen Bryant

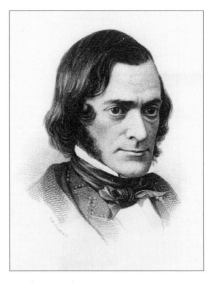

Andrew Jackson Downing

River, would make an ideal location. Featuring rocky outcroppings and sparkling streams, Jones Wood was already a de facto park, a popular haunt for botanists, picnickers, and seekers of solitude. "Nothing is wanting," he wrote, "but to cut winding paths through it, leaving the woods as they now are and introducing here and there a jet from the Croton Aqueduct, the streams from which would make their own waterfalls over the rocks, and keep the brooks running through the place always fresh and full."*

On the heels of Bryant's advocacy, after returning from a trip to England in 1850, Hudson River Valley nurseryman–turned–landscape designer Andrew Jackson Downing (1815–1852) also proposed the creation of a public park worthy of the citizenry of a metropolis-in-the-making. In his magazine *The Horticulturist,* Downing touched the tender nerve of his American readers' cultural inferiority complex with these words: "What are called parks in New York are not even

---

* When Bryant wrote these words, the city, with its population of six hundred thousand, had scarcely a hundred acres of parkland. Washington Square and Madison Square, before they became parks, had served as potter's fields and had been used to bury the victims of the cholera epidemics that periodically scourged the city. There were a handful of other residential squares—Tompkins, Union, and Gramercy south of Forty-Second Street, and Mount Morris in Harlem. The only true parks were Bowling Green, City Hall Park, and Battery Park, which was built on landfill from nearby building excavations. .

apologies for the thing; they are only squares or paddocks." A year later outspoken newspaper editor, politician, and social reformer Horace Greeley announced in his *New-York Tribune:* "The parks, squares and public gardens of London beat us clear out of sight."

Legislative Debate

Spurred by such publicity, the popularity of the park cause grew among civic-minded New Yorkers, becoming a political issue in the mayoral campaign of 1850. Both candidates endorsed it, and in 1851 the winner, Ambrose C. Kingsland, issued a message to the Common Council calling for "the purchase and laying out of a park, on a scale which will be worthy of the city." With the concurrence of the council, a bill was sent to Albany recommending Jones Wood as the most desirable site for a new park, and on July 11, 1851, legislation authorizing the taking of that property was passed.

Aghast that potentially valuable commercial water frontage would be set aside for a non-economic use, business interests sought to have the bill rescinded. The park's champions responded with an alternate suggestion: a larger park on another site. Indeed, Downing thought Jones Wood ridiculously small to meet New York's future recreational needs. "It is only a child's playground!" he cried. "Five hundred acres is the smallest area that should be reserved for the future wants of such a city, now, while it may be obtained." While Bryant felt that the beauties and waterfront location of Jones Wood made it a particularly apt choice for a park, he did not believe that it was the only suitable location; in fact, he thought it would be a fine idea if the public were to gain both Jones Wood and an additional property known as "the central reservation." Stretching northward from Fifty-Ninth Street for nearly two and a half miles, the reservation encompassed the land that had been set aside for the construction of an additional reservoir within the midpoint of the system of basins built to hold water from the recently constructed Croton Aqueduct.[*]

---

[*] This is the reservoir we see in the park today; the then-existing reservoir was a rectangular one immediately south of the Eighty-Sixth Street Transverse Road. It was drained and

A select committee of the state senate was appointed to consider the comparative merits of the two locations. Expert testimony was collected. The botanist John Torrey, who had frequented Jones Wood since boyhood, told the committee of its "fine specimens of oaks, tulip trees, liquidambar, hickories, birch, and some cedars," and he said he preferred Jones Wood to the "more bald and unpicturesque" central site. Others who appeared before the committee remarked on its rocky barrenness, since many trees in the southern half of the park had been cut down for firewood and those in the center removed to make room for a receiving reservoir when the Croton Aqueduct system of water distribution had been built ten years earlier. However, it was agreed that with a large expenditure for draining, topsoil, and tree planting, the land around the planned reservoir could become a park. Furthermore, it would increase the value of property surrounding it. After weighing what it had heard, the committee recommended that both parks be acquired, but urged that Jones Wood be developed first, since its landscape attractions were immediate rather than long-range. With humane pragmatism, the authors of the report summarizing the committee's findings argued:

> The panting and crowded families of the less wealthy, whose children fill the bills of mortality, are entitled to ask, what has posterity done for us? Why should they be taxed now to plant groves, which seventy years hence may shelter those who come after them, when health and pure air, wafted from the breezy river, through ample shades, are within their present grasp?

The passage of the 1851 bill by the state legislature in Albany authorizing the acquisition of Jones Wood and the counterproposal to acquire a larger site in the center of Manhattan resulted in the creation of a special committee of the city's board of aldermen, to study their

---

filled in during the 1930s, after which it was designed as the oval greensward known as the Great Lawn. The southernmost reservoir, impounding water from the first-constructed of the three present-day tunnels linked with a network of pipes distributing water throughout the city, was filled in earlier and became the site of the present-day New York Public Library and Bryant Park.

respective merits with regard to "Extent, Convenience of Locality, Availability, and Probable Cost."

In their January 2, 1852, "Report Relative to Laying Out a New Park in the Upper Part of the City," the committee members foresightedly argued that "Central Park would probably be one of the largest city parks in the world, but not too large for the use of a city destined, in all probability, to exceed in population every other," thereby concluding that "the proposition of Central Park is greatly to be preferred." In addition to its greater size compared with Jones Wood, Central Park's long and narrow rectilinear shape was no defect in their eyes, since such a park "was capable from its extent, of being laid out in a very great length of serpentine road, which a judicious engineer can so contrive as not only to produce startling effects of the distant landscape, and also bring the peculiar natural and artificial beauties of the place into the best points of view, but at the same time, to turn and wind this road through the place, so as to allow a very long drive through constantly varied scenery."

Being in the middle of Manhattan rather than on the waterfront, like Jones Wood, was a further asset in their eyes, inasmuch as Central Park would be surrounded on all sides by Manhattan's street grid and therefore have multiple points of access from four sides when the platted streets were constructed, whereas Jones Wood was a half-mile-square parcel with single-side accessibility in an out-of-the way locality that would necessarily be bisected by the construction of Second Avenue. Moreover, they maintained that the proposed alternative site was not deficient in scenic potential, being "so diversified in surface, abounding so much in hill and dale, and intersected by so many natural streams." They thought as well that the location within its precincts of the reservoir that was part of the recently constructed Croton Aqueduct's distribution system, far from being an obstacle, was an asset because it would provide an unlimited supply of water for artificial lakes and fountains within the park. Capping their argument in its favor, they noted that since the tops of the large outcrops of Manhattan schist were elevated above the surrounding landscape, they would be able to serve as platforms from which to gain magnificent views in all directions.

The committee reasoned that, whereas thinning many of the vener-

Egbert Viele

able trees of Jones Wood would be necessary to create a park, "Central Park will be furnished, of course, with a very choice assortment and great variety of new trees, much more ornamental, and casting more agreeable shade than the natural forest trees, [and] besides, a proper variety of park scenery requires that certain large portions should be improved as sloping lawns, or mounds for statuary and monuments, and points of view for distant landscapes—all of which allow no trees whatsoever."

Acting on the report, the state legislature in 1853 passed two bills, one authorizing the designation of Jones Wood as future parkland, and the other the acquisition of 760 acres extending from 59th to 106th Streets between Fifth and Eighth Avenues (subsequently increased to 843 acres when the northern park boundary was extended to 110th Street). A board of commissioners, along with an advisory board chaired by Washington Irving, was established to oversee the design and development of the park. A civil engineer, Egbert Viele (1825–1902), made a topographical survey of the site and a general plan for its development in the hope that he could eventually receive "compensation suitable to the time and skill . . . expended on the work." Since the clearance of the site was already under way, candidates were interviewed for the position of superintendent of the land-clearing operations that had begun under Viele's direction. They included thirty-six-year-old Frederick Law Olmsted (1822–1903), a farmer-turned-journalist-turned-author-and-publisher.

In an autobiographical fragment written after he had gained eminence as the founder of the profession of landscape architecture in America, Olmsted tried to explain the forces of destiny that shaped the uncharted career path upon which he embarked at the age of thirty-six. Only in retrospect, as in my own case a hundred years later, did the journey make sense. The scion of an old New England family and son of a successful Hartford merchant, Olmsted enjoyed a happy and

secure middle-class childhood in which
he imbibed a love of nature and scenery.
As a boy, he would ramble in the woods
and fields surrounding his Connecticut
home, and it was of no concern to him or
his family when, lost in the woods after
sunset, he would seek overnight shelter in the homes of friends. In addition,
carriage drives with his father and stepmother through the countryside with
no purpose other than the enjoyment of
scenery added an aesthetic dimension to
this unconscious preparation for what lay
ahead. "It was my fortune at this period,"
he remarked, "to be taken on numerous
journeys [in the Connecticut River Val-

Frederick Law Olmsted

ley and along the coast of Maine] in company with people neither
literary, scientific, nor artistic, but more than ordinarily susceptible to
beauty of scenery and who with little talking about it, and none for
my instruction, plainly shaped their courses and their customs with
reference to the enjoyment of it."

At the age of fourteen Olmsted suffered an acute case of sumac poi-
soning, resulting in an eye disorder that caused doctors to advise him
against pursuing formal study. For this reason, he tells us, "it followed
that at the time my schoolmates were entering college I was nomi-
nally the pupil of a topographical engineer but really for the most part
given over to a decently restrained vagabond life, generally pursued
under the guise of an angler, a fowler or a dabbler on the shallowest
shores of the deep sea of the natural sciences." He did manage to read
on his own, however, and the books that most interested him were,
significantly in light of later events, those of Uvedale Price and William Gilpin, eighteenth-century English theorists of the aesthetic of
the Picturesque as applied to landscape scenery.

Upon reaching his majority, Olmsted decided to become a farmer,
and with financial aid from his father, in 1846 he purchased a seventy-
acre farm at Sachem's Head in Guilford, Connecticut, on the rocky
edge of Long Island Sound. Soon, however, he decided to exchange

this location for a more congenial one on Staten Island where he could pursue with greater success the new agricultural methods that were then coming into practice. As it turned out, what interested him as much as or more than his experiments in cultivating fruit trees were considerations regarding the layout of his farm and those of the neighbors who sometimes solicited his advice. Here is what he wrote as he reflected on this chapter of his life:

> All this time interest in certain modest practical principles of landscape architecture was growing in me. Applications I mean, for example, to the choice of a neighborhood, of the position and aspect of a homestead, the placing, grouping and relationships with the dwelling of barns, stables and minor outbuildings . . . Application also . . . to the determination of lines of out-look and of in-look and the removal or planting accordingly of trees, screens, bridges, windbreaks and so on, with some consideration for unity of foreground, middle ground and back ground, some consideration for sceneric [*sic*] effect from without as well as from within the field of actual operations.

When he realized how he could further his self-education in the most advanced agricultural technologies of the day, such as the laying of subsurface clay tiles to drain standing water, and at the same time observe landscapes designed in the Picturesque style, he was able to persuade his father to allow him to accompany his brother John on an extended trip to England following John's graduation from Yale. The result of this travel experience was a diaristic account of the customs and habits as well as the sights he saw in England. Publication in 1852 of his first book, *Walks and Talks of an American Farmer in England,* was followed by a commission from the *New York Daily Times* to travel in the South in order to gather firsthand impressions and data showing the comparative unprofitability of the Southern slave economy as opposed to farming employing free labor. For this reason, he chose as his byline the word "Yeoman."

Olmsted's first journey took him to plantations in the older Southern states; his second was a tour in the region west of the Alleghenies; and his third a trip to Texas in the company of his brother John. With the publication of his *Times* newspaper dispatches in three successive books—*A Journey in the Seaboard Slave States* (1856), *A Journey Through Texas* (1857), and *A Journey in the Back Country in the Winter of 1853–4* (1860)—Olmsted gave up the notion of being a farmer and began to pursue a career in publishing. After affiliating himself with the firm of Dix, Edwards & Company and becoming managing editor of *Putnam's Monthly* magazine, he enjoyed his new identity as a man of letters and member of the "literary republic of New York." Although pleased with the opportunity this gave him to solicit books and articles from the likes of Emerson, Irving, Longfellow, Stowe, Melville, and Thoreau, the uncertainty forced on the publishing industry by the financial panic of 1857 did not bode well for his future as an editor and author.

As it happened, a state-appointed commission had recently been formed to oversee the construction of the public park in New York City that Bryant and Downing had championed. When approached with the information that the commissioners were seeking a man to work under the direction of the chief engineer as superintendent of the preliminary clearing operations, Olmsted said that he was interested in applying for the job. Although ill-fitted in the opinion of some because he was not considered to be a "practical man"—that is, unqualified because he refused to engage in patronage politics—and of others who saw him as a gentleman inexperienced in this line of work, he was nevertheless able to obtain the position and was soon successfully transforming an army of ward heelers into an efficient workforce.

Now it was my turn to be tested, not by Tammany Hall but in a similar fashion as Olmsted had been. Stigmatized as an elitist, a woman no less, with an impractical vision that impinged on the existing civil service management system, I found myself confronting a unionized labor force that was reluctant to work alongside volunteers and outside hires whom they considered a threat to their jobs. Within the parks administration itself, I experienced polite tolerance but no enthusiastic buy-in to the notion of incorporating a private-sector partner into its existing bureaucratic operational structure. With only my newly minted title of administrator and the backing of Commissioner Davis, I would, in spite of this opposition, carry the banner of the neophyte Central Park Conservancy into battle, marshaling necessary forces along the way.

Chapter Three

LOOKING BACK

As a writer–turned–park administrator like Olmsted, my only instruction, as was also true in his case, was to be found on the job—a job for which there was as yet no description. Let me quickly add that the comparison between Olmsted and me should not be over-extended. Olmsted faced the challenge of converting what was still a ragged 843-acre wasteland into a pleasure ground that is a masterpiece of landscape design and paragon of social beneficence, while my task was not to build such an extraordinary civic amenity but to develop a plan and find the means to rescue this underappreciated, wholly original tour de force from further destruction—a less remarkable but nevertheless important feat.

But, digging deeper into our respective pasts, one can find a ser-endipitous similarity mitigating our common status of inexperienced novice when it came to assuming responsibilities for which we were both patently unprepared. Just as Olmsted had as a boy roamed the fields around his Connecticut home responding to the beauties of nature and appreciating picturesque scenery on carriage drives with his father and stepmother, I had a similarly subliminal preparation for the job that I was about to create. This included the same freedom to explore the outdoors as a child that he had enjoyed and, through the later education of my aesthetic eye, the development of an appreciation of landscape scenery as a combination of nature and art.

Childhood Idylls

Growing up in San Antonio, Texas, in Alamo Heights, a suburb on the northern outskirts of town, I was the unconscious recipient of an ecologically richer and safer world than the one most children know today. Nature was my actual playground, not its digital representation in an adventure game computer application, and my parents felt there was no danger in allowing me to wander at will outdoors.

In memory's eye I see a pretty white fence at the edge of our lawn of sturdy semitropical St. Augustine grass (*Axonopus*), or "carpet grass," as everyone called it, which reaches its northern limit of growth in the southern part of Texas. Shading this lawn is a tangle of live-oak trees somewhat more stunted than those found in the moister states of the Deep South, yet a distinguishing and much-appreciated asset to residential properties in this new part of town, trees to climb and swing from. I can recall the sensation of rough bark against the tender skin of a bare stomach as I scrambled up and down their trunks and sinuous branches. I remember, too, my pleasure in examining the population of a front-yard insect universe and my particular delight in capturing pill bugs, or roly-polys, and watching these small crustaceans curl up like gray pellets in my hand. I also recollect a favorite trick: holding a broad, flat blade of carpet grass taut between my two thumbs and blowing through the aperture between my pressed-together knuckles to make a shrill whistling sound. Later, when I was old enough to crave sophistication, I would cut sticks from a large grapevine that hung from a tree beside our driveway and smoke pretend cigarettes with my neighborhood playfellows. These will seem to have been boring amusements compared with those enjoyed by a generation that can indulge in the kind of Indiana Jones–style adventures offered by iPhone apps connected by Bluetooth to virtual reality goggles. Nevertheless, such self-concocted local encounters with actual nature, tame as mine were, seem more rewarding in retrospect than the most exciting forays into the universe of virtual reality.

Our house was situated at what was then the northern edge of town, on a slope leading down to a grassy gully in which a few feathery-leaved honey mesquite and several Texas mountain laurel trees with their drooping clusters of fragrant bluish-lavender flowers—both indigenous species like the live oak—grew. This patch of nature was actually a median strip in the divided street embracing it, which is why it was called, rather too grandly, La Jara *Boulevard,* and it was one of the principal domains of my outdoor adventures. With neighbor children, I scrambled through the concrete culverts that punctuated the green median at various street crossings and discovered beside the trickle of water that ran through it after a rain a streak of gritty clay firm enough for modeling crude figurines.

If La Jara was my green valley, the vacant lot opposite our home on Castano Avenue—another extravagant designation for a still unpaved street—was my fairy-tale forest, heavily treed with live oaks like our lawn but forming a denser tangle. It was possible for a child to enter this half acre and completely lose sight of the houses on Castano. I always referred to this place as "the deep, deep woods." For me the deep, deep woods were full of epiphanies, both divine and natural, a setting for revelations. For instance, after a Sunday School lesson on Jacob, the son of Isaac and Rebecca and twin brother of Esau, I envisioned his dream of the ladder rising to heaven as taking place in a familiar live-oak copse, a logical setting, I thought, for this Old Testament biblical story. It was in the deep, deep woods that, with the help of my father, I captured an abandoned baby owl that became my ferocious short-term pet, and there, too, that I discovered, with a child's capacity for awe proportionate to Howard Carter's thrill on unearthing Pharaoh Tutankhamen's tomb at Thebes, a small gravesite marked with a circle of stones and a whitewashed rock bearing the crudely lettered inscription "Here Lies Spot."

In 1942 my father bought a ranch in the Texas Hill Country four miles east of Johnson City. Although he bred a small herd of cattle, the place was essentially our family's weekend and summer getaway. In addition to going to the barn, putting a bridle on my horse Peewee, and racing bareback with my cousins Kenneth and Martha across the pasture in front of the ranch house, I would take walks to Honey-cutt Creek, a tributary of the Pedernales River running between the two ridges that defined the boundaries of the property. Like the other creeks in this area, it is one of the typical features within a karst formation—in geological terms, a stratum of limestone that has been internally eroded by the dissolution of pockets of calcium so as to become a porous Swiss cheese–like rock filled with sinkholes, fissures, and caves colonized by bats. Because this type of geological formation traps water, it is in essence a huge underground aquifer, a source of both well water and springs such as the one feeding Honeycutt.

I would always go as far as this spring, which emerges from a crevice beneath a limestone ledge. It was here that my response to nature assumed a spiritual dimension as I stooped to peer into the dark cavity from which a tiny stream runs over two parallel runnels carved in the rock by the force of time. My ritual communion with this place took the form of drinking a few swallows of the clear, pure water that flowed into my cupped palm as it poured out of the ground.

This love of the landscapes of my childhood imprinted me in ways I could not have guessed. Becoming a gardener and an early environmentalist, taking wilderness hikes with my husband Ted and son David and admiring the Hudson River School artists as well as contemporary painters of landscapes—all these affinities must somehow owe their origin to revering the mystery of the spring bubbling out of the aquifer feeding Honeycutt Creek as well as my childhood explorations of the "deep, deep woods." Was this also the origin of my long and continuing love affair with Central Park, a romance that had begun even before I knew where it would lead? Other factors, of course, would come into play.

Leaving Home

By the time I was a teenager, falling in love with boys gained precedence over playing outdoors and exploring the natural world. In addition, I was about to embark on a life journey that was somewhat atypical for a San Antonio girl at that time. This did not mean that I felt estranged from my family, only that I was taking the first step toward discovering a wider world, which would lead to my residence in, and lifetime commitment to, a very different sort of culture and place from the one I had known as a child.

At Wellesley, besides falling in love with boys, I fell in love with the history of art. My courses there, which incidentally took place in an exceptionally well-designed campus setting, have provided me throughout the years untold pleasure by informing my visits to museums and art galleries as well as walks in cities, parks, and gardens throughout the world. As in Olmsted's case, the aesthetic perspective I gained at this age turned out to be a professional asset. This may have been because in those days, before art history became as focused on political subtexts as it is today, my Wellesley art history major taught me to see compositional space, color, and form with a critical eye.

This kind of visual education would become a core value in my job in Central Park as well as in my ability to judge works of landscape design elsewhere. And, like Olmsted, I have continually found myself at pains to make people understand that, as with a painting, an actual landscape should be read in terms of foreground, middle ground, and background. I still continue to talk in this vein, although it is not always easy to get people to realize that both natural and designed landscapes should be seen as holistic compositions in which the spatial frame itself, rather than the objects within it, is preeminent.

Not with any fixed intention at the time of severing my Texas roots, I decided to graduate from Wellesley rather than return home and finish the last two years of my education at the University of Texas. To think of this as a bold resolution seems ridiculous today, but at that time it was common custom for girls like me who had gone to school in the east to follow this conventional route to marriage with a fellow Texan. At the same time, I was not inclined to extend my formal studies in academia or apply for a job. Like almost all my classmates, I was imbued with a "ring-by-spring" mentality, and one month after graduation I married my popular Yale college boyfriend Ed Barlow. His obligatory military service as an ensign in the navy took us to Washington, D.C., where we settled into a small row house in Foggy Bottom. Besides learning to cook and decorating our home with the Danish Modern furniture favored by most young couples at the time, during my first year of marriage I took a course in Italian at the Georgetown University School of Foreign Service on the chance that this would be an asset should I want to study Renaissance art history again someday. In addition, I had a brief stint as a secretary at the Embassy of Thailand. Then, in step with a large number of my college friends, I became a mother by the age of twenty-two.

My sudden overwhelming love for Lisa did not mean that I was any kind of paragon as a mother. A shameful memory remains of the time she playfully spilled her milk on the floor for a third time, and I watched her small pink face pucker up as I screamed at her, "I'll have you know that I went to Wellesley College and was born to be something besides a milk mopper!" There must be a way, I thought, to balance maternal love and responsibility with individual fulfillment and social contribution. No longer able to go to my Italian class, I registered for a University of Chicago correspondence course in creative writing, something a housebound mom could do while baby napped or played nearby.*

After Ed became a first-year student at Yale Law School in 1961 and Lisa was enrolled in kindergarten in New Haven, I applied to the Yale School of Architecture's city planning program.† Not surprisingly, my focus in planning school was on urban and regional open-space preservation. However, the courses I was offered when I began my city-planning studies were oriented to a modernist super-block, regional shopping mall paradigm, and I was tuned in to a less avant-garde perspective. I owe this to the fact that soon after its publication in 1961 I read Jane Jacobs's *The Death and Life of Great American Cities*. Understandably, I did not particularly find favor with my professors when, with the zeal of a religious convert, I professed Jacobs's prescriptions for urban vibrancy through the preservation of old neighborhoods and historic street patterns, a not-yet-accepted alternative to modernism's notion of comprehensive master planning based on thoroughgoing urban renewal.

---

* To my recent astonishment in light of the turn my life took later, I came across a box of saved papers in which I found the essay I sent off to my professor describing Washington's Rock Creek Park and its importance to the city.

† I might have enrolled in a landscape architecture program instead, but Yale did not offer one at that time.

But planning school offered me a valuable education in other ways. Lewis Mumford's 1961 publication of *The City in History: Its Origins, Its Transformations, and Its Prospects* and Professor Christopher Tunnard's course on the history of cities gave me knowledge of the urban forms of the past. I thus learned how the grid layout with straight thoroughfares and a central agora developed by the fifth-century BCE Greek architect Hippodamus of Miletus became a paradigm for subsequent urban plans, including the 1811 grid plan of New York City. And I could now perceive how the grand boulevards and squares of Baron Eugène Haussmann's monumental mid-nineteenth-century plan for Paris had their origins in André Le Nôtre's tree-lined allées and radial axes at seventeenth-century Versailles. Remembering the days I had spent in the nation's capital during my first three years of marriage, I readily grasped another example of the Versailles influence, first on Pierre L'Enfant, the city's original eighteenth-century planner, and subsequently on the turn-of-the-twentieth-century McMillan Commission, which regularized and augmented the L'Enfant plan according to the neoclassical principles of the City Beautiful movement.

In addition to falling under the influence of Jane Jacobs's now-classic book, when it was first published in 1962 I read Rachel Carson's *Silent Spring,* the clarion call that inaugurated the environmental movement. Besides propelling the ban on the use of pesticides on cropland, this seminal work gave impetus to the notion of protecting natural landscapes from overdevelopment. For this reason I became particularly interested in the Garden City movement Ebenezer Howard initiated in the United Kingdom in 1898, the ancestor of the trend toward American planned communities such as Reston, Virginia, and Greenbelt, Maryland, which were being laid out during the time I was in planning school.

A third then-revolutionary publication, Betty Friedan's 1963 *The Feminine Mystique,* was a summons for me as well as for many other women who were living lives on the cusp of social change. I can remember how riveted I was standing in one of the book aisles of the Yale Co-op devouring her words: "We can no longer ignore that voice within women that says: 'I want something more than my husband and my children and my home.'" "Yes," replied a loud voice inside me, in spite of the remorse I still felt for shouting in rage at Lisa when she was a baby as I gave vent to my frustration over being a home-bound "milk mopper."

As our respective graduations from Yale in June 1964 approached, Ed, who was a member of *The Yale Law Journal,* had several offers from legal firms, including prestigious ones in Los Angeles and San Francisco as well as New York. We traveled to the West Coast the weekend following John F. Kennedy's assassination on November 22, 1963, for interviews with two of them, but, as far as I was concerned, there was only one right choice as to the city in which we should make our future home. I therefore encouraged him to accept the position he had been offered at the Wall Street firm of Cravath, Swaine & Moore.

Such was my transit from happy Texas girlhood to Wellesley-educated young woman with a love of nature and art and a master's degree in city planning. Now I faced the question of what fulfilling avenue I could pursue after we had settled into our apartment on East End Avenue and Lisa was enrolled in first grade at the Chapin School. It would be ten years before I began my Central Park career. During that time I pursued varied interests, all of which, though I could not have guessed it at the time, would have a bearing on that most important chapter of my life.

Chapter Four

MOVING FORWARD

I have always found it a source of happiness and pride to be one of the millions of non-native New Yorkers who have come to this cosmopolitan city to find a greater degree of challenge and acceptance than would be possible elsewhere—or at least such was the case back in 1964 when I moved to this world-class metropolis as a member of the generation of young Americans living on the brink of huge societal change. There was no way for me to shed my identity as a young Wall Street lawyer's wife, nor did I particularly wish to divorce myself from the values of my youth. I was therefore conscientious in fulfilling the duties of a mother and homemaker that I had been raised to honor, but at the same time I was eager—well, driven actually—to find my niche within the world of work.

With six-year-old Lisa at home and pre–Martha Stewart pleasure in the domestic arts—cooking, gardening, home decorating—I chose the path of volunteerism. My first civic affiliation was a small organization called the Parks Association (later the Parks Council and now New Yorkers for Parks). As the head of its Budget and Planning Committee, I had to conquer my fear of public speaking and testify at City Hall hearings on the need for more financial support of the city's parks. I wrote an occasional letter to the editor of *The New York Times* protesting encroachments on parklands and even sent a promptly rebutted epistle to Robert Moses objecting to his rimming the city's waterfront with highways. I traveled to the outer boroughs, where I could see the landfill operations that were blanketing the city's once-extensive wetlands with garbage, and joined the fight to prevent a Moses highway from destroying the forested Staten Island Greenbelt. Thus it was that I came to write my first book, *The Forests and Wetlands of New York City*.

It was not difficult to decide what my next book would be after I realized that Central Park was much more than a nature preserve in the middle of New York City. The name of Frederick Law Olmsted, who along with Calvert Vaux designed this extraordinary masterpiece of landscape architecture, was barely remembered back then, but by happy coincidence his life and work had become a subject for research by others besides me. Of primary significance, the transcription and publication of the Olmsted papers in the Library of Congress under the editorship of historian and Olmsted scholar Charles McLaughlin was just getting under way. In a remarkable act of scholarly generosity, Charlie loaned me an original typescript of the doctoral thesis he had written when he was a PhD candidate at Harvard, which he was then revising as the biographical portion of what was to become the initial volume of Olmsted's papers.*

Standing in the Argosy Book Store on Fifty-Eighth Street and Lexington Avenue one day, I spotted a first edition of Olmsted's *A Journey Through Texas*. I browsed its pages with proprietary desire, relishing descriptions of the prosperous free-labor farms of the mid-nineteenth-century German immigrant settlers in the Texas Hill Country, where I had spent happy childhood summers and weekends on the family ranch outside of Johnson City. Fifty dollars seemed like a very large price for me to pay for a book in those days, but I was soon the proud owner of the first work in my collection of historical landscape travel

---

* From its inception in 1972, the Frederick Law Olmsted Papers Project has undertaken to identify the most significant of these writings and to present them in context in a readable twelve-volume format. Volumes 1 through 9 and Supplementary Series Volume 1 have been serially published by Johns Hopkins University Press—presenting the most significant of Olmsted's writings and major reports on public parks drawn from his entire career.

books, treatises, and folios of engravings. In the library I also read Olmsted's *A Journey in the Seaboard Slave States* and *A Journey in the Back Country*. It was from these sources that I first comprehended how many discerning descriptions of scenery were embedded in the newspaper travel dispatches he had written with the primary intention of proving the diseconomies of the system of Southern slavery as a means of agricultural production. I also learned that, in collaboration with Calvert Vaux, Olmsted had designed not only Central Park but also Brooklyn's Prospect Park and Fort Greene Park, as well as Morningside Park in northern Manhattan, and that they had conceived a new kind of thoroughfare, the parkway, to unite parks and the surrounding cityscape in a comprehensive urban plan. The fruit of this research was my second book, *Frederick Law Olmsted's New York,* published in 1972 on the occasion of an exhibition at the Whitney Museum of American Art celebrating the sesquicentennial of Olmsted's birth.

An even happier event occurred that year with the birth of Lisa's brother, David. After this my primary contact with Central Park was pushing my toddler to the playground in his stroller. When he was old enough, he enjoyed playing the role of *Star Wars* archaeologist digging for plastic toy figurines of Darth Vader, Han Solo, and Luke Skywalker in the sandbox in what is now known as the Ancient Playground because of its proximity to the wing of

David with his sister, Lisa, in Central Park, 1976

the Metropolitan Museum housing the Temple of Dendur. Even more fun was climbing the park's rock outcrops, sledding on Pilgrim Hill, and exploring the Ramble's "deep, deep woods" with me.*

---

* The Ramble was reputedly, and in reality, still dangerous in those days, but we managed to escape an attempted mugging unscathed and with the money still in my wallet.

By 1974 I was able to juggle my responsibilities as a mother with writing scripts for the narrator of a Time-Life documentary television series called *Wild, Wild World of Animals*. As discussed previously, Central Park was something of a wild, wild world itself then, at least in terms of social behavior and physical condition, and its reputation as a lawless, vandalized, crime-ridden, and derelict place had become a byword for New York City's fall from its pinnacle of urban pride.

First Steps

My involvement with the fate of the park began at the same time that Abraham Beame was elected mayor in 1974 and Edwin Weisel Jr., a contributor to his campaign, was appointed parks commissioner. Things looked faintly promising when, based on a telephone interview, Weisel asked James Marston Fitch, the founder of the historic preservation program at Columbia University's School of Architecture, to direct a task force with the mandate to spearhead the restoration of Central Park according to Fitch's prescription that any proposal for a modification of the park landscape should be "judged against a coherent master plan based on what the park looked like when Olmsted left." In a position paper explaining the significance of the park as a great work of landscape design, Fitch wrote, "It is a tribute to the soundness of the original concept that, although it has lost almost all of its original botanical material and is still defaced by the scar tissue of this neglect, it has never lost its sheer scenographic splendor." To help undertake the daunting task of restoring that splendor, Fitch hired Bruce Kelly, a young landscape architect trained at the University of Georgia and a recent graduate of his program at Columbia, to become a member of the small staff now officially named the Central Park Task Force.

After a dinner-party conversation with Adele Auchincloss, wife of the well-known novelist Louis Auchincloss and a good friend from my Parks Association days, Weisel appointed her deputy parks commissioner and gave her the job of overseeing the work of the Task Force. Socially well connected, she was the first person to seek private funding for the historic preservation of Central Park. Three women philanthropists—Brooke Astor, Iphigene Sulzberger, and Lucy Moses (later the first donors to the Central Park Conservancy)— responded to her solicitations with sufficient funds to enable initial steps to be taken toward developing a preliminary plan to restore the park.

For no other reason than friendship, and the fact of my recent publication of *Frederick Law Olmsted's New York,* Adele asked me to run a Central Park Task Force youth employment program funded by Mrs. Sulzberger. I loved the idea that this privately supported phil-

Bruce Kelly

anthropic initiative could provide kids with outdoor summer jobs and that, thanks to a gift from Mrs. Astor, it could at the same time undertake a restoration planning process to spearhead a vision for the park's renaissance. The admiration I felt for Olmsted's accomplishment as I walked through the park almost daily with Bruce nurtured my vision of what needed to be done to restore it. This did not, of course, prepare me in any way to run a youth-employment program in the park for the twenty teenagers recruited as summer interns from high schools in poor neighborhoods across the city. I gamely rose to the challenge and now reflect on those days as perhaps the happiest I spent during the twenty years when my daily life was professionally intertwined with that of the park.

Within less than a year after he had been appointed historic preservation consultant to the parks commissioner and director of the Central Park Task Force, Professor Fitch, who was known to be an outspoken activist, ran afoul of agency politics and was relieved of his position. Also impolitic, Weisel told the mayor that he wasn't going to give out any more patronage jobs in the Parks Department at the behest of

Geraldine Weinstein

City Hall, whereupon he, too, was required to resign. This meant that his deputy commissioners, including Adele, were also forced to leave office.

With Adele's departure the leadership of the Task Force fell on my shoulders. Now it was my turn to learn about fund-raising and to keep the candle of hope lit in the darkness of the park's precipitous decline. I managed to continue occupying an office in the Parks Department headquarters in the Arsenal, and with Brooke Astor's continued support of the Task Force, I began to assemble the resources necessary to give substance to a comprehensive landscape plan for the restoration of Central Park.

"Bruce has the eye," said Geraldine Weinstein, the horticulturist I hired to work part-time with volunteers and summer interns to bring back the Parks Department's discontinued landscape management practices. And, if it was Bruce who improved my own Olmstedian eye on our many walks in different sections of the park, it was Gerry who helped me take the preliminary steps toward improving the park's maintenance. One day as we were driving through the park in the Task Force pickup, she said, "If we can get Mrs. Sulzberger to let us transfer her support of summer interns to hiring graduates of local degree-granting programs in horticulture to work full-time, we can start to do some serious maintenance on a year-round basis."

As it turned out, I was not forced to terminate the summer intern program. Additional funding was found, and I hired Marie Ruby, a young woman with a background in horticulture, to set high school students to work pulling weeds, pruning undergrowth, and removing the pernicious *Convolvulus* vines that were rampantly smothering entire shrubs.

Dire Disarray

Clearly, back in the 1970s and 1980s, many parts of Central Park—notoriously the Ramble and the North End—were considered too dangerous and scary for park visitors to enter. Even Parks Department workers were reluctant to go into these places, and tourists were told at hotel desks to avoid Central Park altogether.

This deplorable situation stemmed from the fact that the entire administration of the Parks Department was so disorganized that no qualified outsider could be found who was willing to accept the job of commissioner. The agency was therefore being run in a revolving-door fashion by a series of commissioners composed of superannuated civil servants willing to continue their city employment with salary and benefits for a year or two beyond their retirement dates. Park

Central Park Task Force summer interns

workers and their supervisors belonged to the same union, and there was a general consensus among them that their jobs were an entitlement that required not much more than showing up for work and getting their time cards stamped.

Thus began my first lesson in municipal government politics. As indicated above, in those days before public-private parks partnerships had become widely accepted, the formation of a day-to-day working alliance between city officials and private citizens within a single management structure was viewed with considerable skepticism. In some quarters this amounted to anathema, which could be summarized in the inelegant metaphor of the human body's automatic rejection of a life-saving organ in a transplant operation. There was no overt animus on the part of government and certainly no objection to receiving private funds. After all, contributions from private citizens to the campaigns of candidates for public office were the lifeblood of elections. But here it was a question of authority. Who would control the money—the city comptroller or the board of an outside philanthropic entity? The answer to that question came when Martin Lang, former head of the Sanitation Department and at that time one of Mayor Beame's stopgap parks commissioners, decided that he should have control of the Astor Foundation's Task Force grant. Naturally it was a great day for me when Mrs. Astor, wearing her milliner-made hat, genuine pearls, and tweed designer suit, came in person to meet with the two of us in the conference room of the Arsenal. "You mean you want *her* to be in charge of the money?" he demanded. "Yes, Commissioner," she replied, "that is right." He thereupon banished me to a small bottom-floor office, but at least the Central Park Task Force remained under my control.

To measure the distance that has been traveled with regard to the city's embrace of public-private park partnerships as a welcome and necessary part of government, one must look back to their inception during the first term of Ed Koch's mayoralty. Moreover, the concept of civic betterment by means of public-private partnerships in New York City would not be thriving to such a degree had it not been endorsed by Mayor Michael Bloomberg, a former Conservancy board member, even before he took office in 2002. The fact that his administration was based on merit appointments of agency commissioners rather than on patronage paybacks was significant. In the case of parks, this meant selecting a savvy and dedicated up-through-the-ranks veteran, Adrian Benepe, as commissioner. Continuing to build upon the previous success of the public-private modus operandi, the current parks commissioner, Mitchell Silver, today champions the Conservancy's Institute for Urban Parks, which provides workshops and training sessions for staff and volunteers in parks citywide.

For these reasons it is now hard to believe just how much whistling in the dark there was during the five years before the birth of the Conservancy, when, as head of the Task Force, I promoted the mission of saving Central Park with nothing more than optimistic determination. But my zeal was only half the story. There was an immense reservoir of love for Central Park, even in its derelict condition, and I was immensely buoyed up by how readily it could be tapped. As I went about envisioning the park reborn, having a background as a writer and journalist proved to be an important asset, and on June 14, 1976, *New York* magazine published an article of mine titled "32 Ways Your Time and Money Can Rescue Central Park." Although the management and restoration plan would not crystallize as a planning document until 1985, after the Conservancy had been founded and become capable of funding a team of landscape architects and consultants to study the park in a comprehensive manner, I could offer willing donors such obvious gift opportunities as this sampling: "Improve the Lake Shore," "Organize a Weed Patrol," "Provide Tools for Volunteers," "Rebuild the Belvedere Castle," "Refurbish the Dairy," "Repair the Wisteria Pergola," "Restore the Shrub Beds," "Save the Stone Arches," and "Work with the Zoo Animals" (the New York Wildlife Conservation Society had not yet taken over the remodeling and running of the deplorable old zoo).

The week after the article appeared, letters containing checks began to arrive on my desk. Even more gratifying than these gifts—totaling $25,000 in one week—was the outpouring of memories and appreciation of the role the park played in people's lives. I can still recall some of the sentiments these letters expressed. From a first-generation immigrant there was this: "When I was a girl Mama used to take me to the park at the end of the day when she got home from work, and while the park attendant at the Conservatory Garden lowered the

American flag, I would say the pledge of allegiance." From a woman who now lived in Arizona: "I used to push the baby carriage with the twins through the zoo." From a New York man with sweet memories: "I proposed to my wife on the Mall." None of these people had ever heard of the Central Park Task Force, but here was a group of far-flung correspondents and local constituents with faith in its preliminary efforts to rescue from ruin New York City's crown jewel.

As gratifying as this outpouring of monetary gifts and heartfelt tributes was the response I received when the Central Park Task Force started its program for volunteers. Bulb planting, weeding, and bench repainting were some of the tasks they performed. The New York Fern Society even sent a group of its members to plant ferns in the Ramble.

It was now imperative for me to become a fund-raiser for real, and soon my principal literary endeavor was preparing grant proposals. I was very pleased when, after obtaining the guidelines of the National Endowment for the Humanities, I wrote one that resulted in a $140,000

Volunteers planting ferns in the Ramble

grant to permit the Task Force to extend its educational efforts into nearby schools.

Simultaneously, our first corporate gift, a challenge grant from Exxon, enabled us to sponsor an outreach program called Double Your Green, whereby the company's foundation matched the funds we raised from park neighbors. Exxon further supported the publication of *The Central Park Book,* which I edited and partly wrote. Intended primarily for teachers whose curriculum consisted of regular Task Force–sponsored field trips, it has chapters written by authorities on Central Park's geology, botany, and birdlife. At the same time I wanted it to be something more than a natural science handbook. Therefore, for readers with a literary inclination like mine, it has a chapter with excerpts from novels, essays, and short stories in which Central Park plays a role, and for people interested in history there is a chapter on the park's original Olmstedian design and early years as a social institution in the life of New York City.

Those who look at the park today as a model of professional care will be surprised to see that among the suggested activities at the end of each of *The Central Park Book*'s chapters, the one on park botany is focused on food foraging. Gary Lincoff, an expert on wild provender who now teaches a mycology course at the New York Botanical Garden, made the following contribution: "While no one should ever pick the flowers or branches of trees and shrubs growing in any public park, it is permissible to pick certain edible weeds, providing you can identify them positively and know for a fact that they are non-poisonous, not contaminated by automobile fumes and do not grow in a known dog run." Following these cautionary words, he provides a series of recipes for Central Park foraged fare. I can attest to the fact that the crabapple cake is a lot easier to make than acorn bread, which requires leaching acorns by boiling them for two hours to remove the bitter-tasting tannic acid, shelling and drying them in a hundred-degree oven, and then grinding them in a food processor.

In addition to supporting the Task Force's work with teachers from nearby schools, the grant from the National Endowment for the Humanities enabled me to use the skills I had learned during my stint as a documentary film writer. For this endeavor I was able to hire a *Sesame Street* cinematographer, Marc Brugnoni, to shoot sequences showing the park as both a nature sanctuary and a place for recreation and self-expression. Composer and songwriter Joe Raposo provided a theme song, and Joanne Woodward narrated the script I had written. Simply titled *The Park,* the film was aired twice on PBS Channel Thirteen.

In contrast to the unfrequented Ramble and the North End woodlands, which were simply derelict, open areas of the park such as the Sheep Meadow, Great Lawn, East Green, North Meadow, East Meadow, and almost every scrap of lawn in between were heavily damaged because of unregulated sports activity and grass-trampling hoards streaming across the park during mass events. Although upon taking over the reins of office in 1978 Gordon Davis had instituted certain crowd-control regulations, the park remained the venue of choice as a place of assembly for demonstrations and other large gatherings. And now that Gordon had appointed me Central Park administrator and the Task Force's mission had been subsumed by that of the Central Park Conservancy, it was incumbent on me to face these matters head-on.

Litter-strewn compacted ground with an oil drum overflowing with uncollected garbage following a concert in the 1970s

New Dawn

The challenge of getting the Conservancy off the ground was immediate. With no authority over park workers, no city funds to hire new ones, and no way to reform existing union rules linked to narrowly defined civil service job titles, I had to find private money for a parallel management structure. It would necessarily be small at first and only able to grow through private donations. Gerry Weinstein, who had supervised the Task Force's teacher-education program and cadre of volunteer gardeners, became my head of horticulture. To form the Central Park Conservancy's first planting and tree-pruning crews, she recruited graduates from SUNY Cobleskill's School of Agriculture, SUNY Farmingdale's degree-granting program in Agricultural Management, and the New York Botanical Garden's Certificate Program. Thanks to the ongoing support of Brooke Astor, I hired landscape architect Bruce Kelly to continue to serve as principal consultant on the comprehensive park restoration plan initiated by the Task Force.

In terms of capital construction, our first gifts for major architectural projects enabled us to undertake the restoration of the Dairy and the Belvedere. The Dairy, shorn of its handsome Victorian loggia, had been converted into a Parks Department supply depot for everything from rakes and shovels to lifeguard bathing suits. Located near the easily accessible southeastern entrance to the park at Fifth Avenue and Fifty-Ninth Street and in the same vicinity as an elaborate rustic summerhouse situated atop a large glacially polished schist outcrop christened the Kinderberg—a perfect-for-climbing "children's mountain"—the Dairy's original function was serving milk and dispensing toys. After we had restored the building to its original appearance and reopened it as the Central Park Visitor Center, I asked Marie Ruby, my former Task Force summer intern supervisor, to serve as its program director. She responded by organizing several Sunday afternoon concerts as well as educational programs in park history. At the same time, the rebuilt Belvedere became a classroom for environmental education.

The next step that needed to be taken was the formation of a board of directors. Luckily, I was successful in recruiting William S. Bei-

*William S. Beinecke, first chairman of the Central Park
Conservancy, 1983*

necke, a recently retired corporate CEO, as chairman. Thanks to
his contacts in the New York business community, we were able to
recruit other prominent heads of corporations. At the suggestion of a
young Morgan Stanley investment banker who had learned about the
Conservancy's board-in-formation, I met with Lewis Bernard, later
the firm's chief administrative and financial officer. Lewis agreed to
join the board and served for more than a decade as its vice chairman.

In addition to the Central Park Task Force, there was another organization that was a forerunner of the Central Park Conservancy. This
was the Central Park Community Fund. Founded by Richard Gilder
and George Soros, its mission was to reorganize park workers' job
responsibilities, provide needed maintenance equipment, and reform
the Parks Department's overall management policies. Toward this end
Dick and George commissioned Steve Savas, a Columbia University
business analyst, to undertake a survey of current conditions and prepare a report. Published in 1976, it pointed out the park's fractured
management system, which at the time consisted of twelve park fore-
men in twelve different districts, with separate crews handling general maintenance, grounds care, and equipment repair. Some of these
were based in Central Park, while others had responsibilities elsewhere
throughout the city's five boroughs. It was nearly impossible to coor-
dinate personnel, schedule work efficiently, or track costs.

In his report Savas recommended a more active role for community groups and philanthropies and stressed the importance of harnessing constituency support and private-sector resources to bolster the Parks Department's limited public funds and inadequate staff. The report also promoted the notion of officially sanctioned public-private park support groups and encouraged the Central Park Task Force and the Central Park Community Fund to merge into a new organization he provisionally named Central Park Guardians.

Now that the Central Park Conservancy had been founded, it would become that united organization, thereby combining my vision of park restoration with the Community Fund's mission of management reform. Representatives from the now disbanded boards of the Task Force and the Community Fund were invited to join the Conservancy's board-in-formation. Recruiting Gilder, as it turned out, would provide the nascent organization generous philanthropic support and sound financial advice throughout the ensuing years.

Another preliminary board member of importance must be mentioned here. This is Ted Rogers, one of the corporate executives recruited by Bill Beinecke. His acceptance of Bill's invitation to participate in the formation of the Central Park Conservancy marked a major turning point in my life.

Love Story

For almost three years after Ed and I were divorced in 1979, I dated various men but without much likelihood of remarriage. After meeting Ted, I thought to myself, "Oh dear, isn't it too bad that all the good ones my own age already have wives!" Happily for me, Ted had an opposite reaction. After having recently accepted the offer to become the CEO of NL Industries, a Fortune 500 company, he had moved into a large apartment overlooking the East River; however, since his wife Adele had discovered that she did not like New York, she had returned to Houston, where Ted commuted back and forth on weekends. He, on the other hand, enthusiastically adopted New York City as his new home. Settling into a weekday bachelor existence, he plunged into big-city life with gusto, walking to work every day and marveling at the Chrysler Building and other prominent landmarks. Having earlier run the New York City Marathon, which finishes in Central Park, he had already decided that he would like the foundation arm of his corporation to support the organization-in-formation that was proposing to reverse the park's plight. In addition, even before he had been invited by Bill to become a board member, he agreed to help the Conservancy identify other corporations around the park from which to solicit support.

A story Ted likes to tell involves a photograph of me in *Avenue,* the giveaway magazine for socialites then being distributed in upscale neighborhoods. In one of the issues that arrived in the lobby of his Sutton Place apartment building shortly after he moved in there was an article about the Conservancy, which was accompanied by a photograph of me standing on the recently resodded Sheep Meadow. He claims that this is what prompted him to say yes when Bill asked him to join the board.

Afterward, as Ted and I toured the park together to look at projects that needed funding, we stopped at the Conservatory Garden at 104th Street and Fifth Avenue. Built in 1936 on the site of the park's nineteenth-century conservatory, it had once been a horticultural showcase but was now overgrown, neglected, and devoid of visitors other than vandals. Here was where my friend Lynden Miller, who is both an artist and a gardener, had accepted my challenge that she undertake the revival of its planting beds, central greensward, and wisteria pergola. Ted's pledge of $25,000, the Conservancy's first gift from a corporate foundation, to initiate this project was, unbeknownst to me, the beginning of our courtship.

Ted was interested in dance and was a regular theatergoer. I was naturally happy to accept his invitations to attend performances of the New York City Ballet and be his date to see plays. It was a Cinderella experience for me to be chauffeured to these events in the company Mercedes. Occasionally he would hold my hand, but at this point there was nothing more than a friendly peck on the cheek when we said good night. Our hesitant romance, however, gave us time to get to know one another as friends. When he gave me books he particularly liked, I was happy to note that he was an avid reader and had always been something of a closet intellectual as he moved up through the ranks of corporate America. And he was not a convivial joiner of country clubs and all-male social groups. It was clear from the way he treated me and how he spoke of other women in the workplace that, whether or not he used the word, he was a feminist.

As I got to know Ted better, he told me about his background as a son of the industrial Midwest, where his father had begun his lifetime employment at United States Steel's plant in Lorain, Ohio, as a brakeman on a narrow-gauge railroad delivering raw materials to the factory floor. Ted's life remained rooted in his working-class origins, even when the family moved to the nearby small town of Amherst after his parents were able to buy a car and his father could commute to work. Upon graduating from high school in Amherst, he was awarded a navy scholarship at Miami University, and after four years, his diploma and marriage license, like mine, were issued almost simultaneously. As an officer in the navy, he began learning the ways of a gentleman and had aspirations to go to law school upon completing his three-year tour of duty. He applied and was accepted at Columbia, but his plans to enroll in the fall of 1959 were abruptly canceled when Adele discovered that she was pregnant. They happened to be in Middletown, Ohio, attending the wedding of a friend when they received the news.

Imbued with our generation's ethos in which husbands were called breadwinners and wives stayed at home and raised children, without hesitating, instead of enrolling in law school Ted marched up to the company headquarters of Armco Steel in Middletown and got a job in its training program. Thus began his rise from plant manager in Mexico City to salesman in Milwaukee to sales manager in Baltimore to president of an Armco-owned company in Los Angeles, to president of National Supply, another Armco subsidiary in Houston whose business was servicing the oil industry with drilling rigs and other equipment. In 1980, when the chairman and CEO of NL Industries was planning to retire, Ted was recruited by a headhunter to fill his soon-to-be-vacated position, necessitating the move to the company's headquarters in New York City. Happily, as it turned out for both of us, he accepted the job.

About a year after we had been going out together casually, Ted invited me for dinner at the Four Seasons. Over dessert and coffee, he confided that his marriage had never been rocky or unhappy but that it had always seemed flat. He said that he had married Adele for no other reason than the fact that she was his college sweetheart and it seemed like the right thing to do. He admitted that their interests were not particularly compatible, and now that their daughter Pam and son Ted Jr. were grown and married, he felt that he could ask her for a divorce.

This speech was, of course, a lead-in to what he said next: "I want to marry you." Dizzy with emotion, I remained silent as he picked up the check and we walked to the stairs leading out of the restaurant. Then on impulse I put my arms around him and we embraced and kissed—this time it was a bona fide lovers' kiss—right in front of Julian Niccolini, the maitre d' and co-owner of the Four Seasons, who was standing in his usual place at the reception desk in the Grill Room. And, although it would be two years before Ted was granted his divorce, he sold his Sutton Place apartment and moved in with me. At last, on June 26, 1984, following our wedding at the Madison Avenue Presbyterian Church, we celebrated with our families, personal friends, Parks Department colleagues, and my Central Park Conservancy staff at a reception held in the newly restored Conservatory Garden.

In its current reincarnation according to Lynden's redesign, the garden is a signature statement of the success of the Central Park Conservancy, which is probably one reason why it remains the perennial venue for the Women Committee's annual Frederick Law Olmsted Awards Luncheon. But for me it will always stand for something more: a reminder of the beginning of a marriage that has been, as I often like to say, the best of all the many good things that Central Park has brought my way over the past forty years.

Chapter Five

DESIGN MASTERPIECE

What led British architect Calvert Vaux to propose collaboration with Olmsted in preparing a submission in the design competition for Central Park in 1857 can only be surmised. His own most important credential was the knowledge of landscape design he had acquired after Andrew Jackson Downing recruited him in 1851 as his architectural collaborator on plans for what were then known as rural villas on the grounds he was laying out for the gentry who were purchasing old farms in the Hudson River Valley and converting them into estates. That occupation had ended with Downing's death in 1852, after which Vaux moved to New York with the notion of setting up an independent architectural practice. Two important reasons why Vaux may have approached Olmsted were that he lacked Olmsted's social and professional connections and the latter's experience as a well-known writer. Also in Olmsted's favor was the fact that his new job as on-site super-intendent of clearance operations gave

Calvert Vaux

him intimate knowledge of the future park's terrain. However, perhaps even more important was what Vaux must have perceived as Olmsted's predisposition for viewing landscape with the eyes of a latter-day Romantic, a qualification that may not have seemed as far-fetched then as it might now.

The Picturesque

Beginning in the late eighteenth century, appreciation of landscape as visual experience was grounded in the aesthetic of the Picturesque as propounded in the books by William Gilpin and Uvedale Price that Olmsted had read in the Hartford Public Library in his youth.*
Recollecting many years later their significance on the formation of

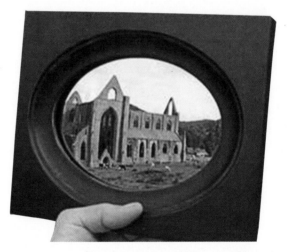

Claude glass reflecting an image of Tintern Abbey

* The Picturesque can be considered as an intermediate category between the Beautiful and the Sublime, as distinguished in Edmund Burke's famous 1757 aesthetic treatise *A Philosophical Enquiry into the Origin of Our Ideas of the Sublime and Beautiful,* in which he dissected and defined the specific characteristics of each—in the case of beauty, such qualities as smallness, delicacy, and smoothness, in contrast to the vastness and magnificence of the infinite of the Sublime, as found in the powerful frisson-inducing grandeur of such elements as majestic mountains or crashing surf. In terms of aesthetic theory this word "Picturesque" with a capital *P* should not be confused with lowercase "picturesque," denoting a landscape or artifact that is merely eye-catching.

his particular sensibility toward landscape, he wrote in a letter to an old friend, Lizzy Baldwin, "I esteem [them] so much more than any published since, as stimulating the exercise of judgment in matters of my art, that I put them in the hands of my pupils as soon as they come into our office, saying, 'You are to read these seriously, as a student of law would read Blackstone.' "

Such discrimination in looking at landscapes can best be characterized by visualizing a Claude glass, the device reputedly invented by the seventeenth-century landscape painter Claude Lorrain, which became a common accessory for late-eighteenth-century tourists. It is a slightly convex, dark-toned mirror that merges the reflected subject

Tintern Abbey, sketch by Rev. William Gilpin

with its surroundings while also reducing and simplifying the color and tonal range so as to give the entire composition a painterly quality. It is not coincidental that Gilpin illustrated his books with warm-tinted oval aquatints, for whether actual or simply metaphorical, the Claude glass typifies the perception of nature as scenic vignettes—in other words, as art.

Here it is important to remark that Olmsted lived in an era of great botanical discovery, when plant hunters were collecting exotic specimens from the four corners of the globe to propagate and plant in European and American parks and gardens. Nevertheless, like the Picturesque theorists, he looked at trees not so much as a botanist or gardener would, but rather as the arboreal palette of the landscape artist; their forms and tints were the stuff from which scenic effects were made. Significantly, Olmsted took Gilpin's precepts to heart and made them cardinal principles of landscape composition when it came time to design Central Park.

Of course, looking at existing Picturesque landscapes as a tourist was not the same thing as designing a public park. Vaux's opinion of Olmsted's credentials was probably further reinforced by this enthusiastic account in Olmsted's first book, *An American Farmer in England,* of his visit to Birkenhead, Joseph Paxton's recently designed park outside Liverpool:

> Five minutes of admiration, and a few more spent in studying the manner in which art had been employed to obtain from nature so much beauty, and I was ready to admit that in democratic America, there was nothing to be thought of as comparable with this People's Garden. Indeed, gardening had here reached a perfection that I had never before dreamed of. I cannot undertake to describe the effect of so much taste and skill as had evidently been employed; I will only tell you, that we passed by winding paths over acres and acres, with a constant varying surface where on all sides were growing every variety of shrubs and flowers, with more than natural grace, all set in borders of greenest, closest turf, and all kept with the most consummate neatness . . .
>
> But this is but a small part. Besides the cricket and an archery ground, large valleys were made verdant, extensive drives arranged—plantations, clumps, and avenues of trees formed, and a large park laid out. And all this magnificent pleasure-ground is entirely, unreservedly, and forever the people's own.

These words were written in 1852, when Olmsted had no inkling of the turn his life would take five years later. Pertinently, there was no such thing as a profession of landscape architect in America at the time of the Central Park design competition in which Vaux wished to collaborate with Olmsted—the two would be the ones to later coin the term—and it would be from Vaux, with his training and experience as an architect, that Olmsted would learn drafting and other necessary professional skills that would allow him subsequently to enter into a highly successful practice on his own. The basis for Vaux's assessment of Olmsted as a pragmatic thinker as well as a sensitive observer of landscape was confirmed by Olmsted himself many years later in an autobiographical fragment about the period he spent in London following the publication of his three books on Southern slavery.* Still thinking of himself as a "literary man," he had taken a position in a publishing firm, a business that took him upon occasion to London, where he had frequent opportunities to visit the city's Royal Parks.

> Hardly a day passed in which I did not ramble in one a little. On holidays I went to Kew and Bushy and Richmond & Windsor. I [came] to look at public grounds critically but not at all from the official point of view or a gardener's point of view but from that of a citizen seeking rest, refreshment, recreation in [them]. So it happened that when Central Park was to be laid out & managed it is quite possible that I was more intimate with public parks and had a better understanding of what they should be than any other man of American birth and breeding.

Still, Olmsted was initially hesitant to accept Vaux's proposal, since his boss, Central Park engineer in chief Egbert Viele, had already made a topographical survey of the site along with a general plan for its development. He decided to put the matter before Viele, and when Viele retorted that it was a matter of indifference to him whether Olmsted entered the competition or not, Olmsted agreed to go ahead and collaborate with Vaux. Though neither realized it at the time, they were launching what would become the most influential partnership in the history of American landscape design.

---

* Olmsted was engaged in compiling these into a single volume titled *The Cotton Kingdom: A Traveller's Observations on Cotton and Slavery in the American Slave States* when he interrupted this labor in order to accept the position of superintendent of the clearing operations in Central Park.

Design Competition

A hitherto wasteland on the northern fringe of the then-built city, the land reserved for the new park had become a place where squatters built shanties and grazed goats and recycling entrepreneurs erected boiling works where the carcasses of horses and other dead animals were rendered down into carbon for sugar refining and other uses. Because of Olmsted's daily duties as supervisor, he and Vaux worked on their plan primarily in the evening hours. To further their aim of producing a Romantic landscape devoted to scenic recreation, they paced almost every square foot of the park's surface, appreciating the monumental beauty of its mica-flecked schist outcrops, noting the ones that would remain as bold presences in the landscape and those that would impede the construction of open meadows. In this way they gained an intimate understanding of the park's topography. They discussed the excavation, grading, and filling that would have to be undertaken to create rolling meadows, picturesque streams, and natu-ralistic lakes. They debated the alignment of carriage drives and foot-paths with respect to view lines and looked for elevated vantage points for broad vistas. Vaux, with his training in architecture, was in a posi-tion to assist Olmsted, who still felt himself to be primarily a man of letters, in developing the practical design skills necessary to turn these scenic ideals into plans.

Eventually it was time to sit down at the drafting table in Vaux's house at 136 East Eighteenth Street and render their design on paper. Downing Vaux, who was a small boy at the time, later remembered his father hard at work on the project. "There was," he said, "a great deal of grass to be put in the usual small dots and dashes, and it became the friendly thing for callers to help in the work by joining in and 'adding some grass to Central Park.'" Perhaps the trouble expended in drawing so much grass is what prompted the designers to call their plan "Greensward." Labeled number thirty-three out of thirty-three entries, it was delivered to the park board on April 1, 1858, the last day of the competition. Subsequently judged the winning design, "Green-sward" became the official plan for Central Park, entitling its authors to a prize of two thousand dollars.

Although we do not have all of the other thirty-two plans for comparison, we can be grateful today for the commissioners' farsighted choice. What Olmsted and Vaux accomplished was an extraordinary feat. They combined complex engineering with naturalistic scenery so skillfully that visitors today are barely aware of the park's intricate infrastructure.

Their achievement was particularly remarkable given that the land reserved for the park was, as we have seen, a relatively narrow elongated rectangle. As such, it was not the asset that the Board of Aldermen's special committee claimed it to be. Its shape and location may have made it easily accessible from all directions, but it definitely hindered the realization of the designers' aesthetic goals. Much of their Greensward plan was therefore directed toward the remediation of this defect. For instance, providing an "umbrageous horizon line" to screen out buildings that were destined to spring up around the park's periphery called for a line of trees surrounding the entire park between its perimeter wall and the street. The designers also stipulated that shrubs and trees be massed along the inner side of the wall as well.

The reservoir occupying the area between Seventy-Ninth and Eighty-Sixth Streets, the site of the present-day Great Lawn, offered a particular challenge. Although it would become, as the report of the special committee claimed, a copious source of water for ponds, lakes, and fountains, the severe geometrical lines of this rectangle within the rectangular confines of the park were at odds with Olmsted and Vaux's Picturesque style of design. Instead of straight paths they envisioned gently curving ones that took the visitor past meadows, through woods, and alongside various irregularly shaped water bodies. The purpose of this type of circulation system was to allow the park visitor to behold a sequence of alternating views, with here and there an architectural feature for visual interest. Ideally, no structures would be so large and conspicuous as to intrude on the park's broad vistas, which were scenically framed like the views found in landscape paintings.

Because of the nature of Olmsted and Vaux's design, the illusion of a landscape with distant prospects implying that the park was a distant rural retreat was maintained until the twentieth century, when the uptown march of the city included the construction of high-rise buildings around the park's perimeter. Because these soaring towers give dramatic visual definition to its boundaries, the designers' original notion of Central Park as a rus in urbe has taken on emphatic meaning. The views from on high are onto the rus, rather than the other way around, and standing in the park, an aesthetician could come to the conclusion that the urbe has subsumed the Olmstedian Picturesque into its sister category the Romantic Sublime, in which skyscrapers substitute for towering mountains as awesome wonders.

The rectangular shape of the reservoir was only one of the impediments to the creation of this objective. Between Eighty-Sixth and Ninety-Second Streets, 106 acres, or one-eighth of the park, were reserved for an even larger reservoir, the one with which we are familiar today. Although it would have an irregular, lake-like shape, its embankments had to be elevated several feet above the surrounding grade in order to create a deep-enough basin to impound an ample supply of water. In addition, its eastern perimeter was so close to Fifth Avenue that there remained only a strip of land to accommodate the route of a carriage drive and a companion bridle trail connecting the northern and southern halves of the park. Olmsted and Vaux considered this unavoidable proximity to the park's urban edge a serious drawback militating against their desired illusion of the park as unbounded rural countryside.

There was another non-park necessity to test Olmsted and Vaux's artistry: the four roadways to carry the city's traffic across the park, which had been mandated by the commissioners' competition guidelines. Severing of the site by four east-west thoroughfares meant that Central Park would be in effect five discrete parks. Designing transverse roads that would not compromise the visitor's experience of a unified landscape required a signal feat of engineering ingenuity. Olmsted and Vaux's solution was to sink their roadbeds below the grade of the rest of the park. Where necessary, they further screened these crosstown arteries from view with well-vegetated berms. To give their design additional coherence and unity, they delineated other nonconflicting modes of circulation throughout the park, carrying pedestrians over bridle paths via ornate cast-iron bridges and under carriage drives through carved-stone and ornamental-brick archways. Thus,

Sunken transverse road for non-park-related crosstown traffic

Cast-iron bridge for carrying pedestrians over the bridle trail near the south gatehouse of the Reservoir

nowhere in the park were there any dangerous crossings. Only after Olmsted and Vaux had conceived of these measures to mitigate what they considered the site's defects and planned the lines for the park's entire circulation system could they set about realizing their primary goal of creating a pastoral and picturesque semblance of rural country-side within the city.

The designers' desire for Romantic rusticity was given full rein in the Ramble, a miniature, man-made forest in the heart of the park. They made this small woodland seem more extensive than it was by creating a series of indirect, winding paths that would foster a pleasant sense of disorientation, making structural features and views come as an agreeable surprise. To heighten the dramatic potential of this section of the park, they envisioned an elongated arch of rough-hewn stone blocks; a partially concealed cave at the far end of one of the Lake's coves; and, atop Vista Rock at the Ramble's northern edge, the Belvedere, a Victorian Gothic tower with sweeping views in several directions. To further enhance the Ramble's wildwood character, an

Rustic arch, Ramble

The Belvedere in the early 1900s

Historic view of the Cascade   *The Cascade today*

artificial stream named the Gill would cut across it before tumbling in a waterfall over a mass of boulders into the Lake.

In the park's northern end, a preexisting stream known as Montayne's Rivulet, which the designers renamed the Loch, took its course through the Ravine. Near the West 100th Street entrance to the park, they planned a pool. Like the park's other water bodies, it would be connected to the city's new Croton Reservoir system through a series of pipes and valves artfully concealed behind piles of large rocks gleaned from Manhattan schist outcrops that had been leveled during the process of construction. Beginning at the Cascade on its eastern bank, the water from the Pool flowed beneath the West Drive, where it spilled over another mass of tumbled boulders to become the Loch. From here it flowed beneath a massive arch built of rough-hewn Manhattan schist and was punctuated by two smaller waterfalls at it took its eastward course to the mouth of the Harlem Meer, the lake to be created by excavating swampy ground at the park's northeastern edge.

Unfortunately, in 1962 the mouth of the Loch was buried underneath the Lasker Rink and Pool—the last major park encroachment during the Moses era—which means that today the beautiful rivulet simply ends abruptly where its water flows into a drain adjacent to

Loch, first waterfall, nineteenth century

Loch, first waterfall today

Loch, third waterfall, nineteenth century

Loch, third waterfall today

Loch flowing into the Harlem Meer, nineteenth century

Subterranean drain carrying water beneath Lasker Rink today

the parking lot behind this obtrusive structure. More than any other encroachment, this eyesore exemplifies the opposition between the modernist aesthetic of the mid-twentieth century and the nineteenth-century Olmstedian Picturesque.

Here in the North End Olmsted and Vaux used the existing glacier-polished rock outcrops as design assets. Since the views in this section of the park are more sweeping than those in the southern half, they emphasized in the report accompanying the Greensward plan that a unity of treatment should prevail and "formal and architectural effects, unless on a very grand scale, must be avoided."

Some existing architectural features in this area of the park did remain, at least for the time being. The most prominent was the school run by the Sisters of Charity of Mount St. Vincent, which had been constructed in 1848 on the high bluff overlooking the Harlem Meer. After the land on which it stood was acquired by the city, its buildings were used as offices for park commissioners.[*]

Also located on the same ridge were the sites of a chain of forts built as lookouts during the American Revolution, when the area had been occupied by British and Hessian mercenary troops. The easternmost, Fort Clinton, was connected to Nutter's Battery, named for Valentin Nutter, a local landowner. This earth-and-wood redoubt was linked to Fort Fish by earthworks along the Old Post Road, running from the upper reaches of Manhattan to the Bronx. At the line of present-day 107th Street and Lenox Aveune, the succession of fortifications incorporated the gatehouse on the site known as McGowan's Pass. From here they progressed up a rocky hill to Fort Clinton. The venerable Blue Bell tavern beside Kingsbridge Road, which remained until its demolition in 1917, was still a popular hostelry at the time the park was being built.

The North End was the scene of another chapter in military history. Following the American rout by the British in the Battle of Long Island on August 27, 1776, General Washington ordered his troops to retreat to the Harlem Heights, where, pursued by the British, they

---

[*] Since 1924 the offices of the Parks Department have been in the Arsenal, which had been built between 1847 and 1851 by the State of New York as a storage repository for munitions.

fought again at McGowan's Pass. With the redcoat victory and the evacuation of all of Manhattan by American soldiers, the garrison next to McGowan's Pass continued to be manned by a small regiment of British mercenaries until the end of the war in 1783. Then, for the next thirty years, the area surrounding the abandoned outpost reverted to forest and was avoided by all but hunters who came there to bag such game as woodcock, snipe, foxes, rabbits, and squirrels.

But as the nation was thrown into the grips of another war with England between 1812 and 1814, New Yorkers realized that the enemy could strike from the north. Quickly the section of land that would forty years later be designated as the uppermost limit of Central Park was remilitarized as the call went out for able-bodied volunteers to strengthen the old line of defense on the rocky Harlem bluffs. Medical students, men from the Society of Tammany, the Marine Society, and the Society of Tallow Chandlers, butchers, members of the bar, Free Masons, firemen, and Sons of Erin worked by daylight and moonlight to resurrect Nutter's Battery as well as Fort Clinton and Fort Fish.

Carrying a banner with the slogan "Friends of Our Country / Free Trade and Butchers' Rights / From Brooklyn's Fields to Harlem Heights," a contingent from the Master Butchers Association from Brooklyn joined the Manhattan volunteers and went to work constructing a thirty-foot-square stone tower known as Blockhouse Number 1. Open to the sky today, it originally had a sunken wooden platform for a roof, from which a heavy traversing gun could be

Blockhouse Number 1

Bethesda Fountain

The Mall, circa 1900

mounted to fire over the parapet in all directions. With these relics of the past and an overall wild woodland character, the North End remains the part of the park that most approximates a nondesigned landscape.

By contrast, Olmsted and Vaux felt that the southern half of the park, having more interrupted views, lent itself to a greater diversity of features. Near the main gate leading into the park at Fifty-Ninth Street and Fifth Avenue, they considered it appropriate to break away from carefully orchestrated passages of smooth meadow turf alternating with rocky forested heights and introduce a straight axis to form the formal promenade they called the Grand Mall. It was set on a slight diagonal to the park's boundaries in order to face the Ramble's wooded acres on the opposite shore of the Lake, with the Belvedere as a focal point in the distant background. A grand staircase under the Seventy-Second Street cross-park drive permitted promenaders to descend from the Mall and pass through an arcade with an ornamental tile ceiling and three carved stone arches opening onto Bethesda Terrace. The Terrace's centerpiece was to be an impressive fountain.

In 1873, *The Angel of the Waters,* by sculptor Emma Stebbins, added

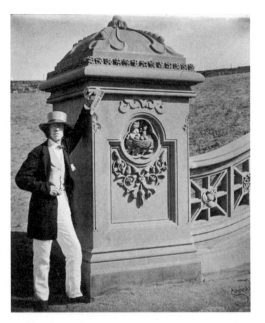

*Bethesda Terrace, detail of staircase carving by
Jacob Wrey Mould*

emblematic meaning to the fountain, which was intended as a reminder
of the public health victory that occurred in 1842 when New York
City was freed by the opening of the Croton Aqueduct from diseases
caused by contaminated well water.*

In Construction

The Greensward plan was merely a preliminary design of the park's
landscape. While it defined the drives, paths, and transverse roads and

---

* See John 5:2–4 (King James Version): "Now there is in Jerusalem by the Sheep Gate a
pool, which is called in Hebrew, Bethesda, having five porches. In these lay a great mul-
titude of sick people, blind, lame, paralyzed, waiting for the moving of the water. For an
angel went down at a certain time into the pool and stirred up the water; then whoever
stepped in first, after the stirring of the water, was made well of whatever disease he had."
In 1982, when the fountain no longer spilled water into the basin beneath the foot of the
angel and the pool surrounding it was dry, it had another meaning for me: I thought of it
then as an emblem of the newly fledged Conservancy spreading beneficent and protective
wings over the park.

outlined the areas that would be excavated to form ponds and lakes, much of the task of creating Central Park was carried out pragmatically in situ by a team of men with complementary abilities. Olmsted, who now bore the official title of landscape architect, oversaw this vast project in association with Vaux, his codesigner and the principal architect for most of the structures within the park. Architect Jacob Wrey Mould (1825–1886) assisted Vaux, providing many of the carved stone details at Bethesda Terrace and elsewhere.

Civil engineer George Waring (1833–1898) was responsible for making the park a triumph of nineteenth-century technology. Its landscape seemed to be nature's own accomplishment only because of the complex underlying infrastructure of irrigation, drainage, and sewer pipes. Aboveground, chief landscape gardener Ignaz Anton Pilát gave the park much of its naturalistic appearance. An Austrian who had served as a gardener to Prince Metternich and immigrated to America when that statesman fell out of favor during the revolutionary wars in Europe in 1848, Pilát had a solid working knowledge of botany and horticulture, which helped him implement the Picturesque planting vision Olmsted had in his mind's eye.

Good soil was a critical consideration. Since the park was previously the ragged edge of the growing city, its southern section retained organic waste from market gardens and the offal of dead animals. Some of this material could be incorporated into earth as fertilizer, and sludge from the swampy areas that were excavated to create the Pond and the Lake could be added as well. But elsewhere, especially in the northern part of the park, there was only a thin layer of soil, which had to be loosened and enriched in order to make it suitable for planting.

Beyond these measures, a vast quantity of new soil was imported into the park to remodel the topography into a rolling terrain of hills and dales. As a next step, five million trees, shrubs, and vines were ordered from commercial nurseries or propagated in the two nurseries set up within the park to cultivate seedling plants. To fertilize planting beds, the park's maintenance force composted horse manure on site.

During this time the park was like a giant quarry, for much of its building material was chopped out of the local Manhattan schist. Sometime when you are driving on one of the sunken transverse

Mall in construction, 1859

roads, look at the rough-hewn blocks of stone on either side, several
with grooves where cylinders of gunpowder were used to fracture the
parent rock; on your next walk in the Ramble or the Ravine in the
North Woods, observe how the waterfalls that punctuate the courses
of the Gill and the Loch cascade over great slabs of fragmented rock
and tumbled boulders placed in their streambeds; when you find your-
self standing by Turtle Pond at the south end of the Great Lawn, look
up at the Belvedere and study the way it is built of rusticated stone cut
and dressed from the identical coarse-grained metamorphic formation
as Vista Rock on which it stands; if you have occasion to stroll on the
sidewalks along Fifth Avenue, Central Park West, Fifty-Ninth Street,
or 110th Street, notice how the park perimeter's wall is constructed
from blocks cut from the park's very bedrock.

Thus was Central Park's hardscape constructed of locally derived
stone at the same time that its landscape was being dug, graded, and
sculpted into ponds, meadows, and hillocks. Here is how diarist
George Templeton Strong described the scene of the park in construction on June 11, 1859:

Improved the day by leaving Wall Street early with George Anthon
and Johnny to explore the Central Park, which will be a feature of the

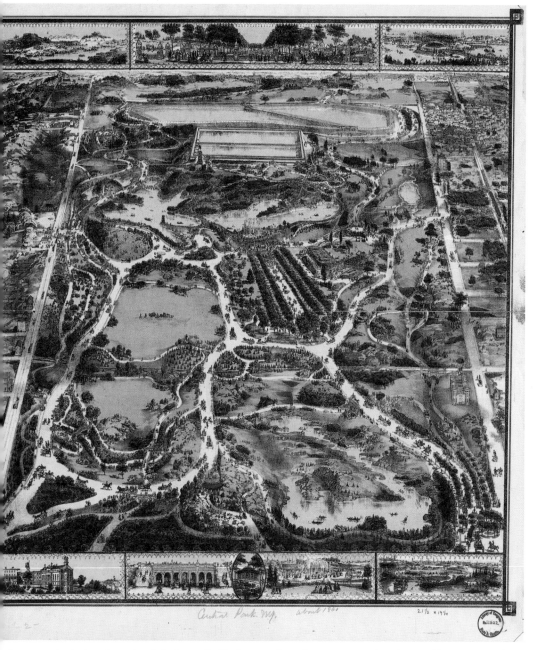

A perspectival view in 1860 of the lower half of Central Park as envisioned and partially constructed

city within five years and a lovely place in A.D. 1900, when its trees
will have acquired dignity and appreciable diameters. . . . Reached
the park a little before four, just as the red flag was hoisted—the signal for the blasts of the day. They were all around for some twenty
minutes, now booming far off in the north, now quite near, now
distant again, like a desultory "affair" between advanced posts of two
great armies.

As discussed above, what remained after the dynamite charges had
gone off was not ordinary rubble to be carted away, like the rocky
debris from the street-grading operations around the park, but rather
stone to be cut and dressed or hoisted, moved, and repositioned in
order to create the park's scenery and architectural structures.

Strong's diary entry continues:

We entered the park at Seventy-first Street, on its east side, and made
for the "Ramble," a patch just below the upper reservoir [the Old
Reservoir]. Its footpaths and plantations are finished, more or less,
and it is the first section of the ground that has been polished and
made presentable. It promises very well. So does the lower park,
though now in most ragged condition: long lines of incomplete
macadamization, "lakes" without water, mounds of compost, piles
of blasted stone, acres of what may be greensward hereafter but are
now brown earth; groves of slender young transplanted maples and
locusts, undecided between life and death with here and there an
arboricultural experiment that has failed utterly and is a mere broom-
stick with ramifications. Celts, caravans of dirt carts, derricks, steam
engines, these are the elements out of which our future Pleasaunce
is rapidly developing. The work is being pushed with vigor and system, and as far as it has gone, looks thorough and substantial. . . .
Narrowness is its chief drawback. One sees quite across this Rus in
Urbe at many points. This will be less felt as the trees grow. The tract
seems to have been judiciously laid out. Roads and paths twist about
in curves of artistic tortuosity. A broad avenue [the Mall], exceptionally straight . . . with a quadruple row of elms, will look Versailles-y
by A.D. 1950.

It is hard to envision the amount of sheer backbreaking labor that went into what Strong saw at the outset of the construction of Central Park, and few today realize that it is almost entirely a man-made creation. Think about it: sculpting the park's surface by moving hundreds of tons of rocks and earth, enriching poor soil with sufficient organic matter, procuring and installing the myriad plants necessary to revegetate it. Consider the channeling of artificial streams spilling over piled rocks to create waterfalls that flow into naturalistic ponds and lakes. Behold rolling meadows of green turf, beds of shrubs, carved stone arches, and cast-iron bridges. Observe how the Belvedere, the Dairy, and several rustic gazebos appear as integral elements within the general landscape rather than as a miscellany of structures superimposed upon it.

It is astonishing to learn that the building of Central Park was in large part completed within only fifteen years. Remember, too, that its construction was accomplished by horsepower and human brawn in the days before the advent of modern fuel-powered earth-moving and construction machinery. The revitalization of Central Park's management and the restoration of the spirit if not letter of its original design required an understanding of this stupendous accomplishment and close study of the park's original Greensward plan. Even as this analysis was under way, it was necessary to take steps to make visible the Conservancy's commitment to succeed.

First Priorities

The park's architectural heart, the Mall and its extension as Bethesda Terrace, was a central priority of the Conservancy from its inception. To repair the broken Terrace Fountain with its Angel of Bethesda sculptural centerpiece was for me, as indicated above, symbolic of our mission to heal the park. For this reason I chose as our young organization's logo an image of the fountain. My selection of this emblem was substantiated by a gift from the W. Alton Jones Foundation, which enabled the restoration of the Terrace and its eroded surrounding slopes at the same time that the renovation of the foun-

Children holding Conservancy flag with Bethesda Angel logo

tain was occurring thanks to the support of my early benefactor Lucy Moses.

A word about Mrs. Moses is due here. Over the years I was able to form lasting personal friendships with several Conservancy donors, but none was more important to me than hers. She ranks alongside Brooke Astor and Iphigene Sulzberger as one of the benefactors I continue to think of as my triumvirate of "Great Park Ladies." Their belief from the earliest days of the Task Force that another woman could reclaim the park from ruin should be recorded in the annals of Central Park's history.

There is an anecdote connected with the dedication of the restoration of Bethesda Fountain, so I will digress momentarily to say that Mrs. Moses—Lucy was so venerable a nonagenarian that I did not call her by her first name—lived to be 104, and in her latter years she was prone to lapses of memory. When I called on her one day to discuss how we should celebrate the completion of the project she had funded—repairs of the fountain's broken plumbing, cleaning of its stone basin and supporting cherub sculptures, and repatinating of the bronze Angel of Bethesda crowning it—I showed her a vintage postcard with a picture of a gondola on the Lake being rowed by a gondolier with the fountain in the background. "A gorgeous gondola!"

she exclaimed. "That's what we must have when we dedicate the fountain!"

Thinking no more about it, I was surprised a few days later when I received a call from Hedy Giusti-Lanham, a native of Venice and former director of the Italian Cultural Institute of New York. "Your troubles are over," she announced. "I have arranged for the two champion gondoliers from last year's regatta to row your gondola." It turned out that she had also called on Mrs. Moses after we had been fantasizing about being transported in a gondola across the Lake to the fountain for the dedication ceremony. She was no doubt surprised when I explained that we had no gondola, only rental rowboats on the Lake. But before telling Mrs. Moses that the whole notion

Horticultural intern wearing Conservancy T-shirt with Bethesda Fountain logo

was just an idle dream, I decided to call Henry Schneider, her lawyer and representative on the Conservancy's board, to see if she would fund the purchase and shipment of a gondola from Venice to New York. What a far-fetched idea that was and what a rigmarole ensued as we entered into negotiations with an Italian lawyer! But such was my affection for Mrs. Moses that I persevered, with the result that we were at last able to buy a gondola that had been retired from service on the canals of La Serenissima. It duly arrived and was docked at the Central Park Boathouse.

The fact that it was in need of considerable repair did not make it impossible for the two Venetian gondoliers, who had come over for the purpose, to row Mrs. Moses and me across the Lake on the day of the dedication. Beyond this extravagance, costs continued to mount— fortunately underwritten by Mrs. Moses—as the gondoliers were put up in a hotel for an extra week and a translator was hired in order for a Parks Department employee and a member of the Boathouse concessionaire's staff to receive instruction in the unfamiliar technique of standing upright while rowing backward and forward with a single thirty-six-foot-long oar resting in an elaborately shaped wooden

Betsy Rogers and Lucy Moses celebrating the restoration of Bethesda Fountain

oarlock called a *forcola*. The reward for the entire comedy of errors is knowing today that the Central Park gondola has witnessed countless marriage proposals as dating couples have taken romantic excursions on the Lake.

Beyond the restoration of Bethesda Fountain, Mrs. Moses's philanthropy extended to caring for the trees in Central Park. Her several gifts for this purpose enabled us to increase the size of the tree crew, which allowed us to provide the kind of systematic arboricultural care the park had not received in many years. One of its first tasks was to inspect the trees on the Mall for signs of Dutch elm disease, take laboratory samples of wood suspected of infection, and remove limbs, or in some cases whole trees, where the fungus spread by the elm-bark beetle had reached pathological proportions.

Our newly formed graffiti-removal crew had as its first assignment the elimination of the spray-painted moniker tags covering almost every square foot of the ornamental carving of the architecture of Bethesda Terrace—a task made especially difficult because the Terrace is built of relatively soft sandstone, a material that absorbs liquid to greater depth than a hard surface such as granite. Besides being defaced by graffiti, the panels of the staircases leading down to the level of the Terrace had been mutilated. Many of the sculpted birds that nested, perched, or flew amid their carved vines, flowers, and fruits had been decapitated, and the Terrace's retaining walls were being dislodged by the accumulated erosion debris that washed down from the surrounding slopes.

Studying historic paintings and engravings of the coping where the Terrace meets the Lake at the same time that the newly formed Conservancy restoration crew began cleaning and repairing it, I observed the elegant Venetian-style gonfalons—long fishtail banners—that once streamed on either side. The carved stone bases for the missing bronze stanchions were still there, and as we were removing the graffiti that obscured the ornamental beauty of the bases, I conceived the idea of refabricating the twenty-two-foot-high stanchions from which replicas of the original gonfalons could be hoisted aloft.

One might ask, why undertake such an icing-on-the-cake type of project when there was still such a lot of plain flour-and-yeast bread to bake throughout the park? I reasoned that if Bethesda Terrace was the park's centerpiece and the adopted symbol of its renaissance under the auspices of the Conservancy, then we should try to find a prospective donor to fund the refabrication and installation of these two grand exclamation points—one orange, bearing the seal of the City of New York, and the other green, with the logo of the Department of Parks—someone inclined to be as generous as Mrs. Moses had been in underwriting the renovation of Bethesda Fountain. Lawyer, real-estate investor, and philanthropist Lawrence Wien liked the uncon-

Venetian gondoliers rowing on Central Park Lake

Restored Bethesda Terrace with replicas of its original gonfalons

ventionality of our proposal, and through his generosity we were able to add replicas of the gonfalons as a finishing touch to the restoration of Bethesda Terrace.

As important as these strong signals of the reborn park were, a comprehensive management and restoration plan for the entire park of which they were a part was an even greater priority. But to think that the restoration of the twentieth-century park could reproduce with strict fidelity the appearance of the nineteenth was neither possible nor desirable. Strong as was my admiration of Olmsted and Vaux's original Greensward plan, I realized that historic landscape preservation does not mean reproducing in faithful detail designs of the past. Central Park's restoration was and remains an exercise in honoring the principles and spirit of the original plan while melding into its footprint as harmoniously as possible those elements that have altered it but should not be removed because they still serve the desires and needs of contemporary users.

Thus, in moving forward, it was important for the Conservancy to take into account the fact that the park is a layered landscape whose current appearance reflects the ethos of different periods as well as the random acts of history that gave it its contemporary form. And, as I was to learn, public taste and popular opinion have always governed the fate of Central Park.

Chapter Six

MULTIPLE LIVES

Reading the landscape of Central Park means looking backward through the telescope of time. Such an exercise is replete with stories of ideals and egos, approbation and vilification, good intentions and opportunistic exploitation.

Olden Days

The cultural climate animating the first era of Central Park's existence was expressed by the ideals of its original proponents and designers. Olmsted strongly believed that the pastoral beauty of the park would bring refinement and happiness to all the city's inhabitants. Summing up his philosophy, he wrote:

> It is not simply to give the people of the city an opportunity for getting fresh air and exercise . . . It is not simply to make a place of amusement or for the gratification of curiosity or for gaining knowledge. The main object and justification is simply to produce a certain influence in the minds of people and through this to make life in the city healthier and happier. The character of this influence is a poetic

one and it is to be produced by means of scenes, through which the mind may be more or less lifted out of moods and habits into which it is, under the ordinary conditions of life in the city, likely to fall.

The pride the city took in Central Park was evident in tourist guides of the period, and engravings and stereopticon photographs showing park scenery were widely sold. The enjoyment the public felt was reflected in the attendance records, and by 1872, the year its initial construction campaign ended, ten million people were counted as they entered by one of the twenty gates, which were named for social and occupational groups—Girls, Boys, Children, Women, Warriors, Inventors, Woodmen, Pioneers, Hunters, Artists, Artisans, Engineers, Naturalists, Scholars, Miners, Merchants, Mariners, Strangers, Farmers, All Saints. After entering the park, visitors discovered a geography defined by such names such as Kinderberg, Loch, and Dene.

Although the park would wear another face eventually, scenic recreation was its primary purpose in the beginning. The visitors who thronged there promenaded on the Mall, wended their way through the wooded Ramble, rode in carriages along the curving drives, cantered on horseback on the cinder bridle trail, and boated on the Lake. Besides these pleasant pastimes, there was one particularly popular activity that harked back to an earlier era. Throughout the eighteenth century, ice skating had been popular on the tidal channel that severed the tip of Manhattan from the rest of the island,[*] as well as on adjacent Collect Pond—which became optimistically known as Fresh Water Pond.[†]

---

[*] After the marsh through which the channel flowed was drained in order to create firm land, its subsistence spurred the digging of a forty-foot-wide, eight-foot-deep ditch for carrying off excess water. The ditch subsequently became an open sewer, and covering it over without air traps resulted in noxious air quality in the surrounding areas. With remedial renovation, in 1820 it became Canal Street, which, following its checkered history as an area known for rampant crime, became the lively thoroughfare that we know today.

[†] Forty-eight acres in surface area and sixty feet deep, Collect Pond was fed by an underground stream that served as the city's main water supply for two centuries, until it became too contaminated with wastes to be potable. After it was filled in, its bed of sediments proved to be an unstable foundation upon which to erect buildings, and the area remained unsanitary as well as unsavory in reputation.

A skating scene in Central Park by Currier and Ives

After 1811, when both the channel and the pond were filled in and repurposed as dry, albeit excessively boggy land for construction, that experience was only a dim memory. With the vigorous uptown growth of the city, there were soon no other water bodies large enough for winter skating. The creation of Central Park changed all that. The seemingly natural ponds and lakes provided smooth, hard ice, and the city's merchants were soon stocking quantities of skates as practically every able-bodied New Yorker took up the new craze. Indeed, in the early years more visitors were recorded in January than in July, a fact that can only be explained by the popularity of skating.

This idyll did not last long. Looking back a hundred years, one can see that the indifference to the preservation of the park's landscape that had predominated during the Lindsay administration in the 1960s and the financial disarray and inept management of the Beame period in the first half of the 1970s were an old story. Just as these more recent eras marred the park through wanton destruction, the shenanigans of Tammany Hall politicians a hundred years earlier left their marks of municipal corruption on its landscape. In 1868 Boss William Magear

Tweed's henchman A. Oakey Hall won the mayoralty contest, and another member of the Tweed ring, John T. Hoffman, became governor of New York State. Andrew Haswell Green, a member of the original Central Park Board of Commissioners and its comptroller of finances, was ignored and his office overridden as the park was turned into a sinkhole of patronage and graft. In 1870 Tweed drew up a new city charter that enlarged the opportunities for fraud by creating a Department of Public Works, of which he was appointed head. His crony Peter B. Sweeny was appointed president of the Department of Parks, the entity with which Tweed replaced the Central Park Board of Commissioners.

The ties between politicians and the building trades were blatantly dishonest. Every member of the Tweed ring had a brother, nephew, or friend ready to be enriched by a grossly inflated construction contract. Olmsted and Vaux's vision of the park as a quiet, rustic retreat was obviously at odds with Tweed's objective of filling it with superfluous public works that would be remunerative to cronies, contractors, and ward heelers.

Soon there was a plethora of make-work projects, including pruning trees into bare poles, grubbing out vines, and otherwise undoing many of the carefully conceived Romantic landscape effects that had been achieved by Olmsted, Vaux, and Pilát. Park Keepers, an independent park police force under Olmsted's supervision, was replaced by a cadre of political hacks. Fortunately for the park, however, Boss Tweed's reign was brief. Some members of the press not in his pay sensed scandal and mounted an attack that culminated in Tweed's trial for graft. The result was a hung jury, but a retrial sent him to jail, where he retained sufficient power to live in comfort until he could exert his influence to arrange an escape. His flight from prison took him to Cuba and eventually Spain. There he was tracked down, extradited, and returned to New York, where he was incarcerated until his death in 1878.

After Tweed's downfall, Olmsted and Vaux resumed their previous positions, but it was not easy remedying the amount of destruction the park had suffered. Fortunately, almost none of the grandiose buildings contemplated by the Tweed ring had been built, but the unnecessary grubbing up of plants had destroyed banks of shrubs, and the hard winter of 1871–72 had killed almost eight thousand trees. To make matters worse, the Tweed ring's graft had left the Parks Department badly in debt. Now, hampered by budgetary constraints and bickering among politicians over power and patronage, the design partners were understandably dismayed. Olmsted's irritation with the inadequate funding allotted for the park caused him to complain that "the Park is going to the devil and I have grave doubt whether a rural recreation ground in the midst of a city like this was not a mistake." But, in spite of his despair and frequent bouts of debilitating illness, he never ceased to believe in the therapeutic value of Central Park as a scenic counterpoint to the noise and stress of the rapidly expanding city.

Still, however much Olmsted may have wished to reassert his influence and burnish this tarnished ideal, he was hamstrung by the fact that Tweed had appropriated mayoral power over city property by politically engineering the passage by the New York State legislature of a home-rule city charter, thereby transferring the stewardship of Central Park from the original Board of Commissioners to a newly formed Department of Public Parks. In this situation Olmsted was allowed to retain the title of landscape architect with the duty of superintendence, and Vaux was appointed consulting landscape architect. As time went on, Olmsted's high-minded honesty and idealistic vision of the park as an as-yet-unfinished work of landscape art were increasingly troublesome to the new park administration, which performed its responsibilities according to "that form of tyranny known as influence and advice and that form of bribery known as patronage," as Olmsted wrote long afterward in an acerbic essay titled "Spoils of the Park." He was equally frank during the time he remained on the job in his criticism that there was now less attention paid to the needs of the park than to the jobs the park created. As a result, there were attempts to oust him, with one official declaring that his "position is merely a sinecure. We have to retrench somewhere and I think it would be infinitely better to cut off these high-toned fellows and help the poor laborers to work." Under these circumstances, and probably for personal reasons as well, the relationship between Olmsted and

Vaux became frayed, and in 1872 they decided for "reasons of mutual convenience" to dissolve their professional partnership.

Two years later, when Olmsted was forced to take a vacation on his doctor's orders, his office was summarily abolished. As a sop he was appointed the Parks Department's consulting architect, a title of practically no significance, since he was consulted infrequently. Green, a holdover commissioner from the park's prior administration, had previously antagonized Olmsted with his micromanagement of park finances and yet fought on his side. Now his civic weal and integrity counted for nothing, and he was out of office by 1876. Embittered, Olmsted left New York and in 1883 took up residence in Brookline, Massachusetts, where he established a private practice. With numerous commissions, he went on to build a firm that included his sons, who also helped found and nurture the profession of landscape architecture in America.

After Olmsted's departure, Vaux served as landscape architect to the Department of Public Parks from 1881 to 1883 and again from 1888 until his death in 1895. He was succeeded in 1898 by Samuel B. Parsons Jr., son of the Flushing nurseryman who had helped provide so many of the park's fine trees throughout the period of its construction. Although Olmsted and Vaux were gone and the Department of Public Parks was now an agency of city government and no longer under the authority of an independent board of commissioners solely accountable to the state of New York, Parsons was nevertheless able to perpetuate important elements of the original Greensward vision.

Trained as a landscape architect with a nurseryman's background, Parsons desired to make the park a botanical showcase for the many new species coming into cultivation at this time, an intention somewhat at odds with Olmsted's original Picturesque ideal. But in terms of routine maintenance protocols—removing dying trees (Dutch elm disease had by this time been identified as a blight); resoiling lawns; grubbing out invasive weeds; installing new drainage infrastructure; dredging silted ponds; resurfacing bridle trails with fresh gravel and drives with bitumen because of their increasing use by motorists; planting trees and shrubs; and even repairing and building new houses for squirrels—during Parsons's term of service as the department's official landscape architect, Central Park was still a well-managed landscape.*

Shifting Tastes

Although no longer being performed according to the Greensward plan's Picturesque principles, routine park management did not suffer unduly in the wake of Parsons's dismissal in 1911. But the Romantic ideal of scenic experience as its primary purpose was being superseded by an entirely new concept of what a park should be. Due to Progressive Era efforts to provide recreational opportunities for immigrant children, the Parks Department had an increasingly citywide focus. Several new "midget grounds"[†] with sand piles and swings were installed on the Lower East Side in order to give slum children an alternative to street life. Playgrounds for a wide range of games including baseball, volleyball, basketball, ring toss, shuffleboard, tag, croquet, jump rope, and folk dancing were built throughout the city and a cadre of municipal employees hired to organize recreational activities. This populist pulse naturally affected Central Park. As the park transitioned from sylvan retreat to recreational arena, its meadows began to accommodate organized sports such as lawn tennis and baseball.

---

* By way of example, according to the 1912 Parks Department Annual Report, "Three thousand creeping roses (*R. multiflora, R. wichuriana,* and *R. setigera*) were set out among the rocks on the promontory over the lake and on the steep banks at the upper end of the lake. Over 30,000 flowering shrubs of all the principal varieties were planted in this section of the park alone. . . . At the Harlem Meer from 106th Street north to 110th Street, and from 5th Avenue along 110th Street to Lenox Avenue, the lawn areas were seeded and enclosed in 6-foot wire mesh fence. A path was laid out between the north side of the Harlem Meer and the 110th Street wall north of the existing walk. . . . On the north shore of the Harlem Meer a dry rubble slope wall was built to protect the shore at this point. A quantity of additional shrubs and trees were planted in this area."

† This term was coined to signify grounds for small children, since the word "playground," as it was then used, referred to grounds for athletic activities. According to the 1914 Parks Department Annual Report, "New York's playgrounds contain about one hundred (100) baseball diamonds where the youngsters and young men can practice and play. The science of the game is easily acquired and comes as a natural instinct to the American boy."

Tennis on the East Meadow, circa 1900

Playground (now Heckscher Ballfields) with the Boys' Ballplayers House in the background, circa 1900

There was an increase in the orchestral concerts held in the music pavilion on the Mall, and the 1910 Parks Department budget allocated a handsome thirty thousand dollars for the 314 performances held that year. Unlike the band concerts of earlier days, these performances offered more than casual entertainment. Indeed, in his report the supervisor of music maintained that the orchestral music concerts on the Mall were a powerful acculturating influence, promoting "a popular musical civilization in New York surpassing, in breadth of horizon, that of any city of the old world."

The picture was not a completely rosy one, however. With words that sound all too familiar to those who saw the condition of Central Park in the 1970s, the 1913 annual report lamented that "the damage done during one season through vandalism is almost incredible. Trees planted in the spring are torn up by the roots, or the branches and even the trunk broken off before summer; shrubs newly set out are pulled to pieces to furnish switches for play. Bronze railings, decorative tablets, or fittings of any character are pried from fences, monuments or walks, apparently to be sold."* To overcome the problem of inadequate security, a company of "Auxiliary Boy Police" was formed in order to patrol defined districts within the park. Headquartered in an abandoned wooden structure adjacent to the Conservatory, they were given badges and written permits authorizing them to enforce Parks Department regulations. Not surprisingly, the boys were harassed by the vandals, thereby adding to, rather than eliminating, the woes of the park.

Memorial Grounds

During the same years that accommodation to physical recreation in Central Park was being made, the impulse to erect large memorials on

---

* The theft of the four bronze plaques from the pedestal of the Seventh Regiment statue, one from the statue of Simón Bolívar, and the ornamental decorations of the large horse-drinking fountain at Cherry Hill in the early twentieth century was paralleled by the same sort of market-driven vandalism that was occuring at the time of the formation of the Central Park Conservancy.

the perimeter gathered force. Earlier, when Beaux Arts–trained architect Richard Morris Hunt had drawn up a plan to erect a series of gates at park entrances, Olmsted had vociferously deplored the shift from a Picturesque aesthetic to one of neoclassical grandeur. The plan for the gates was abandoned, but in 1895, sensing that another battle of styles was at hand, Olmsted wrote to a friend, "Now I want you to take my assurance that there is a strenuous fight coming on between those of our side and those who are disposed to revise every body of public land that has been laid out with the object of transforming it as far as possible into a field of architectural beauty."

His words were prophetic. At the 1893 World's Columbian Exposition in Chicago, Daniel Burnham's plan for the fairgrounds popularized monumental urbanism, an inspirational spur to the City Beautiful movement. The neoclassical Beaux Arts style supplanted the Victorians' Queen Anne Gothic. Augustus Saint-Gaudens's 1903 equestrian monument to General William Tecumseh Sherman at Grand Army Plaza, the forepart of the Fifth Avenue and Fifty-Ninth Street Scholars' Gate entrance, is a conspicuous legacy of the City Beautiful era. Its similarly patriotic counterpart, located at the nexus of Eighth Avenue (Central Park West), Broadway, and Fifty-Ninth Street (now Columbus Circle), boasts the sixty-nine-foot-tall monument to Christopher Columbus. It is a column of granite with bronze reliefs surmounted by Gaetano Russo's 1892 Carrara marble statue of the Italian navigator, who according to legend is the "discoverer" of America.

The park's southwest corner entrance, named Merchants' Gate, is the site of H. Van Buren Magonigle and Attilio Piccirilli's grandiose 1913 *Maine* Monument, which was commissioned by newspaper editor William Randolph Hearst to honor the 260 American sailors who perished in 1898 when the USS *Maine* exploded while in harbor in Havana, Cuba. An example of the Beaux Arts style at its most baroque, it consists of a massive pylon with a fountain base surrounded by stone sculptures carved by the Italian-American sculptor Piccirilli. This imposing structure serves as a pedestal for a group of gilded cast-bronze figures representing Columbia Triumphant leading a seashell chariot of three sea horses.

When it came to architecture within the park proper, the Parks Department's 1914 Annual Report announced that preliminary plans for a new boat and skate house in Central Park had been drawn up "in a Spanish Mission style of architecture, constructed of terra cotta blocks, stuccoed, and a Spanish metal tile roof" to replace the deteriorating original nineteenth-century structure built of wood. Olmsted's notion of the park as a *rus in urbe* was also compromised by its use as a receptacle for numerous commemorative works of art. Although he vociferously opposed the placement of sculptures within it, it proved impossible to curb the popular desire to use the park as the venue of choice for this purpose. Among the numerous bronze memorials that found a home there during his lifetime were a bust of Johann Christoph Friedrich von Schiller by G. L. Richter (1859); three works by John Quincy Adams Ward—*William Shakespeare* (1864), *Indian Hunter* (1869), and the Seventh Regiment Civil War Monument (1874); Thomas Ball's thirty-foot-high memorial to Daniel Webster (1876); and Jeronimo Suñol's statue of Christopher Columbus (1892).

More egregiously, the park was increasingly viewed as a suitable site for a heterogeneous array of non-park uses. An 1892 proposal for a so-called speedway—a track for horse races—encircling the entire park was defeated only after prolonged controversy. However, this victory did not alter the fact that meadows and lawns continued to be looked upon as unencumbered open space ready to serve as sites for a plethora of encroachments. Now that the city's residential population was moving uptown, it was even suggested in 1904 that the park should be divided into building lots.

In 1910 an opera house and an aquatic facility with baths and pools were proposed; by 1911 the list included a checkerboard grid of paths to replace the original curvilinear circulation system, a huge outdoor stadium, and a playground for "noisy sports." During World War I a full-scale replica of the kind of trenches dug by troops before the 1916 Battle of Verdun was put forth as a publicity scheme for selling Third Liberty Loan war bonds. Other proposals included a landing field for aircraft, a central fire station, and a burial ground for war heroes.

While routine maintenance continued during this period, it was obvious that, with the complete loss of Olmsted and Vaux's vision of a scenic counterpoint to the surrounding urban bustle, the existence of the park qua park was in jeopardy. Fortunately, none of these proposals were realized. To preserve Central Park while at the same time radically transforming it according to a vision completely at odds with the Greensward plan would take the temperament of an autocrat.

Chapter Seven

POWER PLAYER

With the exception of Olmsted and Vaux, Robert Moses (1888–1981) has had greater impact on the physical outlines of Central Park than anyone else in its 150-year history. His authority, moreover, was exercised throughout New York City's five boroughs.

Robert Moses

Iron Fist

Immediately upon becoming parks commissioner on January 18, 1934, Moses issued a memorandum outlining the consolidation of the department. No more was there to be a commissioner, deputy commissioner, superintendent, chief engineer, and their attendant secretaries and stenographers for each of New York City's five boroughs. Now there would be only one commissioner—himself—one general superintendent, one consulting park engineer, one part-time consulting landscape architect, one part-time consulting architect, one secretary of the department, one assistant and a secretary to the commissioner, one chief park designer, and one senior park designer, all reporting directly to Moses.

To implement his vision for an entirely new park system, Moses would personally initiate and supervise every new project. His primary motive was to accelerate and institutionalize the growing trend toward *active* recreation with the construction of new facilities for games, sports, and supervised play. With an astute understanding of New Deal funding sources, he was quick to appropriate federal Works Progress Administration (WPA) funds to carry out new construction and revamp a workforce that he declared to be "undisciplined, in most instances working under untrained and unskilled supervision and with no orderly plan of operation," into one with definite lines of responsibility. To do so, he initiated a complete reform of Parks Department field management.

Now, according to the 1934 Parks Department Annual Report:

Unskilled laborers whose sole qualification for their jobs in the past have been their ability to lift a 50-pound weight over their heads are being replaced with laborer-gardeners drawn from the competitive class of the Municipal Civil Service. Climbers and pruners who were physically unfit to leave the ground are being replaced by expert arboriculturists. Playgrounds that were opened in the middle of the morning and closed in the middle of the afternoon are being operated from 9 o'clock in the morning until dark. This is a general rule applying to every playground in the Department. The 34 new playgrounds that are or will be opened before the end of the year are being equipped with floodlights to be operated at night. Comfort stations that were closed at the end of an eight-hour shift of a laborer are being manned by Civil Service attendants and kept open during the evenings. The employment of laborers in place of attendants for the operation of comfort stations is a violation of Civil Service Law. The work of rehabilitating these worn-out parks will be entirely wasted unless they are properly manned and operated with intelligence.

Since during the Great Depression numerous skilled gardeners on Long Island and Westchester County estates had been let go, Moses had no trouble finding men with the qualifications he sought. The same was true with trained architects and engineers, whose commissions for private-sector building construction had diminished seriously during the 1930s. To replace prior personnel in charge of design and construction within individual boroughs, he was able to create a hierarchy of technical employees with various job titles, whose citywide projects were to be approved by a consulting architect (Aymar Embury II), a consulting landscape architect (Gilmore D. Clarke), and consulting engineers. Funds for 453 of these new hires were provided through the New York State director of the federal Civil Works Administration. The staff that Moses assembled was derived from lists provided by the National Engineers Society, the Architectural League, the General Contracting Association, and the American Association of Landscape Architects. Significantly, senior personnel were assigned office space on the first floor of the Arsenal. This proximity to the commissioner's office on the third floor meant that all future park designs would be reviewed by Moses before construction approval was given.

Summing up his achievements during his first year in office, Moses proclaimed in the Parks Department 1934 Annual Report:[*]

The Department of Parks took over a dilapidated system of parks and parkways in the City, staffed with inefficient, undisciplined and

---

[*] The practice of publishing Parks Department annual reports was suspended after 1934 and replaced by issuing a constant stream of press releases during the course of the year.

untrained employees. The able employees in the staff were identified and placed in positions of responsibility commensurate with their abilities. Experts in park design and operation were employed at less than half the cost of the previous overhead administration. Unsafe and unsuitable construction was demolished and the rest rehabilitated. The staff was reorganized and those who did not fit into a scheme of good management were discharged. The 1935 departmental estimate is still lower than the period between 1929 and 1933. The playground areas have been doubled and 1,000 acres have been added to the park system. The season of 1934 was largely spent in correcting the mistakes and neglect of past administrations and in expanding the park system, and the operating season of 1935 will afford the first opportunity to the citizens of the City to use the new facilities and take advantage of its parks.

In spite of the high park maintenance standards and improved public service ethic Moses established, it is not hard to deplore his autocratic manner and ruthless efficiency. But the truth is that, in light of his times, which spanned the Great Depression and post–World War II years, his vision for the city's entire park system was enthusiastically welcomed. Whether poor during the 1930s or on the road to prosperity after the war, Americans wanted to have fun. With the shorter workweek, the word "leisure" came into common parlance. Moreover, it must be realized that Moses's social philosophy was both idealistic and pragmatic. He was a son of the reform movement called Progressivism, an outgrowth of the nineteenth-century crusade for improving the harsh lot of the poor. Charles Loring Brace, Olmsted's good friend from the days of his youth, can be counted as a pioneer of the humanitarian crusade through his efforts to place outcasts and orphans in "newsboys' lodging houses" and to send homeless children on "Orphan Trains" to live with farm families in the Midwest. This led to the campaign by early-twentieth-century women and men such as Jacob Riis, who were dedicated to replacing crowded, airless tenements with better housing and congested, dirty streets with open spaces for children's play. The Parks Department was a natural avenue for fostering this objective by converting vacant land into playgrounds, community recreation centers, and school farms. It is in this regard that we must look at the transformation of Central Park during the Moses years between 1934 and 1961, while adding this important caveat: Central Park was not vacant land but a landscape with already established forms of recreation and a historic design of signal beauty.

Total Transformation

Nowhere was Moses's radical new recreational agenda more immediately apparent than in Central Park. Clearly the park would no longer wear its old sylvan and pastoral face. The shorelines of lakes and ponds would be regularized by riprap embankments, asphalt paths increased in number and edged with concrete curbing, and concessions to motor vehicles made by realigning portions of the drives and supplanting certain conveniently located historic landscape features with parking lots.* In the future, all statuary would be commissioned or approved by Moses, and all of the encroachments onto the park's green acres would be initiated and implemented by him without outside review.

So far Central Park had been considered simply as a place for such activities as community singing and games and pageants held according to the season of the year. Popular winter activities such as ice-skating and sledding and the temporary use of meadows as sites for lawn tennis took place without much impact on the landscape. Now, in addition to providing numerous new parks and playgrounds on the Lower East Side and elsewhere throughout the city, Moses fostered the growing trend toward active recreation by converting many parts of Central Park's multiuse landscape into playgrounds and other single-purpose recreation facilities, including three sets of ball fields with several diamonds each and two ice-skating rinks, one doubling as a swimming pool in the summer.

Such public benefactions provided a new way of life for a grateful

---

* An early project of the Central Park Conservancy was to convert the carriage turn-around at the top of Cherry Hill from a parking lot back into its original form, with the restoration of its soft-surface paving and ornamental horse-drinking fountain.

populace. Since the master builder was also a master of public relations, newspaper stories trumpeted his success in bringing good times to the people of New York City. On November 23, 1934, Moses announced that "the building of the new Zoo in Central Park, which replaces the former jangle of unsightly firetraps that had stood for sixty-four years," was to be dedicated the following week. The program for the dedication ceremony, with Mayor Fiorello La Guardia and former governor Alfred Smith in attendance along with the chairman of the Temporary Emergency Relief Administration of New York State and the city's commissioner of the Department of Public Welfare, was described in another press release, which did not fail to mention that the new zoo had been constructed entirely by Work Relief forces with material supplied by the Department of Welfare.

In his prepared address for delivery at the ceremony on December 2, Mayor La Guardia recounted the history of the old zoo with its ornamental buildings, one for carnivores and one for birds and monkeys; sheds for bears, wolves, and other large mammals; open-air cages for eagles, domestic fowls, and other avian species; and enclosed structures for elephants, camels, and various tropical animals. Detailing their defects, he continued:

> The light was poor and they were unsanitary firetraps. The Monkey House had been converted into a hot dog stand and the bear dens perched on the side of a rock outcropping. There was no orderly arrangement or supervision of animals. The hippopotami shared the same quarters with the lions.

Moses had demolished all of these decrepit wooden structures, and the new zoo (the one that many visitors today call the old zoo and still remember from before it was put under the management of the Wildlife Conservation Society, rebuilt, and reopened in 1988) was constructed from masonry. It had been designed by Aymar Embury II, with the assistance of the staff of architects of the Parks Department. Its exterior walls were made of brick and adorned with sculptural limestone friezes depicting various animals. Tile-covered interior walls made the cages easier to clean.

One of eighteen playgrounds built around the park's perimeter in 1934

The reconstruction of the old zoo was only one of the many projects accomplished in Moses's whirlwind year of 1934. Significantly, in Central Park twenty fence-encircled playgrounds had also materialized. The eighteen around the park's perimeter had large sandboxes—"places where children can dig," as Moses characterized these then-novel features—slides, swings, and gymnastic paraphernalia. In total, including the preexisting Heckscher Playground in the park's south end, the park now boasted twenty-one playgrounds. Enthusiastically adopted by mothers and children, they were touted by Moses as a way to preserve the surrounding scenery. To further discourage romping on the grass, he encircled lawns with pipe-rail fencing, posted "Keep Off the Grass" signs, and made infractions punishable by fine.

There was no public review process in those days to discuss the appropriateness of Moses's incursions on the park's landscape. His authority to overwrite the historic Greensward plan in whatever way he wished was unquestioned. Moreover, park structures that today would be protected as architectural landmarks were in Moses's eye

The Casino, early 1900s

obsolete, and he promptly quelled any voices raised in opposition to their demolition.

Such was the case in 1936 when he proposed to tear down Calvert Vaux's 1862 Casino, originally called the Ladies Refreshment Salon, in order to build a playground for older children in the interior of the park. A popular eatery in the nineteenth century, by the 1920s it had been converted into a nightclub patronized by the Tammany Hall–supported New York City mayor, playboy, and songwriter James J. ("Gentleman" Jimmy) Walker. Capitalizing on the unsavory reputation of this Casino habitué (Walker had been thrown out of office in 1932 on charges of graft), Moses was probably right in characterizing the restaurant as an elite establishment no longer in keeping with the purposes of the park. However, according to many people at that time and now, he was wrong in maintaining that the Casino could not be restored as a regular food service and that its site could be better used as an interior playground to supplement the numerous outdoor ones he had already constructed around the perimeter of the park.

Such was the view of those who still had fond memories of the old pre-nightclub Casino and did not want to see the historic building torn down. Firmly gripping the reins of power, Moses answered their letters of protest with alacrity and arrogance. To Mrs. Lionel Sutro's proposal that the Casino should be used as a sheltered indoor play space for children, he responded: "The building is a white elephant and is of no use for legitimate park purposes." Others wondered why Moses did not simply get a new concessionaire to run a remodeled, less exclusive dining facility. Mrs. Donald McIntosh pleaded, "Surely you, Commissioner, you who have such outstanding ability, such understanding of the peoples' needs, must realize too the needs of the 'in-betweens.' The very rich, the socially prominent are always safe—for those who haven't the entrée to smart clubs but who do enjoy gracious living the Casino provides an escape into that gracious world." But Moses, who had recently converted the sheepfold that housed the flock he had removed from the Sheep Meadow into a restaurant he christened Tavern on the Green, replied: "I am convinced that no restaurant is required in this place, that none could be operated successfully, and that the proper use for this area is for a playground for children of the group between the very small ones for whom we are providing new playgrounds at the outskirts of the park and the larger ones who play in the Mall and elsewhere."

Iphigene Ochs Sulzberger of the *New York Times* newspaper dynasty, who much later became an early supporter of the Central Park Conservancy, was at that time president of the Parks Association. But even she could not reason with the strong-willed commissioner when she wrote on behalf of that respected civic organization:

Sheep grazing on Sheep Meadow, circa 1902

I know comparatively small acreage in Central Park is set aside for playgrounds, but I do not think that to say all the rest is for adults, answers the problem of the old people and the invalids. I believe I know Central Park very well, and the only section I can recall which fills this need is a part of the Ramble and a small section around the 59th Street Lake. The Casino site is somewhat off the beaten path and being elevated, would make a delightful retreat [for them].

Moses turned a deaf ear, and the Casino was demolished and replaced by a playground bearing the name of philanthropist Mary Harriman Rumsey, sister of Averell Harriman, who was a Democratic party politician, wealthy scion of a railroad baron, future governor of New York State, and a man whose political support Moses cultivated assiduously.

Thus it became increasingly clear that Moses was determined to give over as much of Central Park as possible to a series of facilities designed for specific constituencies and to demolish whatever historic park structures and multipurpose landscapes impinged on this goal.

The Great Lawn as viewed from the Belvedere, 1936

Using the royal, first-person-plural pronoun, he proclaimed: "We are providing [fields in the south end of the park] for soft ball playing and others for hard ball in the area to the north. There will be two diamonds for regular baseball. We have provided additional baseball fields in the North Meadow . . . and there will be more good facilities for baseball playing in the park today than ever before." A horse stable next to the North Meadow ball fields was converted into a recreation center. The crest of the Great Hill was encircled with a wide path for roller-skating. Inside this asphalt ring, hard sand courts for roque, a version of croquet, were laid out, and wickets for regular croquet were set up on nearby lawns.

The Old Reservoir between the Seventy-Ninth and Eighty-Sixth Street Transverse Roads that predated the park's creation had been drained in 1931 when a new water tunnel made it obsolete. The American Society of Landscape Architects' previous design to turn the site into what is now the Great Lawn was carried out in 1936, with only modest modification by Moses's appointed landscape architect, Gilmore Clarke. Although the teams that enjoy this popular sports amenity today would not concur, Clarke was understandably dismayed when Moses decided to convert the smooth grass inside his encircling oval path into nine ball fields.

Not surprisingly, the remaining remnant of the now-filled-in Old Reservoir between the north end of Great Lawn's oval path and the Eighty-Sixth Street Transverse Road received a symmetrical pair of circular playgrounds. The one at the northwest side of what is now a narrow rectangular strip of parkland occupied by the Arthur Ross Pinetum had a wading pool, seesaws, swings, and a jungle gym, whereas the other leftover undesignated piece next to the Great Lawn's northeastern perimeter was furnished with basketball courts and an encircling roller-skating track intended to serve teenagers.

Vaux's stable fronting the Eighty-Sixth Street Transverse Road was divided into a shop for repairs and a police station from which the officers who enforced Moses's rules were deployed. At Fifth Avenue and 104th Street, Moses tore down the 1899 Conservatory and had the surrounding six acres transformed into the Conservatory Garden. As with the Great Lawn, Beaux Arts symmetry prevailed. A central lawn

Conservatory Garden in construction

bordered by allées of crabapple trees was terminated by a fountain jet, behind which semicircular hedges rose in tiers to a terrace crowned with a wrought-iron wisteria pergola. A circular garden to the north with formal beds for seasonal display was balanced by an English-style garden of flowering shrubs and perennials to the south. In 1936 Bessie Potter Vonnoh's fountain sculpture of Mary and Dickon, the protagonists in Frances Hodgson Burnett's well-loved children's story *The Secret Garden,* was installed in the south garden's center pool. In 1947 another fountain featuring jets of water splashing on a bronze sculpture of three dancing maidens was placed in the pool in the north garden.[*]

During the 1940s, federal funds that Moses had used so adroitly to help finance these and other park projects throughout the city were directed toward the war effort. However, within the limits of the city budget, Parks Department employees were able to undertake a number of routine maintenance operations and perform small capital projects intended to enhance security, increase safety, and augment

---

[*] Known today as the Untermyer Fountain, it was originally created in 1910 for the Samuel Untermyer Gardens in Yonkers by sculptor Walter Schott.

*Frances Hodgston Burnett Fountain by
Bessie Potter Vonnah, Conservatory Garden*

automobile access. These included the reseeding of lawns, the repaving of asphalt paths and parking lots, and the repair of broken benches and lights.

After the war years many more elements of the park's historic plan continued to be sacrificed with impunity. Nature lovers protested the destruction of its picturesque and pastoral elements, but the architects, landscape architects, and engineers working under Moses's direction did not heed the objections of these early park preservationists. In realigning park roadways in 1941 for the convenience of automobile traffic, Marble Arch—the below-grade pedestrian passageway beneath the East Drive at Sixty-Fifth Street and the south end of the Mall—was buried. On the heights above the Meer, in the areas surrounding the forts built during the American Revolution and reinforced by militiamen at the onset of the War of 1812, flagpoles, pavement, and benches were substituted for trees.

A skilled fund-raiser, Moses found time to take walks in Central Park with Judge Samuel J. Harris, the lawyer for Kate Wollman and principal trustee of the William J. Wollman Foundation, named in honor of the brother whose fortune Miss Wollman had inherited. To replace the tradition of skating on the natural ice of the Lake and Pond, Moses, with the help of his friend the judge, persuaded Miss Wollman to give $600,000 toward the $800,000 cost of building an ice-skating rink over the northern lobe of the pond.

Most of the capital projects Moses had so far undertaken in Central Park had received generally favorable press, but not everyone welcomed this latest initiative. In an article in *The New Yorker* written at the time of the opening of Wollman Rink in 1949, Lewis Mumford, the most eminent architectural critic of the day, complained:

> H. G. Wells once described Sidney Webb, the trenchant British bureaucrat, as the kind of person who would hack down growing trees and substitute sanitary green glass umbrellas. There is someone in the planning office of our Parks Department whose mind works the same way. Even in a romantic setting, he favors firm, manmade boundaries—iron fences, concrete curbs, heavy wooden barriers,

Wollman Rink, December 1950

devices that Olmsted and his architect-partner, Calvert Vaux, except in such formal layouts as the Mall, did their best to avoid. As for the borders of the lake, instead of planting them thickly with sedge and iris, the Parks Department designer has tried to combine beauty with ease of maintenance by planting them, too, with slabs of stone. The result is damnably neat, but that is about all, for the wide, asphalted paths and stone embankments completely counteract the natural loveliness of the landscape.

Fun Time

Throughout the 1950s Moses combined private philanthropic dollars with city appropriations to build other projects in Central Park: small buildings for concessionaires, more playgrounds, and comfort stations. He adroitly steered prospective donors toward the kind of sculpture and architecture he liked and told artists and designers exactly what he wanted: playful statues and sound, functional, conservatively designed modern structures with touches of whimsy. Aymar Embury, his architectural consultant, was the principal author of this style of disciplined playfulness. His buildings, unlike the rustic wooden structures they replaced, were as sturdy and vandal-proof as the house of the wisest of the Three Little Pigs. Their exterior walls were of red brick patterned with bands of white limestone; their floors were polygonal in plan; and their roofs were almost invariably topped with cupolas.

In 1950 a fire destroyed the Carousel, a longtime favorite park concession. Moses soon located a handsome, forty-year-old Coney Island carousel with horses carved of applewood by the noted Brooklyn carousel makers Sol Stein and Harry Goldstein. He had a new motor installed and used a two-thousand-dollar philanthropic gift to purchase a Wurlitzer band organ. The Parks Department's director of mechanical maintenance oversaw the repainting of the carousel's fifty-seven prancing steeds in what he called "real horsy colors." Moses then obtained another gift from the Michael Friedsam Foundation to erect the brick-and-limestone-striped octagonal building that houses the restored carousel, still one of the park's most popular attractions.

Historic rustic summerhouse

Chess and Checkers House

Next Moses turned to the financier, presidential adviser, and statesman Bernard Baruch (1870–1965), whose favorite spot for discussing
governmental affairs was a bench in Central Park. This time he was
seeking funding for the Chess and Checkers House that he wished to
erect on the site of the largest and most elaborate of the park's rustic
summerhouses. Shorn of its wooden Victorian loggia, the adjacent
Dairy, one of Vaux's original buildings, was converted into a storage
depot for workers' tools and other supplies.

In 1954, when Jeanne Kerbs, who lived in an apartment house overlooking the Conservatory Water near Fifth Avenue at Seventy-Fourth

Mineral Springs Pavilion, 1890s

Street, wished to memorialize her parents, Moses solicited her dona-
tion for the construction of a boathouse for model yachts. Relatively
small in scale, this typical Moses building has brick walls with limestone quoins and a steeply pitched, gently curving hip roof of cop-
per crowned by an elongated cupola. Also in 1954, in order to replace
the original wooden boathouse on the northeast arm of the Lake, the
energetic commissioner successfully sought construction funds from
investment banker Carl M. Loeb, who donated $250,000, almost the
entire amount needed. In 1957 Moses demolished the original Mineral

Springs Pavilion at the northwest corner of Sheep Meadow, replacing it with another concession structure built according to his standard design paradigm.

During Moses's administration, sculptures continued to accumulate in the park, but instead of commemorating figures in military, literary, and political history, they were in large measure based on children's books. In 1938 Moses used WPA funds to erect a granite statue of Mother Goose by Frederick Roth next to the Rumsey Playground. The statue's bas-relief base depicts Little Jack Horner, Humpty Dumpty, and Little Bo Peep. Additionally, near the entrance to the Heckscher Playground in the south end of the park, Moses placed a granite drinking fountain decorated with bas-reliefs of characters from *Alice in Wonderland*.* Dedicated as a memorial to social worker Sophie Irene Loeb (1876–1929), it was relocated to the playground near the Fifth Avenue and Seventy-Sixth Street park entrance by the Central Park Conservancy during the playground's restoration in memory of James Michael Levin. In 1937 Moses had a playful pair of life-size bronzes, *Dancing Bear* and *Dancing Goat,* also by Roth, installed at the entrance to the zoo he had built three years earlier. In 1953 he accepted a gift of $75,000 raised by the Danish-American Women's Association for a bronze statue of Hans Christian Andersen by Georg Lober. Dedicated in 1956 and placed on the west side of the Conservatory Water opposite the Kerbs Model Yacht Boathouse, the sculpture of the storyteller depicts the Ugly Duckling advancing toward the larger-than-life-size bronze figure of the genial author, dressed in a frock coat and seated with an open book in his lap. His knees and the invitingly spread pages of his book gleam where generations of climbing children have polished their surface to the same high gloss as that of a shiny new penny.

The northern end of the Conservatory Water received José de Creeft's *Alice in Wonderland,* given in 1959 by George T. Delacorte, the millionaire founder of the Dell Publishing Company, in memory of his wife, Margarita. The March Hare, Mad Hatter, and Dormouse

---

* Like the Tennis House and North Meadow Recreation Center, which were built in 1930, the Heckscher Playground, built in 1927, was created prior to Moses's appointment as parks commissioner.

crowding around Alice, who is enthroned on a huge mushroom, resemble those in John Tenniel's illustrations for the original edition of Lewis Carroll's famous book. However, the Mad Hatter possesses Delacorte's features, and Alice is thought to resemble de Creeft's daughter Maria. Although at least one art critic characterized Moses's taste in public art as puerile, the bright luster of the surfaces of the bronze mushroom and Alice's outstretched arms and fingers testifies to the perennial popularity of the statue.

In 1952 a memorial playground honoring William Church Osborn (1862–1951), a former president of the Metropolitan Museum of Art, was built at Fifth Avenue and Eighty-Fourth Street. Sculptor Paul Manship designed its handsome bronze entrance gates, which depict the Tortoise and Hare and the Wolf and Lamb, along with other animals from *Aesop's Fables*. The gates were removed when the playground was demolished in 1978 to make way for the addition to the Metropolitan Museum that now houses the Temple of Dendur. Recently cleaned and repaired by the Central Park Conservancy, they have been installed at the entrance to the Ancient Playground at Fifth Avenue and Eighty-Fifth Street.

In 1957 the Irving and Estelle Levy Foundation provided funds for

Dedication of Alice in Wonderland *sculpture by José de Creeft in 1959*

a small rectangular playground to be built south of the Metropolitan Museum near the Seventy-Ninth Street Transverse Road. Like the Osborn Playground, it was furnished with standard play equipment—swings, slide, seesaws, sandbox—and it was entered through specially commissioned, animal-ornamented bronze gates designed by sculptor A. Walter Beretta and architect John Wilson. When the playground was replaced in 1990 by the Pat Hoffman Friedman Playground, situated closer to Fifth Avenue, the Levy gates were integrated into its design, along with Conservancy donor Samuel Friedman's gift of Manship's 1960 *Group of Bears*.

In 1961, just north of the Central Park Zoo, Moses sought to build a children's zoo in which live animals could be penned and petted. This time he encouraged Governor Smith's successor, Herbert H. Lehman, and his wife, Edith, to underwrite the project in honor of their fiftieth anniversary. The resulting design was a juvenile stage set containing such appurtenances as a large plaster whale and a candy-colored Hansel and Gretel witch's cottage. Here Manship's entrance gates, depicting a youth dancing to the music of panpipes, were of incomparably higher artistic quality than the theme-park-like exhibits.[*]

Protestors' Voices

By the mid-1950s neither Moses's arrogant sarcasm nor his political power was enough to mute the voices of those who could no longer tolerate his autocratic style. The unchallenged authority he had enjoyed for so long began to erode. Nascent environmental and historic-preservation organizations attacked his preference for facilities over scenery. Civic organizations such as the Parks Association, which had raised objections to projects such as the Rumsey Playground with polite diffidence in the 1930s, now called the recreational projects Moses continued to add to Central Park egregious encroachments.

The Ramble proved to be the field where opponents fought their first major battle in 1955. The thirty-eight-acre woodland was weedy

---

[*] When the Lehman zoo was redesigned in 1996 after it was put under the management of the Wildlife Conservation Society, the gates were retained.

and eroded because of lack of maintenance, and its proposed reland-
scaping was to be accomplished with $200,000 from the city budget.
Following prevailing Parks Department design guidelines, some paths
were repaved and lined with London plane trees, standard construction elements such as pipe railings and concrete retaining walls were
installed, and a parking lot was built beside the East Drive. However,
when Moses sought to fence the area to exclude "anti-social persons,"
by which he meant the men who frequented this well-established gay
cruising area, he discovered that the Ramble had another constituency
that had to be taken into account—birdwatchers. The Linnaean Society, which prized the area as an important stopover for migrant species,
assembled enough political backing to quash the plan to tear out the
trees and shrubs that provided privacy for the gay men frequenting the
Ramble's bosky hollows while at the same time serving as an important
source of food and shelter for birds. Unsuccessful in his typical ploy of
countering opposition with dismissive contempt, Moses decreed that
serious birdwatchers would be allowed to enter in the early morning
hours and other "orderly adults" throughout the day.

Things came to a head when the newspapers announced that Moses
wished to build an "Oldsters Center" in the Ramble for persons over
fifty-five. Equipped with a food bar and rooms for TV and music, the
building and its adjacent lawn, which was to be furnished with chess-
and-checkers tables and areas for horseshoe pitching, croquet, and
shuffleboard, would completely transform the woodland character of
the Ramble. The center was to be funded with a gift of $250,000 from
the Albert and Mary Lasker Foundation in honor of Albert's sister,
social worker Fiorina Lasker. But, perceiving a lack of support from
the press and the strength of the political forces against him, Moses
dropped the project.*

An even more contentious issue arose in 1956. Always interested
in making the park more convenient for motorists, Moses wished to
add eighty spaces to the existing parking lot at Tavern on the Green.
A group of mothers whose children frequented the playground on

---

* In 1961 the Lasker gift was redirected to the construction of the ice-skating rink–cum–
swimming pool imposed insensitively on the mouth of the Loch, the little stream that
courses through the Ravine before emptying into the Harlem Meer.

the site got wind of his plans. On April 20 they angrily tried to stop the bulldozer operators who were beginning to clear vegetation. Two days later they received the backing of the Citizens Union. Undeterred, Moses denied the mothers' request for a public hearing and, as a sop, offered their children the right to roller-skate on the proposed parking lot before 5:00 p.m. On April 25, when the women arrived to protest, they found thirty workmen and twenty-five policemen with orders to restrain them from entering the area, which had been cordoned off overnight with snow fencing. The press, which for years had been in thrall to Moses's powerful public-relations machinery, saw mothers marching in front of bulldozers as more than good copy: this was a story that showed that the parks hero they had formerly lauded had feet of clay. The April 26 *New York Times* revealed that "Commissioner Moses, though he did not personally supervise operations, commanded [workers equipped with] one bulldozer, one power shovel, two dump trucks, pneumatic drills, charges of dynamite, gasoline chain saws, pickaxes, shovels, axes, hatchets, and ropes" to clear the site. As one workman finished hacking down a tree, a mother was forcibly restrained by a policeman, other women wept, and photographers took pictures of the scene. In spite of the fact that Moses brushed off the controversy as an inconsequential flap over a mere half-acre and a few trees, the publicity he received went from bad to worse. The mothers opposing him were better connected than the poor people he had displaced elsewhere in city slum-clearance projects. They had lawyer friends help them obtain an injunction to halt work pending a judicial hearing.

While Moses was on vacation, the opposition swelled. More reasons were found to oppose his heretofore unassailable authority over all parkland—authority he had helped to write into the city charter. Echoing Moses's own rationales for proposing the removal of the Casino in 1937, opponents argued that Tavern on the Green was a pricey restaurant that average park visitors could not afford to patronize. Moreover, parking spaces that benefited a private concessionaire were a questionable use of public parkland. A taxpayers' suit was filed. When Moses returned from his holiday, he learned that the city's corporation counsel, Peter Campbell Brown, had worked out an arrangement with the mothers' attorney, Louis N. Field, to delay the case until the furor had subsided and Moses could announce that he was building a playground instead of a parking lot on the site. On July 18 the *Times* ran a story under the headline "Moses Yields to Mothers After Litigation," quoting Field's winner's compliment: "Bob Moses has gone overboard and is going all out to do the right thing." But the public-relations debacle caused by the commissioner's initial intransigence was a blow from which his image as a great park builder never recovered.

Two other authority-undermining skirmishes lay ahead. In 1954 Moses had allowed Joseph Papp, founder of the New York Shakespeare Festival, to hold performances in the park, but after agreeing to support the construction of a permanent summer theater, he subsequently backed away. Stuart Constable, the man whom Moses had appointed as the executive director of the Parks Department, started a smear campaign based on Papp's suspected communism. (Papp had earlier refused to testify at a hearing by the Committee on Un-American Activities of the House of Representatives.) Moses felt compelled to support Constable, and he now tried to block the project through a series of bureaucratic and budgetary maneuvers designed to make the theater, which he had originally been willing to fund with city money, unaffordable for Papp's shoestring organization.

Papp, a child of the slums, was a skilled street fighter with a passionately democratic artistic vision: free Shakespeare. He was able to garner extraordinarily favorable press and, like the playground mothers, took Moses to court. Philanthropist George Delacorte decided to come to the rescue, and litigation was averted with the acceptance of his unsolicited gift of $150,000, the balance needed to supplement the $225,000 appropriation that had previously been approved by the New York City Board of Estimate. On June 18, 1962, the new 2,500-seat, outdoor Delacorte Theater, situated beside Belvedere Lake (today called Turtle Pond), opened with a benefit production of *The Merchant of Venice*. The funds collected were dedicated to support the rest of the summer's free performances. Papp declared the event a people's victory, and Mayor Robert F. Wagner Jr. praised Papp's persistence.

In 1960 Moses made his last stand in Central Park in defense of a proposed gift from Huntington Hartford, the A&P supermarket heir.

Hartford wanted to build a café in the southeast corner of the park, and Moses agreed to accept architect Edward Durell Stone's flat-roofed, two-story concrete structure with sliding glass doors facing the Pond. Intended to serve five hundred diners, it was 240 feet long by 40 feet wide. Four civic organizations protested, but Moses reminded them that the city charter gave the parks commissioner the authority to accept gifts without the approval of any other city official. At the same time, Walter Hoving, chairman of Tiffany's and father of the future parks commissioner Thomas Hoving, together with a group of fellow merchants, filed a lawsuit protesting this park encroachment. Giving voice to the growing notion that Moses was unduly autocratic, Hoving declared: "Some officials in office a long time seem to get a sovereignty complex . . . Not only do they feel they know better than the rest of us taxpayers, but they ride roughshod sometimes, notably Robert Moses, whose fine work for many years I have applauded, but whose habitual arrogance, particularly in this situation, I decry."

By this time Moses was on the verge of retiring as parks commissioner in order to serve as head of the corporation established to build and operate the 1964 World's Fair in Flushing Meadows Park. New-bold Morris, whom he appointed as his successor, was left to deal with the resolution of the café fight. The Court of Appeals, which had long upheld the authority over all parks-related matters given to the parks commissioner by the city charter, did not do so now. On April 27, 1962, it handed down an affirmative verdict for the prosecution that marked a victory for citizen protection of the park as a scenic landscape and the beginning of the era of its historic preservation. This legal opinion was reinforced by the park's designation as a National Historic Landmark in 1964, followed by its classification as a scenic landmark by the New York City Landmarks Commission in 1974, and its listing on the National Register in 1975.

By the mid-1970s, when I became involved with the fortunes of Central Park following the era of Robert Moses, the Greensward plan was only a distant memory. As the Conservancy's mission for restoring the park as a single entity according to Olmstedian principles got under way in the 1980s, it was clear that Moses's recreational facilities were not inherently sympathetic with this goal. However, because of their popularity, no one, including me, would have dreamed of removing them. The Conservancy's restoration planners were there-fore presented with a demanding challenge: to integrate Moses's radi-cal interventions within the framework of a holistic design in which the protection and enhancement of unencroached-upon open space and naturalistic scenery were paramount objectives.

Chapter Eight

LEARNING CURVE

W hat constitutes success? My mother, who was always ambitious for her children to attain public recognition or social status, told me more than once, "You have to look the part if you are to be successful." Although I did try to always look my best, I knew that there was more to it than a great hairstyle and fashionable clothes.

Game Plan?

Someone recently asked me, "What was your game plan?" With an amazed jaw-drop, I replied, "Game plan? It was just a matter of putting one foot in front of the other." Although I was sometimes lacking in diplomacy and political acumen, I was never short of a fervent and articulate vision for a reborn Central Park that was based not so much on a *game* plan as it was on a *physical* plan, the need for which I had grasped from my earliest Central Park Task Force days. Upon taking office as park administrator, I had known that the Conservancy should have a plan for rebuilding the entire park, not merely the restoration project agenda I had put forth in my 1976 *New York* magazine piece.

Encouraged by the board, I was able to raise $500,000 to undertake this three-year effort.

With my degree in city planning as a credential, I turned away offers by outside firms proffering their professional services to prepare a master plan. Instead, I picked four landscape architects with park-design experience—Marianne Cramer, Judith Heintz, Bruce Kelly, and Philip Winslow—to work in concert under my direction. We agreed that the plan should include management strategies as well as restoration projects. One of the advantages of doing the work in-house was our ability to include maintenance staff in meetings. We therefore dropped the term "master plan" and always referred to our program to rebuild Central Park as a "management and restoration plan."

My staff and I, along with outside consultants, would study the park in its entirety in a way that it had not been studied since 1858, when Olmsted and Vaux had won the design competition for Central Park. This meant poring over their pen-and-ink drawings of the Greensward plan hanging in the third-floor conference room in the Arsenal and reviewing all the annual reports of the Central Park Board of Commissioners dating from the park's inception in 1858 until 1872, when its construction was substantially complete. It also meant unearthing in the New York City Municipal Archives a treasure trove of archival images. These consisted of plans, elevations, perspective drawings, and maps, including ones for the park's drainage and water-supply infrastructure. Of special interest were architectural renderings of the Belvedere, Bethesda Terrace, and the park's handsome stone arches, all works by Calvert Vaux. Depictions of ornamental cast-iron bridges along with vanished structures such as the Ballplayers House and the Music and Mineral Springs Pavilions helped us to visualize the park in its original state.

We next outlined the preliminary items of data collection necessary to move forward. Among these was a survey of existing vegetation by a group of horticultural graduate students who recorded the species, age, size, and condition of the park's twenty-six thousand trees and identified and mapped all of its existing shrubs and groundcovers. The planners then prepared graphic documents depicting eroded areas, "desire lines"—off-path dirt trails established by irregular foot traffic—and the extent of the current tree canopy as compared with the historic one.

In addition, we hired outside consultants with expertise in specific areas. These included a soil scientist, a hydrologist, an architect to assess the condition of park structures, and an urban sociologist to survey visitor demographics. Of particular importance was the study and mapping of the existing circulation system, including the bridle trail, carriage drives, paths, stone arches, and cast-iron bridges. Not surprisingly, a large component of this study incorporated paths created by Robert Moses, who had cut additional entrances into the perimeter wall to provide access to the new playgrounds he built.

By looking at the park as a unitary design, the planners were able to chart the repairs needed to restore its infrastructure of transverse roads, carriage drives, paths, bridle trails, cast-iron bridges, stone arches, drains, and conduits. They analyzed the landscape as an interrelated series of scenic experiences and delineated the coordinates of its view lines. They mapped desire lines as well as the large areas of bare, compacted ground throughout the park. They inventoried the park's architecture, which included stone arches, cast-iron bridges, and fountains as well as buildings. They cataloged its approximately twenty-six thousand trees in a database that recorded their species, size, age, and condition. They surveyed the park's visitors and charted types and patterns of park use according to the seasonal calendar and time of day and week. These findings were then analyzed and the results consolidated in the form of a series of park-wide recommendations.

At the same time, they considered the landscape section by section, pinpointing areas where restoration and new management protocols were priorities. Within each they defined specific projects in need of funding, which became in effect a list of gift opportunities for prospective donors. Among the planning team, "The Park Is One" became a kind of mantra as we began to think of its landscape as a jigsaw puzzle in which all of the pieces fitted together to form a single picture, rather than simply serving as a blank slate for heterogeneous projects.

The next step was the public's review of the plan. In 1985 we published a large-format document for presentation to city officials, community groups, and the board of the Conservancy. In it there are maps, drawings, photographs, and text outlining the overall recommendations and zone-by-zone proposals that would guide the series of capital projects and maintenance strategies that continue to the present day.*

While the preparation of the plan was in progress, we were initiating environmental-education programs at the newly restored Dairy and Belvedere. As funding increased, we were able to augment the size of the Conservancy's year-round horticultural, graffiti removal, bronze conservation, and carpentry and masonry repair crews. We also hired supervisors to oversee volunteers and summer interns, which allowed us to accomplish tasks that the regular maintenance workforce could not perform alone.

In the process of subdividing the park into constituent units—the jigsaw puzzle pieces mentioned above—we began to hire zone gardeners accountable for the daily upkeep of designated areas, an important management innovation funded through requests to donors for endowment monies in conjunction with their gifts for specific restoration projects. Regreening the bare ground plane and preventing further erosion were obvious general priorities. A further signal to the public that good park management was under way was renewing standards of cleanliness throughout the park, including those for comfort stations, which often stank of urine and were hardly ever supplied with toilet paper. In addition to the elimination of years of accumulated spray paint, the graffiti-removal crew expunged fresh tags as quickly as they appeared. The cleaning and repatinating of bronze sculpture and the repair of broken fountains were additional means of broadcasting the message of a new level of park care.

Maintenance Maneuvers

With new management protocols and a unified multi-project restoration plan in place by 1985, the Conservancy was in a better position

---

* It is obviously a great satisfaction to me that *Rebuilding Central Park: A Management and Restoration Plan,* published by MIT Press in 1987, two years after we presented our draft version to the public, is still used as a text in landscape architecture courses in this country as well as a guide to organizations seeking to revitalize parks both here and in other parts of the world.

Removing graffiti, early 1980s

to chart its course. It was clear that during the five years since its formation we had made significant strides in terms of developing new operational standards for park maintenance. Nevertheless, a review of my journal recording this period reveals that in these first years of its existence the Conservancy's success was filled with a series of ups and downs, as would be the case when implementation of the plan went forward. Not only was there resistance to overcome both outside and inside the Parks Department, but there was also a steep learning curve for me to climb if I were to be successful in truly fulfilling the Conservancy's mission to make Central Park clean, safe, and beautiful once more.

Probably the most glaring symptom of the park's neglect in 1980 was the estimated fifty thousand square feet of graffiti covering every conceivable hard surface—the park's perimeter walls, rock outcrops, the beautiful carved stonework of Bethesda Terrace, and the brick exteriors of virtually every one of the structures that Moses had built. Its removal would be an enormous task. We therefore had to learn what technology might prove effective and raise funds in order to hire and train a crew for this purpose. To understand what an important step this represented, one must read the account in my journal of the first efforts to eliminate the park's ubiquitous graffiti, which were undertaken four months after I had become Central Park administrator.

SATURDAY, MAY 19, 1979

I decided to be "on duty" this weekend, observing the usual spring throng of Saturday and Sunday visitors along with the management strategies, from garbage to gambling control, their presence entails. But it is raining and thus the park is clean, green, and peaceful as David and I ride around in a truck with Jack Kiley, the Parks Department's head of maintenance and operations in Central Park. The enterprising concessionaire we have selected to open what he has named the Ice Cream Café beside the Model Boat Basin has found a chemical solvent to remove graffiti, something I had noticed yesterday evening when I took my favorite stroll home from the office and stopped to watch the water gather in the last daylight. It was a gratifying surprise to see that the small building at the south end of the pond, a dollhouse-like Robert Moses whimsy, was no longer covered with "Ziggy" and "Crunch" tags. Impressed with this counteroffensive on vandalism, I suggested to Jack that we stop by and take a look, thinking that maybe the Parks Department could put in a purchase order for this miracle product that we could use elsewhere. Alas! Overnight every surface of the little building—the brick walls on the sides and back, and the newly painted, green, roll-down door over the counter (paint color selected by me and paint purchased by the Conservancy)—was emblazoned with graffiti. Yes, "emblazoned" is the right word, "Blazer" being the most prominent culprit. Who the hell is he? How could he have done it for heaven's sake at night and in the rain?

Graffiti was only one of the more conspicuous forms of vandalism that had brought about the ruination of Central Park. Throughout the

1970s the Sheep Meadow had been the site of choice for mass events of all kinds. Crowds trampled grass and event sponsors erected sound systems that disturbed residents in apartment houses adjacent to the park as well as visitors seeking tranquility within it. Often the policies that the new parks administration under Gordon Davis was trying to institute to curb these abuses were resisted on the grounds that they constituted a breach of the First Amendment. The challenge we faced was to reinstitute and defend a policy that made park protection as much a people's right as unregulated public assembly. Damping down the destructiveness of mass events meant drawing the line between what was still acceptable and what was not. The things we were up against in terms of enforcing a policy with regard to events in the park when the ethos of the free-spirited sixties was still very much alive is evident in the following journal entry, written a year and a half before the founding of the Central Park Conservancy:

MAY 2, 1979

My day in court. The group that calls itself Rock Against Racism, successor to Abbie Hoffman's Yippees, wants to hold a two-day concert cum rally on the Sheep Meadow. The Department of Parks is denying the permit application and offering them instead a one-day permit for the Bandshell on the Mall. I have been rehearsed by the Corporation Counsel to testify on the destructiveness of mass events like this to the park, our policy of not permitting additional activities on the Sheep Meadow in anticipation of sodding it, the displacement of people who ordinarily enjoy picnicking and sunbathing on the Sheep Meadow, and so forth. Bill Kunstler, the celebrity lawyer who defended the Chicago Eight in 1968, is Rock Against Racism's lawyer. Long-haired, with a wide Indian-beaded watchband, Kunstler huddles with the plaintiffs. It is the most déjà vu scene I've witnessed in a long time, or at least since I saw the movie *Hair*. One just doesn't expect to see hippies these days—flower children grown older, but still affecting the style of yesteryear. It is ironic to hold an antiracist political event in Central Park, I think to myself. Why,

Central Park is probably the most democratic, least racist place in America!

As it turned out, I did not have to testify and be cross-examined by Kunstler. His militants were mollified, and the matter was settled without a courtroom confrontation. After all, our position was reasonable. We ended up with their agreeing to our terms for damage and behaviorial control and our promising not to cut off the electrical current to their sound system at the Bandshell until 9:00 p.m.

Although I was officially embarked on my career as Central Park administrator, the Task Force was yet to be incorporated into the Conservancy-in-formation, so in the meantime I continued the work begun under its auspices. Here is how I assessed the situation back then:

FRIDAY, AUGUST 17, 1979

Summing up summer. To further the burgeoning enterprise of restoring Central Park, support from the commissioner, colleagues, and sponsors counts for everything. Much hard work and more to come. I am gathering new friends and new skills to match my ambitions.

Crisp, almost autumnal, air after a spell of enervating, torrid weather. The summer interns are filling out their questionnaires. They come, these high school students, to learn to be responsible, hold a job, and receive their first paychecks. Now they have become agents of our vision. They are helping bring back fragments of the old park, the noble pleasure ground of scenic surprises. This year, excavating beneath the knotweed in the north end next to the entrance at 110th Street and Lenox Avenue, they are resurrecting the Lily Pool and the spillway that once fed it. "Real cool," the neighbors shout approvingly.

I watch the grass seed that was planted by my order in the spring beginning to sprout. Last year's mud gulch is green now. A bit of progress. I feel proud. The James Taylor concert held on the Sheep Meadow was billed as a benefit for planting more grass. A Philharmonic concert, also on the Sheep Meadow, with fireworks cascading in a velvet sky to the sprightly notes of a Sousa march was watched by a delighted crowd estimated to number two hundred thousand. The new Sheep Meadow slogan: "Let it grow!"

Our intention is to make this piece of remaining greensward a meadow again for park visitors who like simply to sit on lush turf—a special luxury for Manhattanites. This will mean the enforcement of a new policy to protect the Sheep Meadow if more concerts and ad hoc softball and volleyball games are not to turn it into a dust bowl once more. A total ban on these activities would be justly resisted by many people; therefore the Great Lawn, an established sports area since the days of Robert Moses, will receive a different kind of restoration than the Sheep Meadow.

The Conservancy's recently created design office is now developing a set of plans for the capital project necessary to accomplish this. The worn-out existing ball fields on the Great Lawn will be replaced with the same number of new ones, and infrastructure that never existed before will be installed at its north end where the heavy equipment needed to erect a temporary concert stage will inflict less damage than would be the case if one were put up

Central Park Conservancy Landscape Design Team developing the restoration plan for the Great Lawn

on its southern perimeter in the same haphazard manner as in the past. As with every other restoration project, a post-construction events-management strategy and ongoing maintenance plan will be essential if the turf of the outfields is to remain green and soil compaction from the crowds that gather for concerts minimized.

Necessary Repairs

After the Conservancy's official incorporation as a not-for-profit organization and first board meeting on December 3, 1980, I was able to initiate a few modest but significant improvements that became important indicators of progress. For starters, there are features that are ubiquitous throughout the park, notably more than nine thousand benches, eighteen hundred lights, and seven hundred litter receptacles. When the Conservancy was formed, decrepit benches with missing slats spoke of chronic lack of repair in the same way that graffiti broadcast a message of rampant vandalism. The shattered luminaires on more than half the lampposts signaled that the park was unsafe at night. Litter thrown into rusty fifty-five-gallon oil drums that were randomly strewn across the landscape gave the impression that Central Park lay in a third-world country.

Replacement of the smashed light fixtures was triggered by the mugging of Andrew Stein, the Manhattan borough president, one evening while he was walking in Central Park. As an elected official, his voice was heard in City Hall when he called for redress of the poor lighting situation. However, officials in the Department of Transportation (known by its acronym as DOT), the agency that maintains both street and park lighting throughout the city, said that due to budget cuts it could do nothing other than purchase, at the lowest competitive price, off-the-shelf fixtures from a commercial vendor. When the borough president and I met, he agreed to assist in raising funds for a new Conservancy-designed custom luminaire that would be congruent with the park's historic lampposts. I hired Kent Bloomer, a professor at the Yale School of Architecture, and—unusual for that time— a follower of John Ruskin's structural ornamentation precepts, for this job. In a general way, his design keyed off the vegetal iconography of Henry Bacon's early-twentieth-century lamppost, which has a band of leaves set off by a belt of seed-like beads.

In conjunction with its commission of a new luminaire for Central Park, the Conservancy waged a campaign to replace the light source—high-pressure sodium favored by DOT engineers—with metal halide. The latter, a gaseous mixture of vaporized mercury and halide salts and a combination of metals and halogens, emits a white light providing better illumination and color rendition than pressurized sodium gas, which has a harsh yellowish glare and projects a murky light that gives surrounding vegetation a muddy tonality.

Central Park luminaire designed by Kent Bloomer

I was constantly reminding the staff that "God is in the details," and that the repair and redesign of park furniture not just in one area but throughout the entire park were as important as any individual restoration project. Eventually, the Conservancy was able to replace the rusty, dented oil drums being used as garbage receptacles with dark green four-wheeled plastic litter bins that could be more efficiently emptied. We also repaired thousands of broken slats on park benches and installed replicas of the historic ones where this alternative seemed desirable.*

These were projects that could be done to a large degree under the Conservancy's own initiative. Assuming decision-making authority with regard to larger ones required challenging the Parks Department's current modus operandi.

At this time the Loeb Boathouse served only mediocre, over-the-counter fast food. It was common knowledge that the principal employee of the concessionaire was running a numbers game. Since

---

* The historic model with cast-iron supports and a circular cast-iron arm at each end is called the World's Fair bench, and the other has a continuous run of slats supported by concrete stanchions.

the current contract was soon to expire, I managed to get the head of concessions in the Parks Department to write into the Request for Proposals requirements that would allow for the selection of a concessionaire capable of managing the existing hot-dog, hamburger, and soft-drinks counter and at the same time create a café in another section of the building with fare similar to the popular, then novel, American cuisine pioneered by Alice Waters.

These first signs of the park's renaissance could not have occurred without the support of the commissioner. Gordon Davis's encouragement of my initiatives, however, was no guarantee that longtime agency employees were sympathetic. Within the Parks Department's design and construction division located in Flushing Meadows Park, there was polite resistance to changing the existing rules whereby architects and landscape architects were selected for individual projects from a rotating list of firms. Such a piecemeal approach was antithetical to the consistency of design vision the Conservancy's management and restoration plan called for. Although I was invited to review plans developed by the Parks Department's outside consultants and in-house designers, I was given to believe that I could have no real say in the selection of contractors for capital projects.

The architects and landscape architects within the agency were moreover frequently stymied by bureaucratic procedures. As an example, in September 1981 the reconstruction of Wollman Rink was in a state of paralysis. After much discussion, it had been determined that the pipes laid down for the recommended state-of-the-art freezing equipment had become damaged beyond repair from nearby roadway runoff containing ice-melting salt during the winter construction hiatus. The need for the costly reinstallation of this infrastructure might have been prevented if the contractor had not left the piping exposed until spring, when it would be possible to pour the rink's concrete surface slab. There was a general understanding that the contract should be rebid and a new firm brought in to replace the faulty pipes, but this would involve following departmental regulations that would probably delay the reopening of the rink for at least another year. A faster fix would be to accept the offer that had been thrown on the table by Donald Trump. He maintained that his construction-management experience and ability to fast-track development projects provided a sensible alternative to the Parks Department's cumbersome bidding procedures. The result of the agency's acceptance of Trump's offer was a reopened rink in a matter of months and his company's management of it under a concession license granted by the Parks Department.

It was now clear to me that because of the importance we attached to having representatives of the Conservancy's field operations staff participate in the planning process and a construction supervisor on-site once work was begun, we needed to create a design and construction division of our own. The initial staff was composed of the landscape architects who were already Conservancy employees, plus a growing number of new hires. Gradually we were able to add personnel to oversee the construction bidding process and the subsequent supervision of restoration projects. By demonstrating our capability in this regard, we earned an exemption from old Parks Department rules and were now able to furnish designs, oversee construction, and develop management protocols that ensured ongoing maintenance after projects were completed. I was rightly proud of the fact that the Conservancy now had what could be considered its own in-house design/build/maintain landscape architectural firm.

This did not happen overnight, of course. Inserting new policies emphasizing horticultural care into the existing management system of the Parks Department was an even slower and more difficult task than gaining control over Central Park capital projects. Within its Maintenance and Operations division, there were three separate departments, each with its own chain of command. The regular park workers were not allowed to do what carpenters and mechanics were supposed to do (or couldn't do because they weren't able to get the necessary equipment and supplies from the agency's shops). The same was true of the staff holding the civil service title of gardener, which by the time I became administrator had dwindled to two men whose principal responsibility appeared to be making the oversize annual Christmas wreath for the front of the Parks Department's Arsenal headquarters. Nor was there any coordination of effort among these employees and the men in the forestry division, who planted donated trees (there were no funds for new trees in the parks budget) in a random manner wherever there was an available open space, usually one of the park's Olmstedian meadows or grassy knolls. Moreover, because of the municipal workers' union rules, tree pruning was done in a less-than-efficient manner, since a three-man crew was assigned to each job: a climber to cut off dead limbs, a man on the ground to hoist tools tied to a rope, and an MVO (motor-vehicle operator) who waited in the truck in order to transport the other two men to the next pruning site. Often necessary mechanical equipment was "up against the wall," which meant that it had been sent to the department's repair division on Randall's Island. For this reason, the first permanent Conservancy employee I hired was Andy Knopka, a mechanic whose job was to repair the reel-type lawn mowers we had bought to replace the agency's large, heavy hammer-knife mowers (the kind that are used to mow highway medians). Soon, with the increasing amount of funds the Conservancy was now raising, we were able to employ an assistant to help Andy perform necessary mechanical repairs.

Obstacle Course

Instituting the privately funded Conservancy staff of field workers alongside the Parks Department's existing workforce was not easy, and I was frustrated by the business-as-usual attitude on the part of old-time civil service personnel who felt bound to abide by the work rules of District Council 37 of the Municipal Workers Union. In addition, my ability to guide restoration policy was thwarted by well-intentioned but headstrong donors who had their own ideas regarding the restoration of Central Park in a way that did not follow Olmstedian principles of an integrated holistic landscape. Beyond these impediments, I still had a lot to learn about how to communicate with community groups and existing park constituencies.

One of my first lessons in this regard occurred in 1979, during my first year in office, when I invited a group of headmasters from nearby private boys' schools to a meeting where I hoped to elicit their cooperation in respecting a ban on gym classes using the Sheep Meadow following its resodding. Instead of coming in person, they deputized their sports coaches to attend. I explained that the meadow, which was then still a dust bowl, would henceforth be maintained as green turf.

When I explained that cleated shoes tore up grass, they stared at me in dismay. "Don't worry," one declared. "Just give us clean dirt."

Another early lesson taught me that jocks were not the only ones who were indifferent to my dream of re-creating elements of the former Olmstedian landscape. As grateful as we were to the donors who were helping build the Conservancy, they, too, often had agendas at variance with ours. One example of this occurred when Japanese shipbuilding tycoon Ryoichi Sasakawa wished to use funds allegedly derived from his casino investments to include, among other international image-enhancing philanthropic activities, a gift of cherry trees to Central Park. As far as where to site them, I naturally thought of Cherry Hill. Here one of the Conservancy's first capital projects had been replacing the parking lot Robert Moses had built over an original pedestrian and carriage concourse. This important restoration had included replumbing its broken horse-drinking fountain, refabricating the fountain's missing ornamental bronze centerpiece, removing asphalt paving, and restoring the surrounding landscape sloping toward the Lake. I reasoned that a sprinkling of cherry trees here would not interfere with the views of the Bow Bridge arching over the Lake and the Ramble on the opposite shore.

Rereading the entry describing the dedication of the Sasakawa cherry planting, I see that this was a mistaken assumption:

APRIL 18, 1979

Mayor Koch appears as do a busload of children from the United Nations school who will be singing for the occasion. Photographers and newspaper reporters are there. Gordon waffles a bit when a reporter brings up Sasakawa's alleged criminal past. No one even looks at the restored fountain, and the *Times* gets the story all wrong, confusing Mr. Sasakawa's gift of $150,000 with the erroneous information that 150 trees are being planted when the actual number is thirty-two. But the Japanese apparently now want the place completely plastered with cherry trees. I am told that in Japan there is an old saying: "It is not spring if you can see the sky," meaning the world should be embowered with the blossoms of a veritable forest of cherry trees. I am also told to expect a gift from Japan Airlines, which will greatly increase the cherry presence in the park. Who speaks for the park's landscape and what should be done to it? Apparently not me. But I will, and maybe someday my voice will be heard.

In fact, my voice *was* heard by another Japanese donor, Yoko Ono. Following the death of her husband, the famous Beatles founder and songwriter John Lennon, in 1980, Henry Stern, who was then a member of the City Council—the body that, among other legislative responsibilities, gives honorary names to streets and public spaces—obtained a majority vote for bestowing the designation "Strawberry Fields" on the three-acre portion of Central Park opposite the site of Lennon's assassination in front of the home he and Yoko shared in the Dakota apartment building on Central Park West and Seventy-Second Street. To reinforce this form of commemoration, Yoko sent her lawyer to pay a courtesy call for the purpose of showing me a layout of the full-page spread that would be published the next day in *The New York Times* announcing her proposal to create a "garden of peace" in Strawberry Fields. After reading the copy, I politely demurred, explaining that her invitation to governments of all nations to send gifts of trees and public artifacts associated with their countries ran counter to the current restoration plan in the spirit of the original Olmstedian landscape. I cinched my argument by adding that by law the project would be subject to review by the Parks Department, the Landmarks Commission, and the adjacent community planning board.

Soon after this conversation, I received an invitation to meet with Yoko at her apartment in the Dakota. I was pleased to hear her allow that Olmsted's naturalistic aesthetic was akin to the simplicity of Japanese garden design and grateful that she accepted my suggestion of Bruce Kelly as the right landscape architect for the Strawberry Fields restoration plan. She and Bruce continued to meet over the next several weeks, and while other donors might have demanded a more conspicuous and traditional memorial, such as a bronze portrait bust or life-size sculpture, she only wanted a circular mosaic in the entrance path bearing the single word "Imagine." Unreasonably, this became

"Imagine" mosaic memorializing John Lennon, Strawberry Fields

the only publicly controversial element of the plan. As the debate with Central Park West neighbors raged over this modest memorial, I staunchly supported Yoko in her determination to have the mosaic installed. In its aesthetic quality and because it would not interrupt the integrity of the overall landscape, it would be different from all the previous monuments heretofore erected in the park. Eventually, the uproar subsided, and we were able to proceed with the project. Significantly, with Yoko's gift of one million dollars, in addition to implementing the $600,000 Olmstedian restoration plan Bruce Kelly prepared for Strawberry Fields, we were able to create a $400,000 endowment directed toward hiring our first zone gardener, by definition a horticulturally trained employee dedicated to the upkeep of a specific park area.

The Conservancy was clearly gaining credibility with each visible accomplishment, and with the encouragement of the board I was beginning to form an administration commensurate with the organizational oversight that was now necessary. Rereading my journal from this period, I find myself increasingly immersed in the opera-

tional concerns of the Conservancy as well as the day-to-day business
of park management:

Park blanketed with snow all week. We need sixty more days of
snow or rain to fill the reservoirs. This is unlikely. How will we
plant and water next spring if the city declares a drought emergency? How will we be able to turn on newly repaired fountains?

Worked this week with the existing staff and Pam Tice, the
recently hired Conservancy staff member who will serve as my
second-in-command, assisting me in the preparation of budgets
and grant proposals as well as with organizational administration.
Since I bear the title Central Park administrator, she is called the
executive director of the Conservancy. It is a good division of
leadership and management responsibilities.

Not Now

As a participant in forging park policy with the commissioner, I had
a seat at the conference table when Christo and Jeanne-Claude originally proposed the installation of *The Gates* in Central Park before also
reviewing their plan with Commissioner of Cultural Affairs Henry
Geldzahler, the former curator and critic whose enthusiastic advocacy
of contemporary art made him a prominent figure within the New
York art world.

Although Geldzahler was enthusiastic about the project, Gordon
and I had reservations. So many mass events had occurred in the
recent past and had wrought such damage to the park that anything
that would attract large crowds was a source of consternation. Besides
Hoving's happenings and a popular annual ethnic food festival on the
Mall that drew 250,000 people, there was the legendary concert in June
1967, at which Barbra Streisand sang "Cry Me a River" and "Happy
Days Are Here Again" to an audience of 135,000. Gordon, who was

Christo and Jeanne-Claude presenting drawings of The Gates *to Henry Geldzahler, Commissioner of Cultural Affairs*

under pressure not to turn down another historic rock event, hit upon the idea of inducing the sponsors of the James Taylor concert in July 1979 to dedicate a percentage of the proceeds from record sales, merchandising, and television and video rights to a special fund to restore the Sheep Meadow. Fans screamed as the rock star capped his career singing "Brother Trucker," "Millworker," and "Up on the Roof," but in spite of the euphoria in the air, the impact of so much heavy stage equipment and the number of human feet and bodies on the Sheep Meadow only magnified the challenge that lay ahead.

To illustrate the degree to which things had gotten out of hand, on one Sunday in May 1977 four events were scheduled on the Mall at the same time, including the convening of participants in a bike-a-thon and a foot race, both of which had to cross repeatedly over the line of a parade march as well as the path of vehicles transporting performers, supplies, and floats to a cultural festival. In 1980, when concert promoter and impresario Ron Delsener sought to stage an Elton John concert in Central Park, Gordon was able to shift the site to the Great Lawn (it might more accurately have been called the Great Dust Bowl at the time) and write into the permission agreement a pledge that a specified fraction of the proceeds would go toward its restoration.

Later, in the wake of the concert, some grass seed was dispersed on the trampled compacted ground to remediate the damage caused by a crowd estimated at four hundred thousand (probably an excessive number, even though there were so many people gathered that those who could not find room within the oval circumference of the Great Lawn climbed nearby trees to be in hearing range of the amplifiers). Needless to say, this was not an effective remedy. The Great Lawn remained the dirt plain it had long since become and would be for thirteen more years, as the Conservancy was thwarted in its plan to move forward with the major restoration project our designers already had on their drawing boards—a story for a later chapter. The Sheep Meadow, on the other hand, did get restored, thanks to a grant to the Parks Department from the State of New York.

True, what was now being proposed by Cristo was not a one-day destructive mass concert impacting a single area but a park-wide artwork that would be visited over a period of three weeks. I admired Christo's *Running Fence* and other unique one-time short-term projects accomplished in the face of several years' opposition by government agencies, and I wasn't happy to find myself taking an oppositional role. On the other hand, *The Gates* would exploit the park's conspicuous world-famous location rather than pay homage to its landscape as a great work of art in and of itself. Here was the sticking point as far as I was concerned: Christo versus Olmsted.*

After many months of careful deliberation with members of his staff, including me, in February 1981 Commissioner Davis delivered a 107-page report denying Christo's application. Citing the park's hospitality to many works of public art in the past and the current administration's admiration of contemporary public art in general and openness to the installation of individual, site-specific public art works within Central Park, he nonetheless declared:

---

* I did not know at the time that Robert Smithson, creator of the earthwork *Spiral Jetty*, had been prompted to write his famous essay on Central Park by my 1972 book *Frederick Law Olmsted's New York*. Of course, I concurred when he categorized Olmsted as a great land artist who had put a "sylvan" green overlay on the rugged, barren pre-park landscape. As far as *The Gates* was concerned, from my point of view back then, Smithson had cast his vote on what I considered the right side. (For a detailed discussion of *The Gates* project as finally realized, see Chapter Eighteen.)

Christo's project, if for no other reason than its sheer scale and demanding magnitude, must be evaluated first and foremost from a perspective mindful of Central Park's design and rich history, its precarious past and our hopes for its future. . . . Might it not be better . . . to expend the considerable energy that Christo has sought and required in consideration of a proposal whose principal objective is to improve Central Park directly—for example, components of a restoration master plan or a proposed park use policy—rather than one for which that purpose is only ancillary?

Summarizing, he maintained, "Public architecture and landscape architecture are themselves forms of public art." The decision to deny the application was upheld by Mayor Koch. I remembered, however, that one of the talents of Christo and Jeanne-Claude was their long-term persistence in gaining approval for each of their imaginative, unconventional grand visions. The realization of this extraordinary project twenty-five years later was testimony to the couple's political skills as well as to their fund-raising success within an art world made up of collectors eager to purchase Christo's pre-exhibition drawings of *The Gates*.[*]

As I write these words, I am remembering the day during the February 2005 exhibition when I ran into Jeanne-Claude and Christo beside the Harlem Meer and we greeted one another as old friends. "Betsy," she said, "you know, it was still a dream then. We did not yet have the money!" For me it was, as we shall see in the final chapter of this book, a celebratory reminder of the Conservancy's persistence in fulfilling its own bold dream of bringing Central Park back into the public eye as another and more permanent form of land art.

Lessons Learned

Looking back on this period of my life, I can say that while by nature I embodied the three *P*s—patience, passion, and persistence—that are

[*] All of Christo's multimillion-dollar installations of land art are entirely self-funded through the sale of works on paper illustrating his concepts for their future realization.

quintessential leadership qualities, there are two other intrinsically related *P*s—power and politics—that I had yet to master. Simply put, a public park is government property, and its private-sector partner must operate at the behest of city officials as well as that of the body politic. At the same time, within the dynamics of any public-private partnership, there is another *P*—the purse. In this regard, independent fiduciary responsibility is critical, for without authority to control the funds it has raised, the private partner cannot ensure accountability to its donors nor win cooperation from the city.

This latter achievement was not an easy matter. It is important to explain here that the Conservancy's life began without a formal contract with the city, a circumstance that made the relationship between the public and private partners much cloudier than the one that exists today. The absence of the contractual relationship that now clarifies the respective authority of each partner remained the case throughout the fifteen years I served as an officer within the municipal government of New York City while receiving a single salary paid to me by the Central Park Conservancy for my services as its president. This was a nonissue and indeed a bonus from the perspective of the city, and I never felt any ambiguity in my dual offices as Central Park administrator and president of the Conservancy. On the contrary, for any such public-private partnership, having joint titles invested in a single individual is an essential ingredient of stability and success in overriding the vicissitudes of political change.

However, with only a handshake from Mayor Koch and his letter recognizing this then-novel type of organization's right to exist as an auxiliary arm of city government, I did find it difficult to always practice the required diplomacy. But over time the initial intransigence of the old guard within the Parks Department was overcome, and with its increasing fund-raising success resulting in the mayor and park commissioner's entitlement to take a joint share of the credit for privately funded projects, the Conservancy gradually became institutionalized as an ally of city government as well as a role model for the formation of other public-private partnerships for the improvement of parks elsewhere.

But this would occur only over a period of several years, and there were at first some serious setbacks to the Conservancy's prog-

ress toward acceptance by the world at large. For starters, the notion
that my Olmstedian vision spoke for itself was entirely mistaken.
To undertake the park's restoration according to the design premises
being established by the Conservancy's newly formed team of landscape planners required communication on a project-by-project basis
with various interest groups, community planning boards, and proprietary constituencies who frequently opposed any suggested change.
It was essential for me, therefore, to understand the importance of
good public relations in my job, something I was able to do successfully only after 1989, when I hired Erana Stennett as the Conservancy's
director of community and government relations. Before that time I
had been forced to learn the importance of proactive transparency by
means of an unpleasant tutorial.

This lesson centered upon my staunch support of the Conservancy
landscape architects' carefully analyzed scenic prospects and perspectives as essential components of the management and restoration plan-
in-progress. In comparing the amount of tree canopy depicted on an
1872 map of the park with the one obtained by aerial survey in 1982,
the designers pointed out how over the years the sense of spacious
openness with long vistas from one meadow to another or the sight-
ing of a scenic focal point from a particular angle had been seriously
compromised by the expansion of an ever-denser tree canopy.

To look at a landscape as a scenically varied yet united whole
demands multiple vantage points and view lines. This in turn requires
corridors of sight. Trees in and of themselves need space for mature
growth. These principles were central to Olmsted's design approach. In
1889, long after he had left New York and become a nationally recognized figure in the field of landscape architecture, when asked to pen
a testimony in support of tree removal standard practice, he obliged
with an essay titled "Observations on the Treatment of Public Plantations, More Especially Relating to the Use of the Axe," a lengthy and
thoroughly documented defense of the necessity for tree thinning.
The arguments raised back then by a group of citizens challenging the
Parks Department's removal of some lesser trees that were interfering
with the growth of larger specimens would now echo in my ears.

As I was to find out, a tree war can be a nasty kind of turf battle, since
public spaces such as Central Park have factions who have a powerful

sense of ownership that they will defend as a matter of right. None are more proprietary and passionate than the birdwatchers, who view the Ramble as their special domain. As discussed previously, Robert Moses's drastic plans to reconfigure the Ramble targeted another regular constituency, gay men, who cruised there in order to find partners (these were the days prior to the creation of Internet dating sites). In spite of a couple of nasty incidents when homophobic ruffians went on nighttime bashing sprees and beat up whichever gay men they happened to encounter, the Ramble overcame its general reputation for danger among these two groups, one seeking nature, the other privacy for casual trysts.

The Ramble's character as a unique area designed by Olmsted to be intentionally divorced from the rest of Central Park's circulation system, a discrete miniature wilderness with pleasantly disorienting paths circuitously wending their way through thirty wooded acres, had another meaning for Bruce Kelly and me. We wanted to recover its historic beauty as a special part of the park. Specifically, we wanted to replace the blanket of invasive Japanese knotweed (*Fallopia japonica*) that covered almost every part of the Ramble with a variety of low-growing native species and the kind of berry-producing shrubs that attract birds. While neither of us was prejudiced against homosexuals—Bruce was himself gay—we naturally wished to replant the barren spots that had been turned into hardpan through nocturnal overuse, beginning with the Point, as the little peninsula jutting into the Lake across from Bethesda Terrace is called.

The story of this debacle began with my agreement with Bruce's suggestion that we restore the original view from Bethesda Terrace to the Belvedere, which runs in a direct north-south line across the Point. He drew up a plan that called for the planting of a selection of low-growing native species in barren areas, which our newly hired Conservancy horticultural crew began implementing under the supervision of Gerry Weinstein. At the same time I hired a tree contractor to cut down a dozen or so small-caliper black cherries, a self-propagating species that is almost as successful as Japanese knotweed in its ability to colonize large swaths of parkland. The crew had gotten as far as planting a patch of clethra and witch hazel shrubs when a vociferous controversy arose, after a group of whistle-blowing birdwatchers from the New York City chapter of the Audubon Society discovered what they considered to be a desecration of wildlife habitat. In what amounted to a declaration of war against the Conservancy, someone called *The New York Times,* and the paper assigned reporter Deirdre Carmody to write an article about what had happened. In recounting their side of the story, the birdwatchers she interviewed denigrated the Conservancy's nascent management and restoration plan in its entirety. The editors considered Carmody's piece of sufficient interest to run it on the front page:

MAY 3, 1982

"That plan is 'Mein Kampf,'" said Lewis Rosenberg, a lawyer and director of the New York City Audubon Society. "It has not been approved by the landmarks commission, but the Parks Department has gone ahead and done it all anyway without approval."

"It hasn't been a balanced process," Mr. [Albert Appleton] said. "We're adults. We know you don't get everything you want all the time. What troubles us is that we have no way of getting at the planning process. We hear about it afterward. The hearing process is a mystery."

To my credit, in the same article I admitted to Carmody that I was in error in treating the tree removal as an inconsequential matter:

"I don't think I've handled this brilliantly," Mrs. [Elizabeth Barlow] said. "Bruce Kelly, the landscape architect who did the master plan and who will do the planting around Belvedere, asked me for permission to bring in a tree contractor and do 'a little tree clearing.' He said he would be careful and not take down anything large. I mistakenly said OK."

Other newspapers now saw that the press had a hot story that would interest their readers. There had been such an unobtrusive subtraction from the existing mass of vegetation that the scant evidence of tree removal consisted of some small-caliper, flush-to-the-ground stumps, one of which bore the graffiti epithet "Betsy Barlow is a psycho-slut." (What, I wondered—and still do—is a "psycho-slut"?) A rock emblazoned with a graffiti arrow pointed to the "crime scene," which might have been hard to discover otherwise, since so few trees were gone that the view to the Belvedere that Bruce and I had wanted to open up had not materialized.

Being an object of such vilification when I thought of myself as a nature-loving environmentalist and amateur birdwatcher was a bracing lesson in the importance of ongoing communication with constituent groups—or "stakeholders," as they are now called. The following entry in my journal records the painful experience:

SUNDAY MORNING, MAY 23, 1982

Past two weeks made busier than usual by my notoriety gained through Deirdre Carmody's front-page *New York Times* story. With little understanding of landscape architecture, but a good nose for a hot issue, she polarized the Ramble restoration program into a tale of nature versus historic preservation. Naturally nature won, and editorial-page writer Roger Starr followed up

"Look Over There," graffiti sign on rock at the Point

Birdwatchers in the Ramble, early 1980s

by urging "a little less fidelity to Olmstead [*sic*]." In the mean-time, where the few trees were cut and hundreds of new shrubs installed, there are birds galore. I find the generous and under-standing words of friends consoling, and their nice letters are an antidote to the hate mail I have received since the *Times* article. Nevertheless, "views and vistas" is now a pejorative expression, the word "horticulture" is spoken with disgust, and I am consid-ered guilty of having committed "arboricide."

I subsequently invited Starr to take a walk with me through the Ramble and was heartened when he got the point of the Conservancy's restoration plan-in-progress and wrote another editorial reversing his prior position. But the furor would not die down, and I spent many hours during the summer of 1982 giving tours of the Ramble, explaining how the Conservancy wished to enhance wildlife habitat with more berry-producing shrubbery for birds, and how a greater diversity of tree species and native-plant groundcover in lieu of the monoculture of invasive knotweed would enhance the Ramble's aspect as a natural woodland. The title of a *New York Times* article, "Whose Park Is It, Anyway?," by freelance writer Elizabeth Hawes, highlighted my dilemma and is worth quoting at length because of the portrait it paints of me as I was perceived at the time.

THE NEW YORK TIMES, SEPTEMBER 5, 1982

Central Park is and always has been sacred ground, and New Yorkers feel personal, possessive and protective about the 840-acre oasis of green that was set aside 126 years ago as a public preserve. It is their backyard, their exposure to Nature and, for many, their only accessible alternative to the grid of city life. . . .

The ardor of the various park constituents amounts to a testament of need and affection for the park, but it is also proving a difficult lesson in democracy for the Parks Department as it proceeds with the restoration. When Gordon Davis first came to his post in 1978, the future of the park was in question. Davis, who is 41, black and a graduate of Harvard Law School, held a planning post in the Lindsay administration during the time when then Parks Commissioner Thomas Hoving closed the park to cars and opened it to people, politics and festivals. It was a joyous, circuslike era of eat-ins, be-ins and fat-ins, of political rallies, rock concerts and 12 million annual park users. This was followed by the city's fiscal crisis and the draining of park funds, a series of revolving-door commissioners and the absence of any management policy. By the mid-70's, Central Park had become, in Davis's words, "an unattended Frankenstein" and the post of commissioner was "the lowest of the low." . . .

A master plan, which defenders and detractors alike have called for over the years, still does not exist. But Mrs. Barlow has embarked on one which she expects to be complete by January 1984. The plans for the master plan alone almost defy description: topographical surveys, analyses of ecosystems, historical reports on accessories like signs, lights, benches and playground equipment; studies of vegetation, horticulture and landscaping, past and present; studies of park use; a security analysis and a policy study. Meanwhile, reconstruction continues where designs have been completed, and the people of Central Park, the daily users, rise up, in small and large popular fronts, to advise on and question the work.

There have been conflicts over the southeast corner, the Sheep Meadow and the skating rink, but to date the biggest and most impassioned challenge to the department has arisen over the restoration of the Ramble, a 30-acre miniature forest in the center of the park. On the surface, the issues there are tree-cutting, vistas and preservation of habitat for birds, but deeper, they are the validity of the historic designs, the social function of the area and the process of public review. Inevitably, both the methods and goals of the Parks Department have been brought into question. The focus of the criticism has been the office of the administrator of Central Park, Elizabeth Barlow. Davis represents the whole 24,800-acre New York City parks system; he is the politician, the general; and although he is very involved in Central Park, he delegates authority and treats Betsy Barlow like a commissioner in her own right.

. . . [She] is the first to say that her basic legacy in the park comes from both Olmsted and Moses; she speaks reverently about the designs of Olmsted, more grudgingly about those of Moses. But she recognizes it is a double-faced landscape, with a metaphysical intent on one hand and a recreational one on the other, and it can be difficult to reconcile the parts.

[She] is an able and far-thinking fund-raiser. She also spends a lot of time in Central Park, bird watching, taking educational walks and botany courses. But she is not a politician. And she has underestimated the general populace's desire to be involved in decisions about the park. In architectural projects, which are relatively clear-cut, she has received praise. But in landscape matters, which are interpretive exercises (Olmsted did not have scenic blueprints), she is accused by her critics of being mysterious and arrogant. . . .

Mrs. Barlow expected some degree of resistance over [the Conservancy's project to restore] the Ramble, but the intensity of the current debate surprised and hurt her. "In the newspapers," she says, "there is this feeling that we are doing dastardly deeds. Some people do not see the forest for the trees. We are

trying to see the forest. This is supposed to be healthy land management. The Ramble is such a fragile and delicate area, and so
severely neglected, I thought an interpretive restoration should
be done as a series of small horticultural projects."

The fierce controversy that raged in the Ramble as I continued to
be vilified by the birdwatchers was for me especially galling. Hadn't I
considered myself a naturalist, too? Hadn't I always prized the park's
beautiful trees as well as its open views? Didn't I consider the seasonal
passage of migrating warblers and other birds that I saw in the park on
my walks to work through the Ramble evidence of the miraculous
ubiquity of wildlife within the asphalt, brick, and concrete confines
of New York City?

Although Gordon admitted that the Ramble dispute had temporarily paralyzed the Parks Department, he was nevertheless staunch in
his support of my vision for restoring Central Park in the spirit of its
original designers. "Of course there are lessons," he told Hawes, the
reporter who had written the article quoted above. "Our vision is not
perfect. We are not fanatics in the sense that there is only one right way
to do things. Debate occurs over every blade of grass, and that is the
health of the park."

A different commissioner might not have stood by me as resolutely
as Gordon did during this difficult period, which makes poignant the
journal entry I wrote a few months later as the Ramble controversy
was starting to simmer down:

JANUARY 31, 1983

On Tuesday night I returned from a Philharmonic concert and
was buzzed a few minutes later by the doorman who announced
a Parks Department envelope was riding up on the seat of the
elevator. I tore it open and saw the familiar handwriting: "Call
me immediately when you get in if it is before 1:00 a.m." I made
the call with a sinking anxious heart and heard Gordon tell me
that he was resigning the next day. He continues to play his cards
close to his chest and will not say what he plans to do. (Con-

servancy board member and my good friend Danny Parker has confided to me these past several months that Gordon plans to join a law firm.) With an actor's sense of timing, he knows he should bow out at the crest of his popularity, before his impressive accomplishments as parks commissioner are eroded by the city's increasing budgetary stringency or he burns out from the demands of the job.

How I shall miss his humor and the comradeship and sheer fun of his administration! "No, not Camelot," Gordon corrected another mournful staff member, "just summer camp." He leaves me with many more administrative and political skills than I dreamed of possessing four years ago, and with, despite certain persistent personal faults, a much more mature professional personality.

Boyish yet manly, tough yet sensitive, proud to the point of arrogance but deeply democratic, Gordon is by instinct a natural leader. His complicated attitude about race, which is the strongest emotional chord in his psyche, has made him a champion of non-discrimination against blacks, and his pride in his wife Peggy who is a lawyer is an indication of his openness to placing women in high positions within his administration. Today as a Parks Department team we are biracial and half female, half male. Without the climate of equality he fostered and his confidence in my abilities, could I have succeeded as well as I have in four busy years? With his support and that of the Conservancy's board and my staff, I have created and led a unique kind of public-private partnership that has effectively started to reverse the park's years of decline. Is the Conservancy strong enough—am I?—to continue the momentum under a new commissioner?

Chapter Nine

CHANGING TIMES

I did not go down to City Hall to stand beside Gordon and the mayor at the press conference announcing his resignation. The park has larger meaning than any individual, so with determination to focus on its future, I chose instead to go to our scheduled landscape restoration planning meeting, where I read his letter aloud to my staff. It was good after the fitful night to plunge into the substance of my job and hear the landscape architects argue over the degree to which this or that section of the park should remain a designated sports area or be returned to its original scenic appearance and multipurpose public use.

New Boss

After days of anxious waiting to learn who would be my new boss, Gordon, who remained parks commissioner until the announcement of his successor, walked down the hall to my office and said, "It's Henry." He, of course, meant Henry Stern.

I had known Henry ever since I moved to New York in 1964 and became involved in civic affairs during and after my days as a Parks Association volunteer. In spite of our divergence of opinion on many

Henry Stern

things during his two terms as parks commissioner—from 1983 to 1990 in Mayor Ed Koch's administration (1978–1989) and, following a hiatus during the mayoralty of David Dinkins, the entire tenure of Mayor Rudolph Giuliani (1993–2001)—as fellow lifetime "parkies," we have remained good friends.

To say that Henry Stern is an unusual and remarkable individual is an understatement. The son of Jewish parents, he grew up in northern Manhattan. Born in 1935, he was a wunderkind, graduating from Bronx High School of Science in 1950, from City College in 1954, and in 1957 from Harvard Law School, where he had the distinction of being the youngest member of his class. After law school, he began what he likes to call "going about the people's business," which in his case has meant a lifetime career working in government, first as a law clerk to a New York State Supreme Court justice, then for the City of New York as assistant to two consecutive Manhattan borough presidents, and following that as first deputy to the commissioner of consumer affairs. In 1973 he was elected to the City Council as a councilman-at-large for Manhattan on the Liberal Party line, an office he held until the federal courts abolished the position in 1981. Because of their political connection, which had bloomed into close friendship, it was natural that liberal Democrat Ed Koch would select the recently disempowered Stern as his second parks commissioner.

To understand Henry and how our divergent perspectives frequently put us at loggerheads, it is important to describe the New York City in which he grew up. Born the year after Moses took office, he played in a new Moses playground close to his parents' apartment in the Washington Heights neighborhood, learned to swim in one of the new swimming pools built by Moses, and was taken as a boy of four to the 1939 World's Fair, which had been masterminded by Moses. Thus it might be said that whereas my principal park hero was Frederick Law Olmsted, his was Robert Moses. As evidence, not long after becoming commissioner, he inaugurated an annual Parks Day on January 18, the anniversary of Moses's arrival with his aides in a fleet of chauffeured black Packards to commandeer his office in the Arsenal. Now Henry himself would occupy Moses's old office on the third floor in one of the building's turrets.

To characterize Henry as more than mildly eccentric as well as exceedingly brilliant is no exaggeration. His eccentricity is the product of a phenomenal mind: computational skills like a built-in calculator, a map of every New York City street and every building indelibly imprinted on his brain, a personal telephone directory stored there, too, a speed-reader's ability to absorb the contents of a page in a few seconds, and a historian's memory for dates, even obscure ones such as insignificant anniversaries and near-forgotten people and events. With an encyclopedic memory, his relish of trivia of all kinds, and his expertise in doing difficult crossword puzzles, he is master of an endless array of minutiae. A compulsive counter, he regularly brought his dog, Boomer, to work and clicked a calculator every time someone gave the animal a pat on the head. As an example of his relish of detail and penchant for naming, not long after he took office he ordered green, maple-leaf-incised signs with existing or new commissioner-donated appellations for areas and structures throughout all New York City parks.

Like Robert Moses, Henry recognized the value of publicity. During the first days of his administration, he appointed a deputy for public relations who made sure that press releases were regularly sent to the media. When interviewed directly, his bon mots and aphoristic quips always made good copy for reporters. And, even if he did not wield as much power as Moses, he was able to exercise final authority over the Conservancy's agenda by virtue of his public office. Since he would one day be able to boast that he was the longest-serving parks commissioner in the twentieth century after Moses, our complicated relationship both as lifetime friends and as sometime foes would endure over many years.

As will become apparent in the next chapter, our differences sprang from our divergent perspectives regarding Central Park. With my art historian's background, I looked at the park as a framed landscape in which all of its parts cohere as a scenic entity; for Henry, it was the individual features within the park that counted, and their significance to him was political rather than aesthetic. To illustrate this dichotomy in outlook, I perceived the park as a single composition that is both recreational and spiritually uplifting. Nowadays the Picturesque, a theory discussed at some length in Chapter Five, is a historically outdated aesthetic. Nevertheless, for many visitors, the park's visual unity is appreciated, if only in a subliminal way. Most of us, however, like Henry or Moses, focus on individual park features independent of their scenic context.

Another important piece of background information: since almost all of Henry's career was spent as a public servant, elected official, or mayoral appointee, his knowledge of New York City's political machinery was canny and his loyalty to the existing system of municipal government unequivocal. Although neither of us would say so, judging from the ongoing disputes that characterized our relationship, the idea of private-sector partnering with government was basically antipathetic to him.

Homeschooling

The struggles that I underwent with Henry played no small part in the life of the Conservancy and in my own transition from neophyte to professional, for there were important lessons I still had to learn beyond the ones that had guided me to where I was when Henry took office in 1983. Luck had been on my side so far, and it was apparent that the Conservancy was going to achieve recognition as an established New York City institution. Publicity, reputation, and results were essential, but at this point I realized that, although my leadership ability was solidly grounded, I had yet to mold myself into a good organizational manager. Fortunately, there was help at hand.

When we were married in 1984, Ted stood at the pinnacle of corporate America. As the CEO of NL Industries, he had a decent six-figure salary, although it would seem laughably low to a Wall Street hedge fund investor or top Silicon Valley executive now. Indeed, he was so far from being like the 1 percent reaping a disproportionate amount of the country's wealth today that the only time I ever saw him openly weep was when he was forced to close one of NL's manufacturing plants. "I feel so terrible when I think of how all those people who are now out of work feel tonight," he said to me.

But this was not a shared sentiment in most of the rest of the business world. The mid-1980s was a time rife with hostile takeovers by entrepreneurial investors with junk-bond financing. In 1986, because Ted was doing a good job of managing NL in the best interests of its shareholders, the company's undervalued assets made it ripe for a takeover by a corporate raider. Suddenly, it was "in play" and the raider was moving his pieces around the financial chessboard with unethical adroitness. The upshot was, when the SEC did not blow the whistle on what was going on in this particular case, Ted was out of a job.

Not surprisingly, with his track record in industrial management, he immediately received offers from companies located in Midwestern cities such as Akron and Indianapolis. I would have been reluctant to leave New York because of my job, and also because it would have meant taking my son David out of school and some distance away from his father. But to my lasting gratitude, Ted announced to me, "Your job is more important than mine. We are staying in New York."

His managerial expertise was soon put into pro bono service as chairman of the New York City Ballet during the critical period following George Balanchine's death. At the same time, his friend Richard Bingham, an investment banker, approached him with the then-novel idea of creating a fund for institutional investors in manufacturing enterprises, which the two of them, with their complementary business skills, would run. Thus American Industrial Partners was born in 1988.

Because of Ted's background as an organizational leader, probably the best management tutorials I received occurred at the dinner table. He never lectured me, but due to his long career running industrial plants and the fact that he was affiliated with several nonprofits, he had a perspective on institutional growth that proved very instructive. From him I learned that there is a fairly universal paradigm that follows a biological pattern analogous to the transition from birth to childhood to adolescence to maturity. At each step the growing organization becomes less free and creative and more orderly and systematized. It was now apparent to me that well-defined management protocols would, and should, be nurtured within the institutional framework of the Central Park Conservancy. They did not have to be procedurally hidebound, but written job descriptions and performance standards were essential. Ted put it succinctly: "If you can't measure, you can't manage."

Countering my deficiencies as a manager were my literary skills. I remained, as I had been from the beginning, the voice of the Central Park Conservancy. All grant proposals, all copy in annual reports, all capital campaign literature, and all brochures were written or edited by me. Every year I would write a seven- or eight-page letter to the board recounting the accomplishments of the past twelve months. I wrote and delivered lectures as a means of publicizing the Conservancy's accomplishments. Although I did not put my name on the title page, I authored the text of *Rebuilding Central Park: A Management and Restoration Plan*.

Social Capital

The degree to which money and its corollary social prestige played a role in the success of the Conservancy should not be underestimated. New Yorkers love Central Park, and as the good news of its salvation grew, I was becoming increasingly successful as a fund-raiser. To boost

Marguerite Purnell, Phyllis Wagner, Norma Dana, and Jean Clark, founders of the Women's Committee

Betsy and guests at Frederick Law Olmsted Awards Luncheon

the profile of the Conservancy, and knowing that I lacked the society connections to stage a benefit, I organized what came to be known as the Women's Committee. On May 3, 1982, under the chairmanship of its founders—Marguerite Purnell, Norma Dana, Jean Clark, and Phyllis Wagner—the first Frederick Law Olmsted Awards Luncheon was held. The honorees were the three women who had believed in the possibility of the park's restoration even before the founding of the Conservancy: Lucy Moses, Iphigene Sulzberger, and Lila Wallace, a prominent philanthropist and cofounder, with her husband, DeWitt Wallace, of *Reader's Digest* magazine. I was happy to be able to express my gratitude to each of them with the presentation of one of the bronze medals bearing a bas-relief portrait of Frederick Law Olmsted that I had recently had designed and cast for this purpose. This 1982 luncheon would be the first of a series of subsequent annual high-fashion, hat-featuring fund-raising events held in the Conservatory Garden during the first week in May.

My fashion-conscious San Antonio mother, who was delighted that I appeared to be ascending the social scale, reminded me of her credo, "Looks count," meaning that I was now in need of a designer wardrobe. Complying with her ideal of what constituted appropriate clothes for my duties as a fund-raiser, I gratefully accepted the boxes of beautiful dresses she sent and the financial help she provided in order for me to continue living in my well-appointed Park Avenue apartment following my divorce from Ed. Besides my gratitude and the return of her love for her only daughter, her greatest reward was the pleasure she had in coming to New York every year for the Olmsted Luncheon, which had become one of the major events on the city's social calendar when I penned this journal entry:

WEDNESDAY, MAY 4, 1988

Day of the annual Frederick Law Olmsted Awards Luncheon. I spend the better part of the morning at the hairdresser. Then I don my new peach-colored Adolfo suit and go to the Conservatory Garden early to peep inside the tent at the pretty pink tablecloths and bouquets resembling the flowers that are blooming in the beds that Lynden* has brought to such a state of perfection. The crabapple trees in the twin allées are in the perfect stage of their flowering, the first drifts of petals wafting to the bluestone walks beneath, and in the north garden the pink and lavender and white tulips are all open along with the electric-blue grape hyacinths. There are 950 (!) guests this year—the usual socialite attendees and the loyal park supporters too. Very festive, everyone complimenting the garden and praising the perfect weather. After I made my welcome remarks, Henry took the microphone. He chatted amiably, but his mildly amusing commentary went on too long and the guests became restless. The event chairman, financier Donald Marron, moved over to the microphone and gave a short wrap-up speech as everyone got up from their chairs, accidentally bumped hat brims as they kissed one another hello and good-bye, and strolled out of the tent and down the crabapple allées through the Vanderbilt Gates to the waiting limousines on Fifth Avenue.

But make no mistake: the Women's Committee has done much more than gild the park with remunerative socialite glitter. To wit, they established their own board of officers and developed subcommittees: the Tree Trust, which supports the care of approximately twenty thousand trees; Playground Partners, which raises funds to ensure the quality and cleanliness of Central Park's twenty-one playgrounds; and the Adopt-A-Bench program, a contribution-related means of raising funds for the Conservancy's endowment.† In addition, the Women's Committee initiated the Perimeter Association, which provides fund-

---

* As mentioned above, in 1982 I had persuaded artist-cum-gardener Lynden Miller to develop the planting plan that was necessary to restore the Conservatory Garden at Fifth Avenue and 104th Street. That this horticultural jewel, the Conservancy's first step toward restoring the derelict North End of the park, has remained the Women's Committee's venue of choice for the Frederick Law Olmsted Luncheon is a tribute to its continuing beauty and the sense of safety that now pervades this once reputedly dangerous section of the park.

† There are approximately nine thousand benches in Central Park; today more than four thousand have donors' plaques inscribed with dedications honoring parents, spouses, children, sweethearts, friends, or Central Park itself.

ing for the improvement and maintenance of Central Park's six-mile exterior tree-lined sidewalks in between its encircling wall and the street curb. As part of its mission to educate visitors and prospective Conservancy donors, some members give guided park tours.

The publication of *Rebuilding Central Park: A Management and Restoration Plan* in 1985, marking the culmination of the Conservancy's three-year planning effort, gave us the equivalent of a donor shopping list, and this became our principal fund-raising tool. Since Central Park includes Grand Army Plaza at its Fifth Avenue and Fifty-Ninth Street entrance, in addition to soliciting gifts for projects in the park proper, we undertook a special campaign to replant the plaza's border of trees, replace its broken flagstone paving, and restore its City Beautiful–era centerpiece, the 1902 gilded bronze equestrian statue of General William Tecumseh Sherman by the sculptor Augustus Saint-Gaudens. We further extended the southern boundary of this project to include the replumbing and stonework repair of the 1916 Pulitzer Fountain by architect Thomas Hastings and the removal of the crust of copper-sulfate corroding Karl Bitter's crowning bronze statue of the Goddess of Abundance, also called Pomona.

It is clear from my journal entry below that the party given to raise money for this cause was, like the Women's Committee's luncheon, an example of the Conservancy's growing cachet and the fact that private dollars were helping forge an increasingly viable public-private partnership between our organization and the Parks Department.

SATURDAY, SEPTEMBER 20, 1986

The whole park restoration effort is on a successful course right now, in spite of inevitable bureaucracy and unforeseen setbacks. I am pushing past the Parks Department's inertia barrier, but this has to be done over and over with so much dogged persistence that sometimes I become frustrated and try to imagine another career. But for now I cannot think of work for which I am more suited or which would bring greater satisfaction.

The Bergdorf extravaganza was, by the way, the last word in high-style elegance. The huge white tent over Grand Army Plaza, the softly luxurious and elegant clothes worn by impassively beautiful, thin, sexy models presenting Calvin Klein's first couture collection, the gray silk curtains dramatically parting to reveal the dining area, the tables topped with glass globes filled with white orchids, the thirty-foot-high black urns in the corners of the tent with more white orchids cascading down, the black china with delectable dishes composed like a still life, "Beautiful People" at every table—all extremely glamorous.

The Conservancy's visible success in transforming Central Park boosted its prestige, and now my calendar was filled with dedications of completed projects, fund-raising appointments, personnel matters, board meetings, various administrative chores, and the numerous parties I was expected to attend. In some quarters there was grumbling about "rich people taking over the park"—an unkind characterization of philanthropists with a genuine wish to improve an indispensable public asset and thereby benefit the population at large. I did not like to be referred to as an "elitist," an untrue characterization that rankled. There was another obstacle that had been there all along: the public appetite for controversies, especially ones in which it is a matter of watchdogging and protesting against "them"—that is, governmental or institutional officialdom. As the Conservancy grew in reputation and financial means, I was about to discover what it meant to be one of *them,* as in "Did you hear what *they* are planning to do in Central Park?"

Attuned to the vagaries of City Hall politics and focused more on the publicity surrounding individual projects than on my concept of restoring the park's original scenic beauty, Henry was prone to adopt a noncommittal wait-and-see stance whenever controversy arose. In these situations, our relationship could be considered, as he once characterized it, that of a couple whose lives together are a never-ending series of marital spats.

Chapter Ten

TROUBLED WATERS

My relationship with Henry deserves further analysis, for it strikes at the very heart of the nature of public-private partnerships. The fundamental basis of this special type of institution lies in the necessary division of power between a public agency and a private organization. Accord and cooperation are implicit in the word "partnership," and this alliance is weakened if harmony is breached too often.

Henry and Betsy

Power is a matter of authority, and there are two ways to gain it: it can be either conferred or won. In Henry's case it was conferred by the mayor; in mine it had to be won by public endorsement of the Conservancy's vision to rebuild Central Park. Here is precisely where the friction lay: As the commissioner of parks, Henry was my boss as far as my role as Central Park administrator—my city position—was concerned. However, my presidency of the Conservancy, along with the fact that this private organization paid my salary, gave me a degree of autonomy. Autonomy, however, is not the same thing as authority. Because municipal parks are public property, authority rightfully belongs to the mayor and parks commissioner. Thus, within the terms of the public-private partnership, the city's power is preeminent. For me, this meant that implementation of the elements of the plan that the Conservancy wished to undertake as private funds became available had to be endorsed by Henry.

Reverse Viewpoints

To appreciate Henry's and my differing attitudes toward Central Park's restoration, it is necessary to repeat what has been said above about our opposite perspectives on landscape design and park restoration. Put succinctly into historical terms, ours could be characterized as a rivalry between Olmsted and Moses. On one side there is the ideal of landscape design as an end in itself, in which architectural features are subsumed as inherent elements within an overall plan. On the other there is the perspective of particularity. In the latter case the park is principally a receptacle for a variety of uses, in which objects are sited according to availability of space and convenience of access rather than as elements within a unifying aesthetic.

To analogize principles of Olmstedian aesthetics, we can recall the explanation in Chapter Five of how a Claude glass served the artist or traveler in search of the Picturesque in such a way as to combine elements of scenery into a single visual frame. Similarly, in the 1780s Thomas Gainsborough invented an optical apparatus he called a "show-box" for the display of landscape paintings. Consisting of a number of

glass panels upon which he painted
landscapes, it was lit by three candles
at the back and viewed through an
adjustable magnifying lens in front.
The invention of photography in the
mid-nineteenth century fostered the
creation of another optical device for
perspectival viewing, the stereopticon, a mechanism whereby separate
left-eye and right-eye views of the
same scene merged by means of bin-
ocular vision to form a single image.

Stereopticon

Simultaneous with the creation of Central Park, it became commer-
cially successful to produce two identical photographs of the same
subject, which could be mounted on a bracket fastened at an appropriate focal distance from the eyepiece. The perspectival viewing capability of stereoscopy therefore offers another analogy for seeing the park
not as a collection of discrete objects but rather as objects within a
three-dimensional surrounding space.

Since viewing outdoor scenery is not always a static enterprise but

Stereoscopic photo of Indian Hunter *by John Quincy Adams Ward at the southwest edge of the Mall*

rather one requiring movement through space, an Olmstedian parallel can also be derived by thinking in cinematic terms. Considered in this manner, a walk through Central Park is not unlike the movement of a camera as it pans across a broad area while continuously rolling on a dolly, with frame after frame merging into a unified panorama through which moviegoers perceive themselves to be passing. For yet another comparison, imagine unrolling a Chinese scroll with sequences of scenery all melded into a single linear landscape with a continuous underlying narrative. Think, then, of the Olmstedian experience of Central Park as one of articulated movement. As the author of a recent article titled "Urban Pastorals" in *Art in America* put it, "Central Park is designed to work with human minds and human bodies. From the Great Lawn to the Ramble to the lightly managed wilds of the North Woods, the park's deliberately sculpted topography resonates with our walking feet, scanning eyes, and narrative compulsions. The shifting elevations and vantage points offer up little green scenes from which to construct a variety of memorable images. It all adds up to an immensely rich, layered experience of place."

The point of all of this is not to say that one shouldn't stop and gaze at objects of interest, but rather to emphasize that such park features gain meaning within the context of their environment, and that their presence as well as their siting and visual interrelationships are critical aspects of the art of landscape design. By way of example, view through a stereopticon the dual photographic card depicting John Quincy Adams Ward's *Indian Hunter,* which was installed at the edge of the double row of elms at the southwestern edge of the Mall in 1869. Unlike the lineup of static figures in stationary poses on Literary Walk, the half-crouching Indian stalking his prey is a study in forward motion, and the placement of this early park sculpture off axis beneath the trees may reflect an intention to position it within a sylvan setting. Undeniably, our interest in it is primarily as an object in its own right, a significant work of art by one of America's finest nineteenth-century sculptors, yet viewed within its spatial envelope of park scenery, it has a different kind of presence than would be the case if we saw it in a museum gallery. Adopting an imaginary stereoptic perspective contextualizes this particular work of art in a pleasing way, and it does not appear to visually invade space so much as occupy it.

This digression into the realm of aesthetics is meant to provide the reader with an overview of Olmsted and Vaux's design intentions when they created the Mall and Bethesda Terrace—the Greensward plan's grand architecturally united design centerpiece. It will also help explain my Olmstedian bias and unwavering policy to defend the Conservancy's management and restoration plan rather than readily accede to the politics surrounding individual park projects.

Not so much as a matter of self-vindication, but rather as a means of concretizing my defense of the premium Olmsted placed on view lines and the Conservancy's efforts to restore them in situations in which there was no apparent reason to perpetuate what was obsolete and unsightly, we will examine two opposing attitudes regarding the proposed removal of the Naumburg Bandshell. Here it should be said that there is no definitive right or wrong in deciding what should be regarded as sacrosanct and what should be removed in order to reinstate elements of a historic design. As mentioned earlier, the Conservancy's planning team had considered how best to blend the restoration of Robert Moses's 1930s recreational facilities with the principles underlying Olmsted and Vaux's original Greensward plan. But in the case of the Conservancy's proposal to remove the 1923 Naumberg Bandshell on the eastern edge of the Concert Ground at the northern end of the Mall, there was reason to consider this now-unused and unsightly pre-Moses 1923 addition to Central Park obsolete.

In my text for *Rebuilding Central Park: A Management and Restoration Plan* I summarized the history of the Mall and Concert Ground thus:

> The Mall was one of the first park features to be built. From the beginning, it was as much an axis of motion and activity as it was of directional vistas. Promenaders have strolled and children in goat carts carried along its length. Concerts were originally performed in the octagonal Moorish cast-iron Bandstand that stood in the lawn beneath the west *allée* of trees. These concerts were so popular that eventually they became a daily event, and in 1873 the paved area in front of the Bandstand had to be enlarged to accommodate the crowds that gathered there.

Strollers on Literary Walk at the southern end of the Mall, early twentieth century

Goat carts on the Concert Ground, below the Wisteria Pergola, early twentieth century

Atop a slight rise on the eastern edge of the Concert Ground, visitors would pull off the carriage drive, alight, stop off for refreshment at the Casino, and then walk over to the Wisteria Pergola to enjoy the concert and the sight of the concert goers gathered below in front of the Bandstand. . . . Eventually, it was decided that the Bandstand was acoustically inadequate. In 1923, therefore, it was demolished and replaced by the Naumburg Bandshell. The Concert Ground was enlarged, and its planting islands, gilded bird cages, pools, and fountains were sacrificed to pavement. The Bandshell was oriented so that the audience would not face the western sun during evening concerts, but this effectively destroyed the reciprocal view lines between the Concert Ground and the Wisteria Pergola, thereby rendering the Pergola obsolete as an elevated seating area overlooking the Concert Ground.

Add to this description of the Concert Ground's venerable history the Bandshell's role as the venue of the once-popular Naumburg-sponsored concerts featuring the orchestral music of Beethoven, Schubert, and Tchaikovsky and other classical composers, together with Parks Department–sponsored programs that included music by such contemporary greats as Irving Berlin. Noted bands—Benny Goodman, Duke Ellington, and Victor Herbert—had also played in the Naumburg Bandshell, and during the 1950s couples still swayed beneath the elms on the Concert Ground. Now contemplate the scene after the 1970s, when the park was dirty, unsafe, and unsightly, and when classical concerts and big-band dances were a thing of the past. One-off performances such as Rock Against Racism were also coming to an end under Gordon's administration, although there were still a few random applications to use the stage for non-park-related events, such as the concluding ceremonies of the annual March of Dimes Walk and a Legalize Marijuana rally. Thus, symbolizing the plight of the park, the virtually abandoned Bandshell became a graffiti-covered hub for drug dealing, a little-used and much-abused white elephant.

When the Conservancy made a presentation to the Landmarks Commission of its plan for the restoration of the Concert

Original Bandstand on the western edge of the Concert Ground

Concert at the Naumburg Bandshell, June 6, 1934

Ground, which included removing the Naumburg Bandshell, its members approved the project, stating that the deteriorated structure was not a notable example of Beaux Arts architecture, thereby concurring with the way I had put forth our rationale in *Rebuilding Central Park: A Management and Restoration Plan*:

> The Naumburg Bandshell, which has blocked the view of and from the Wisteria Pergola for over sixty years, has outlived its usefulness as a performance stage. Performers today use electronic sound systems, and the acoustical properties of the Bandshell are therefore redundant. The Bandshell should be removed, and events requiring a stage should take place in a newly designed music pavilion at the location of the original octagonal Victorian structure.
>
> The opening up of the Wisteria Pergola combined with effective security in the area should help put an end to the furtive drug dealing that occurs here. A small paved plaza could be set at the base of the slope leading up to the Pergola, and the bust of Beethoven, now on the west side of the Concert Ground, could be moved to this plaza close to its original position of prominence. The slope should be heavily planted with low-growth shrubs and ground covers, making an important feature out of what is now an eroded embankment with patches of weedy vegetation. Stairways should rise at a gentle incline from the center to both ends of the Pergola.
>
> The Concert Ground's original ample beds with sufficient soil for tree growth and ground-cover underplanting should be restored in order to reestablish the axis of the Mall in its entire length with newly planted elms. Replicas of the original wooden benches with cast-iron stanchions should circumscribe these planting beds. In addition to their historical significance, the benches enclosing the beds will act as a barrier to foot traffic, providing the double benefit of preventing the soil around the elms from being trampled while at the same time providing seating for 550 people. Additional portable benches would enable the space to accommodate audiences of up to 3,000. The two circular fountains that originally stood at the north end of the Mall could be rebuilt and their perimeter edges set at bench height to serve as informal seating.

Guided Tour

The space-object dichotomy I have discussed above is one that can best be understood on a site visit, but as I was to find on the numerous Concert Ground tours I gave for skeptics of the Conservancy's proposal to remove the Bandshell, in the matter of park aesthetics it was not any easier in this case to overcome objections of those who favored maintaining the status quo than it had been during the 1982 tree-removal controversy in the Ramble. This may remain so in these pages as well, but in order to understand why I championed the Olmstedian aesthetic, I would like the reader to accompany me on the following walk, where I will assume once more the role of tour guide.

Although the matter has long since been settled and the Bandshell, which is currently being renovated by the Conservancy, will remain on the Concert Ground for the foreseeable future, our tour will nevertheless provide a useful if purely theoretical exercise by positing the question of which preservation policy should take precedence: that in the spirit of Olmsted and Vaux's concept of the Greensward plan as a cohesion of architectural and scenic elements, or one that opts to take a palimpsestic approach, retaining and restoring a particular feature imposed on the landscape at a later date as a tangible record of the park's alteration over time.

Our route will start from the south, where the Mall begins above the Sixty-Fifth Street Transverse Road at the point where Marble Arch has lain buried since Robert Moses's reconfiguration of the adjacent park drive. Here stroll with me beneath the canopy formed by double rows of American elm trees on either side. Olmsted and Vaux intended their graceful V-shaped branching pattern to resemble the curving ribs supporting the overarching vault of a cathedral nave. Literary Walk (the southern end of the Mall, which was so named when it became lined with statues of famous men of letters) leads to the Concert Ground. This may not be readily apparent, but if you follow the Mall-cathedral analogy, you can think of the way in which the longitudinal axis of this metaphorical elm-tree "nave" is intersected by a cross axis that can be likened to a cathedral transept when you reach the expanded space that forms the Concert Ground.

Wisteria Pergola following restoration by the Central Park Conservancy

Here, if you look to the west, where the Beethoven statue is today, you see the spot where the ornamental cast-iron Music Pavilion once stood. Directly opposite, on the other side of the Concert Ground, the Wisteria Pergola crowns the rocky slope overlooking the Mall. In the nineteenth century, park-goers sitting in the shade of the overhead vines of this open-sided loggia could watch the passing parade of people congregating around the Music Pavilion below and join them in listening to the John Philip Sousa marches, choral concerts, and folk music that were regularly performed.

It is still pleasant today to sit beneath the Pergola—one of our rustic-carpentry crew's earliest restoration projects—especially in

June, when the fragrant wisteria is in bloom. Notice, however, that the view looking west is the blank half-domed curved wall of the back of the Bandshell and toward the east the location where Moses replaced the historic Casino with Rumsey Playground. Since building a replica of the historic Music Pavilion on its original site on the Mall would have been impracticable, the Conservancy sought to erect on the abandoned Rumsey Playground a temporary portable stage that could be disassembled and stored off-site when it was not in use in the winter. It was intended as a performance platform to showcase New York City's multiethnic artistic talent during the summer months; hence "Summerstage" was the name I chose for it. In the meantime, while awaiting public approval of the Concert Ground project and in anticipation of the now disused Rumsey Playground becoming the venue for a new temporary stage, we sponsored a variety of performances in the deteriorated but still functional Bandshell in the hope of dislodging the established drug dealers and providing a taste of the kind of popular park entertainment we planned to sponsor.

With the future of Summerstage in mind, we changed the name "Rumsey Playground" to "Rumsey Playfield," since the rolled, compacted sand fines we proposed to replace its asphalt paving made an

Highway-style "cobra-head" lights, oil-drum litter receptacles, and constricted tree pits on the Concert Ground before installation of new paving, proper drainage, spacious planting beds, and redesigned park furniture

Concert Ground seating before removal of original benches

Replication of the Concert Ground's original continuous bench seating encircling planting beds containing newly planted elm trees and historic lampposts with the Central Park Conservancy's custom-designed luminaires

ideal surface for sports and outdoor games in the fall and spring. As a bonus, the East Green and other nearby lawns would no longer be as vulnerable to abuse from the cleated shoe soles of gym-class students.

This scenario, however, never materialized under the auspices of the Central Park Conservancy. While the project was undergoing the normal review process, Betsy Gotbaum, who had by then succeeded Henry as commissioner of parks, decided that the City Parks Foundation (the Parks Department's in-house not-for-profit fund-raising organization that she had initiated shortly after taking office) would take over the operation of the Conservancy's original Summerstage program. The purportedly temporary stage she acquired and erected on the Rumsey site proved to be a year-round facility. Its tall steel trusses are now permanently anchored in the ground, and during the off-season stage equipment is stored in the comfort station constructed by Robert Moses within the footprint of the demolished Casino.

As stated in the text of the management and restoration plan quoted above, the planned removal of the Naumburg Bandshell was part of a larger project that included a complete renovation of the Mall. Fortunately, this part of the project was carried out. As we stand on the Concert Ground today on our imaginary tour, notice how buckled and cracked asphalt has been replaced with smooth, hexagonal paving blocks and how the generous-sized planting beds resembling the original ones now contain replacements for the dying and dead elm trees whose roots were constricted when the entire Concert Ground was enlarged and paved over in the mid-twentieth century. In addition, notice how we were able to replicate the original decorative bench backing and sculptural supports, making possible the construction of a continuous line of benches such as had formerly encircled and protected the trees and groundcovers in the planting beds. Observe, too, how we replaced the ugly highway-style steel light poles that had been installed on the Concert Ground with traditional cast-iron lampposts containing the Conservancy's custom-designed luminaires.

At the Mall's terminus at the Seventy-Second Street Cross Drive, we are poised to experience a brilliant example of Olmsted and Vaux's genius. Withheld from view until now, Bethesda Terrace, where the elevation drops sharply to the level of the Lake, is accessed through an architecturally elegant underpass below the Cross Drive. If you

Grand stairs descending from the Mall to the Bethesda Terrace Arcade

descend the grand staircase before you, you will have arrived at the ample below-grade Bethesda Terrace Arcade. As you walk beneath its ornamental Victorian tile ceiling, notice how the central arch of its triple-arched entry to the Terrace proper frames Bethesda Fountain. Having been withheld from the vantage point of the Mall, this view of the bronze fountain surmounted by artist Emma Stebbins's sculpture of the Angel of Bethesda supported by four cherubs symbolizing temperance, purity, health, and peace comes as an unexpected surprise.

But say you do not wish to reach Bethesda Terrace by this route. Instead of descending the stairs at the northern terminus of the Mall and entering the Terrace Arcade, you can walk across the Seventy-Second Street cross-park drive, where, standing next to the carved stone parapet, you will have a fine overhead view of the entire Terrace with Bethesda Fountain in its center. By taking one or the other of a pair of grand staircases with ornamental stone side panels carved with vegetal motifs symbolizing the four seasons, you will now be able to descend, admire the angel-surmounted fountain up close, and then stand between the pair of gonfalons fluttering on either side of the carved stone coping at the edge of the Lake. As you gaze toward the Ramble on the opposite shore, notice how the formal lines of Bethesda Terrace have simply dissolved into the surrounding Pictur- esque park landscape. By considering the intentional design sequenc- ing of the promenade you have just taken from the foot of Literary Walk to Bethesda Terrace, you will have gained an understanding of the primary principle of the Olmstedian approach to landscape design as movement through space. The reintegration of this prime example of spatial sequencing with the restoration of the Concert Ground itself was only accomplished, however, after a protracted controversy over whether the Naumburg Bandshell would remain in situ or be removed in order to complete the project according to its original holistic con- cept. Although this never happened, with the restoration of the Mall itself and Bethesda Terrace, the climax of its stately progression, the Conservancy could still claim victory in terms of reanimating the heart of the park. In the meantime, however, much emotional energy was expended on both sides of a hard-fought battle.

Vocal Opposition

Even though the Conservancy had already obtained approval from the Landmarks Commission for its landscape restoration project calling for the removal of the Bandshell, I felt it incumbent on me to speak with Elkan Naumburg's descendants. If reluctant to see a piece of their family's history disappear, the family members with whom I met concurred that it had been several years since the Naumburg concerts had been relocated to Lincoln Center's rear plaza because of the park's lack of safety, the Concert Ground's use as a hangout for drug dealers, and the defacement of the Bandshell by graffiti. I discussed a proposed memorial, which in this case would not only contain a bronze plaque but would be a work of public art in its own right. I showed them a preliminary sketch by sculptor Elyn Zimmerman, with its stepped- down granite seating and a tumble of natural boulders set into the slope between the Concert Ground and the Wisteria Pergola. On the polished surface of one of these there was to be an incised inscription honoring Elkan Naumburg and the family's long association with the site. The meeting ended politely but inconclusively, and I went away feeling encouraged to persist in my advocacy of the project.

I will not try the reader's patience here with a recital of the ensuing Sturm und Drang that went on, in which a younger member of the Naumburg family mounted a campaign that resulted in a 1992 lawsuit against the Central Park Conservancy and the Parks Department. Lacking the support of Henry, who with gadfly insouciance took a politically expedient position in the controversy, saying "this is a matter of taste upon which reasonable people may differ," the Conservancy's cause was a lost one by this time.

Today most people do not know, care, or remember that the Concert Ground was once an ideological battlefield. Indeed, members of the generations dubbed "X" and "Millennial" often look at me with blank expressions when I mention that Central Park was nearly destroyed in the 1970s before many of them were born. It is their park now, and it would be wrong to take issue and suggest mounting another effort to implement the restoration of the site according to the intention laid forth in the Conservancy's 1985 management and restoration plan. I therefore remind myself that Central Park's fundamental design has proved so durable that it has been remarkably able to absorb many compromising encroachments during the past 150 years without entirely losing its scenic integrity.

Taking this historical perspective, one realizes that the park has had many lives and will continue to reflect the cultural values of each period in its history in the same way that it has in the past. When George Templeton Strong penned this entry in his journal on May 28, 1860, the park was in the early phase of its construction:

> The park below the reservoir begins to look intelligible. Unfinished still, and in the process of manufacture, but showing the outline now of what is to be. Many points are already beautiful. What will they be when their trees are grown and I'm dead and forgotten?

Before he died in 1875, Strong must have observed the park when the trees had indeed grown and the place appeared much as Walt Whitman found it when he recorded his impressions in May 1879:

I visit Central Park now almost every day, sitting or slowly rambling, or riding around. The whole place presents its very best appearance this current month—the full flush of the trees, the plentiful white and pink of the flowering shrubs, the emerald green of the grass spreading everywhere, yellow dotted still with dandelions—the specialty of the plentiful gray rocks, peculiar to these grounds, cropping out, miles and miles—and overall the beauty and purity, three days out of four, of our summer skies.

In 1905, when touring his native land as a visiting expatriate, Henry James, adopting the feminine pronoun in reference to the park, gave this account in *The American Scene:*

You are perfectly aware, as you hang about her in May and June, that you *have* as a travelled person, beheld more remarkable scenery and communed with nature in ampler or fairer forms; but it is quite equally definite to you that none of those adventures have counted more to you for experience, for stirred sensibility—inasmuch as you can be, at the best, and in the showiest countries, only thrilled by the pastoral and the awful, and as to pass, in New York, from the discipline of the streets to this so different many-smiling presence is to be thrilled at every turn.

In this book I have tried to conjure these successive lives of Central Park, beginning with its creation in 1858. We have seen how parts of the park have been transformed under the administrations of parks commissioners with little interest in perpetuating the Olmstedian ideal of naturalistic landscape design for the purpose of scenic recreation. We have seen as well how much pleasure some of the park's alterations have brought to new generations of park users. In light of our discussion of the Bandshell controversy, it is worth quoting the following passage from *Here Is New York,* written by E. B. White in 1949:

Another hot night I stop off at the Goldman Band concert in the Mall in Central Park. The people seated on the benches fanned out in front of the band shell are attentive, appreciative. In the trees the night wind stirs, bringing the leaves to life, endowing them with speech;

the electric lights illuminate the green branches from the under side, translating them into a new language. Overhead a plane passes dreamily, its running lights winking. On the bench directly in front of me, a boy sits with his arm around his girl; they are proud of each other and are swathed in music. The cornetist steps forward for a solo, begins, "Drink to me only with thine eyes. . . ." In the wide, warm night the horn is startlingly pure and magical. Then from the North River another horn solo begins—the Queen Mary announcing her intentions. She is not on key; she is a half tone off. The trumpeter in the bandstand never flinches. The horns quarrel savagely, but no one minds having the intimation of travel injected into the pledge of love. "I leave," sobs Mary. "And I will pledge with mine," sighs the trumpeter. Along asphalt paths strollers pass to and fro; they behave considerately, respecting the musical atmosphere. Popsicles are moving well. In the warm grass beyond the fence, forms wriggle in the shadows, and the skirts of the girls approaching on the Mall are ballooned by the breeze, and their bare shoulders catch the lamplight. "Drink to me only with thine eyes." It is a magical occasion, and it's all free.

It is impossible for me to take issue with this or any other form of physical and emotional pleasure offered by Central Park—and they are numerous for me personally as well as for countless others. The issue that arose over the proposed removal of the Bandshell simply highlights my motive to save as much as possible of its original designers' intended scenic effects, as described above by Strong and Whitman and James. This was a preeminent ambition in guiding my career in spearheading the park's restoration, and the continuation of this aesthetic beyond my tenure is for me a source of grateful satisfaction. The belief in the value of natural beauty as a source of spiritual well-being guided me and the other authors of the Conservancy's management and restoration plan in our attempts to recapture the essence of the Greensward plan wherever practicable, and our mission became to meld to the extent possible whatever later additions were still in active use and publicly popular into an integrated landscape that is both scenic and serviceable.

As we have seen, the Moses-era ethos in which the park remained a safe, well-managed place was utterly undermined during the decline of New York City beginning in the 1960s when unregulated use and an absence of decent management drove it toward dereliction. Imagine how shocked E. B. White would have been by the happenings-cum-concerts scheduled at the Concert Ground during the 1970s, when, instead of the sweet plaintive sound of a cornet wafting on the breeze of a summer night, he would have heard loud rock music emanating from amplifiers at the graffiti-covered Bandshell.

But the era in which the Conservancy proposed the removal of the Bandshell and the return of the Concert Ground to its original spatial relationship with the Wisteria Pergola and the rest of the Mall is now gone, too. Today we live in what I take pride in calling Central Park's golden age, when, under the Conservancy's management, the park is no longer dirty and dangerous. Regularly scheduled programmed events once again take place on the Concert Ground, among them a summer series of classical concerts at the Bandshell fittingly sponsored by the Naumburg Foundation. And thanks to increasingly successful fund-raising, the Conservancy's overall park restoration agenda has gained momentum and the formerly decrepit Bandshell is being restored rather than removed. Its continued presence on the Mall because of the Conservancy's earlier failure to bring back the original view lines between the Concert Ground and the Wisteria Pergola does not, however, mean that the park will not continue to be improved and made more scenic by reestablishing view lines elsewhere. Unfortunately, concurrent with the fracas over the Bandshell, a second proposed restoration project, which also involved the replacement of a dilapidated park structure, would not be realized either.

Tennis Anyone?

In 1987 Ira and Miriam Wallach, philanthropists whose generosity spread across several important city institutions, came to my office in the Arsenal to announce that as lifelong New Yorkers they wished to acknowledge their appreciation of Central Park with a gift of a million dollars. I explained to the Wallachs how the Conservancy's management and restoration plan served as a catalog of gift opportunities for prospective donors and offered to drive them around the park to look at several sites for future projects. As we moved at a slow speed along the park pathways in a Conservancy minivan, I pointed out certain potential landscape restorations along the way. When we reached the area between Ninety-Fourth and Ninety-Sixth Streets near the West Drive, I paused next to the tennis courts. Here I explained that the courts had been recently resurfaced but that the 1930 Tennis House next to them was in poor condition. Since Mrs. Wallach had been a tennis player, this was the project that struck her as the one to select. We agreed that it would be better to replace, rather than renovate, this badly deteriorated structure.

The next step was to hire an architect to design the proposed new Tennis House. Based in part on our good working relationship at Bethesda Terrace and the new refreshment pavilion on the site of the historic Ballplayers House (another original building that had been demolished by Robert Moses), we chose Buttrick White & Burtis, a firm known for its conservative yet contemporary style. Harry Buttrick, the founder of the firm, was the lead architect on this project, and his plan for the new Tennis House had an exterior that was responsive to the architectural style of Calvert Vaux and an interior layout with ample new facilities for concession staff and players. His decision to relocate the structure from its low-lying site on the south side of the courts to a knoll overlooking them on the north side would provide views of the players on the courts from a broad, sunny verandah on the front of the building. As with all of the Conservancy's proposed capital projects in Central Park, this one was reviewed by the adjacent community board and the Landmarks and Public Design Commissions, as well as by the design and construction division of the Parks Department. With unanimously favorable approvals in hand, the architects then prepared contract documents, which the Conservancy proceeded to put out to bid.

Less than a week before the construction firm that had been awarded the bid was to break ground for the new building (the old one would remain operable during construction), Henry put the project on hold after receiving a call from Manhattan Borough President David Dinkins, saying that he had heard that a controversy was brewing over the building of a new Tennis House. Thus began a two-year saga in which fence-sitting politicians and Tennis House players with a tacit insiders' monopoly on the use of the courts pushed Conservancy planners toward protracted defeat. Henry publicly dissociated himself from the dispute by telling a *New York Times* reporter that this is "a Betsy Barlow Rogers–Conservancy project." Afterward, he called to apologize and say that he was secretly in favor of it. But, as things dragged on, he enjoined me not to move forward until the matter was settled once and for all. However, as time went on, the project appeared to be in a state of permanent paralysis. Convinced that such was the case, I wrote the following obituary in my journal:

SUNDAY, OCTOBER 10, 1987

The Tennis House project is now dead. Henry justifies his position: "What could I do when Borough President Dinkins called last July and said to wait? How could I disappoint an elected official who votes on every parks project at the Board of Estimate?" I refrain from reminding him it might not have turned out this way if he had told the borough commissioner back in July that this was a desirable, privately funded gift to the people of New York City that was being stymied by a small group of players whose argument that "rich people" were appropriating a public amenity was specious. He would have countered, however, by saying that he could not oppose Dinkins, who was a senior public official, and that this was the reason he had chosen not to become involved in the controversy. I am heartsick since I know that by not allowing the Conservancy to proceed with the project after affirmative resolutions had been passed by every mandated review authority and, with building permit issued, funding in hand, final construction documents prepared, bid awarded, and the contractor ready to break ground, by disassociating himself from the Conservancy Henry has allowed the project to become a popularity contest and media circus, thereby giving the opposition the crucial ingredient for its success: time. Time, that is, to organize, petition, harangue public officials, and develop specious arguments with seemingly reasonable logic. In other words, time to cloud public opinion with doubt. People think that if there is so much fuss, it must be about *something*. The opposition, by its implacable persistence, has won the day. I have now been assured by the chairman of Community Planning Board 7 that if it were to come to a vote now, the members would reason that with such a lot of noise and anger, what is logical and right must in fact be wrong. By stepping aside and not calendaring a vote of resolution by the full board, he wishes to spare me further embarrassment. Henry has said that he will help me think of a way to announce the reversal of plans without appearing to have been overruled.

It turned out, however, that the project was only dying and not yet dead. As we have seen, Borough President Dinkins, who was a tennis player himself, preferred to let the debate be prolonged rather than announce a decision on his part one way or another. Having listened sympathetically to the Tennis House opponents, Henry decided that he now wanted the Conservancy to build a redesigned Tennis House on the site of the old one. He tried to convince me that what was at issue was simply the site. "But the existing site is wrong," I insisted, "and besides, we can't go on and on designing the thing with the disgruntled tennis players acting the role of client, as if they owned the place. Another year of constant meetings with them would be very distasteful."

"Do as you wish," Henry replied. "I can't stop the Conservancy from spending its money however it pleases." I continued to argue my case, urging him to join me in going to the Wallachs for the difficult conversation about our either returning their million-dollar gift or diverting their philanthropy toward a different park restoration project. But he demurred, saying, "Why should I go when I really prefer to have a new Tennis House in the same location as the old one? There's room, after all, for intelligent people to disagree about these things." Reluctantly, I asked the architects to go back to their drawing boards and develop a new design within the footprint of the old Tennis House. But still the project remained in limbo.

It would have been counterproductive for me to become angry or bear a grudge in response to the slow torture I continued to endure before I had to tell the Wallachs that the project was definitely not going forward. Henry and I remained on ostensibly amicable terms, and I was able to sincerely compliment him on a good editorial he received in the *Times* praising his creation of the Historic House Trust, an office to protect the historic-house properties lying within the Parks Department's jurisdiction. That he had so consistently refused to buy into my vision of the restored park and seen the Conservancy as an outside force he needed to thwart rather than an integral asset of his administration was painful but did not cause a serious breach in our friendship. That he cared for New York City's parks in small, noncontroversial, politically safe ways was certainly better than indifference, and as the uncertain outcome of the pending election loomed, in the spirit of "the devil you know" I felt I would rather stick with Henry than try to build a modus vivendi with a new commissioner who would likely be a mayoral patronage appointment. Moreover, there was some merit to be had in trying to emulate Henry's savvy and enjoy his quirky humor, if not his more outré eccentricities and demeaning prejudices.

The lesson from the Bandshell and Tennis House controversies confirmed what I had already learned and then forgotten during my previous bruising battle in 1982 with a group of birdwatchers over the "arborcide" I had purportedly committed in the Ramble. In hewing to the reverse of the saying "might makes right," I had found out once more that my belief in the rightness of the Olmstedian principles that undergird the park's design did not necessarily produce the requisite might to implement them once they became a press-worthy cause célèbre spearheaded by a small but militant opposition.

Happily, the unpleasant controversies discussed above did not discourage donors from continuing to fund the kinds of projects that did in fact restore much of the park to its original scenic beauty. In addition, the Conservancy's annual fund balance for general operations continued to grow. Besides my ongoing job satisfaction as, zone by zone, the jigsaw puzzle pieces of the management and restoration plan began to fit together, I had the gratification of being the creator of a landscape plan over which I had complete control: my own Long Island garden.

Chapter Eleven

GARDENING DAYS

I am one of those non-native New Yorkers who adopt the city as their home with an unshakable degree of attachment, feeling lucky to live in the most vibrant metropolis in the world. I knew, however, at the time I moved there with Ed and Lisa in 1964, that our family would want a weekend and summer-vacation retreat where we could step outside onto grass rather than concrete. With a gift from my parents and the remainder of the trust fund that had enabled me to go to graduate school, the next year I bought a small farmhouse on a two-and-a-half-acre lot in Wainscott, a little one-room-schoolhouse village situated between Bridgehampton and East Hampton on the South Fork of Long Island. In those days, before its transformation into the land of McMansions for the rich, powerful, and famous, the area was simply called "the country," not "the Hamptons." The former term was certainly more in keeping with the character of our house and its surrounding scruffy lawn ending in a crowded tangle of spindly oak and locust second-growth trees, catbrier-clad underbrush, and a stand of pitch pines with charred trunks from an old fire.

Ironically, because it was surrounded by tall oaks of impressive maturity, our house, in spite of its unprepossessing appearance, had been given a social register name, Little Acorns, by the couple who

My farmhouse on Sayres Path, Wainscott, in its original state with an outhouse in back

were its previous owners and precursors of the ensuing gentrification of the area. Although close to the nearby Georgica Association with its rambling turn-of-the-twentieth-century gray-shingled houses with big verandahs, Sayres Path, our street, was a modest thoroughfare. Old Mrs. Emmett, an Englishwoman who lived in a small cottage directly across from us, had been "in service" to a wealthy New York family who summered in East Hampton, and Mr. Niggles three doors down was a mechanic with a car repair shop in his garage.

Built in 1906, our house originally looked something like a child's crayon diagram—a two-story-tall rectangle topped by a triangle representing the gable roof over an attic. During the Second World War, at the time when the Coast Guard was patrolling the shoreline of Long Island's South Fork on the lookout for German submarines, the local farm family who owned it had moved out and an evacuee from the area around Montauk Point was allowed to occupy it.

Put up for sale after the war, the house was bought by Mrs. Emmett as a home for her daughter Rachel, who, with her husband, Ralph, undertook its first stage of improvement. They combined the front parlor and dining room downstairs into a living room with a fireplace, sacrificed one of the three upstairs bedrooms in order to build a pair of indoor bathrooms as replacements for the outhouse in back, and covered the dirt floor of the basement with a concrete slab. They also planted the still-beautiful mountain laurel by the split-rail fence in front of the house. Mr. and Mrs. Lewis, the subsequent owners from whom I bought the place, constructed a modern kitchen, and Mrs. Lewis, who was a gardener, planted a camellia tree[*] in a sheltered location next to the kitchen steps. She also planted a spruce, now grown to towering height, some daffodils, and a vegetable garden where the lawn ended and a second-growth woodland commenced.

S hortly after we moved in for the summer on Memorial Day in 1965, I planted tomatoes, corn, zinnias, marigolds, and dahlias in Mrs. Lewis's abandoned vegetable garden and was so pleased with the result that one evening after dinner I penned this poem:

COUNTRY BOUQUET

Who could paint you, oh you so red dahlias?
Sensual, your hundred whorled crimson tongues
Drink up the evening light
Ruby as opera house upholstery
Theatrical as blood
You glow, all innocent lasciviousness
Young virgins dressed in crimson velvet
Pretending you are
As rich as roses
Simple country bumpkins!
Now bowing over the dinner debris
On the table. Accepting my
Applause

The annual repetition of these modest horticultural endeavors constituted the sum of my gardening activities for the next ten years.

---

[*] A southern species normally found in gardens in and around Charleston, this beautiful Asian shrub with large pink flowers has somehow miraculously survived for more than half a century.

Landscape Art

To bicycle or drive past potato fields with pale lavender spring blossoms and furrowed ridges of loamy soil after the potatoes had been harvested and stored in long rectangular barns was my primary connection to eastern Long Island's landscape beauty back then. The ocean's roar could be heard from the house, and the broad sandy beach stretching in either direction as far as the eye could see was just a scant half-mile from the door. Looking at the scrubby bayberry- and beach-plum-covered dunes and moisture-laden pearly Atlantic light, I could understand why the American Impressionist painter Childe Hassam was drawn to the area. It was equally obvious why other American landscape artists joined him as members of the art colony that grew up in East Hampton in the first years of the twentieth century.

Among the generation of artists on Long Island's South Fork at the time I arrived there, Fairfield Porter, Jane Freilicher, Jane Wilson, Robert Dash, and Sheridan Lord were painting more contemporary versions of the domestic scenes and field-and-ocean landscapes that had drawn their predecessors to the area. Their homes and studios were located in Southampton, Watermill, and Sagaponack, not far from my place in Wainscott, so the subjects of their works on canvas were those of the scenes that I found so pleasing in real life.

The more famous artists of the area at the time were the Abstract Expressionists, members of the New York School—most notably Willem de Kooning and Jackson Pollock, and less prominently Lee Krasner and James Brooks—who had built their studios in the Springs, the blue-collar community beside Acabonack Harbor north of Amagansett. Even though I admired their work and still do, I remain more profoundly attracted to the plein air artists mentioned above.

In those days before I was to discover that my principal artistic endeavor was to occur in Central Park with the restoration, rather than the representation, of a landscape, I briefly engaged in a career of my own as a painter. Following a summer course offered by the Museum of Modern Art in a renovated two-story barge located in the dunes between Amagansett and Montauk, I enrolled in a class at the Art Students League in New York, where I was able to paint from the model. The next summer back in Wainscott, the downstairs room we had built off the living room served as my turpentine-scented studio. I also took up photography in a serious way and began to get some good pictures of the beach and the surrounding Long Island scenery.

Before long, however, I realized that I was a better writer than artist. My first book, *The Forests and Wetlands of New York City,* had received favorable reviews and been nominated for a National Book Award upon its publication in 1971, and my second, *Frederick Law Olmsted's New York,* became the foundation for my mission to recapture some of Central Park's original Olmstedian beauty.

As has been discussed above, in undertaking this daunting venture in 1974 under the auspices of the Central Park Task Force, I found my skill as an author to be a primary asset in articulating its projects and programs as well as a boon when it came to writing grant applications for their funding. Still, I was not ready to give up writing books altogether. Thus, I began a collaboration with Random House editor Jason Epstein on a history and guidebook covering the township of East Hampton. This project started with Jason's interest in the once-thriving whaling industry of Sag Harbor, where he owned a fine old nineteenth-century house just off Main Street, and my simultaneous research on the settlement of Wainscott as a second- and third-generation farming outlier of the original East Hampton settlement.

I enjoyed my role as coauthor with Jason and briefly considered collaborating with him again on a series of similar place-specific historic guidebooks. At the same time, I took a job composing narrations for a Time-Life television series called *Wild Wild World of Animals* and began to seek commissions to write magazine articles. In 1974 when the opportunity to do a book review for *New York* magazine of Nigel Nicolson's *Portrait of a Marriage* about his father, diplomat Harold Nicolson, and mother, the inspired gardener, garden writer, and poet Vita Sackville-West, I seized it. Accompanied by my freshman-year Wellesley College roommate Linton Carter Watts, I visited Sissinghurst, the ancient castle in Kent where the couple had created their now-famous garden in the 1930s. Thus began a new chapter of my life, one that was nurtured by both my love of the beautiful and fertile area around Wainscott as a milieu of art and agriculture and Olmsted's design of Central Park as a combination of art and nature.

Sissinghurst was for me a transformative experience. Guided by Nigel Nicolson, I took note of his father's axial organization of hedges and pathways to form a series of garden rooms and, as a romantic counterpoint to this classical plan, his mother's abundant beds of perennials and heritage roses weaving a brocade in which color, scale, and texture were in perfect harmony. Now I began to understand that gardening is another art form that might be likened to painting, architecture, and sculpture all in one.

After this epiphany there would be no more flashy annuals such as zinnias and marigolds for me! When I returned to my Wainscott garden, I promptly dug up the picket-fenced side yard outside the kitchen, laid out a rectangle of brick walks, filled my planting beds-to-be with good soil, and outlined the square one in the center with box hedging. This small bit of geometry represented the influence of Harold Nicolson's classical order. As for Sackville-West's luxuriant romanticism, I could never match her genius as a plantswoman, but to make a stab in this direction I filled almost an entire bookcase with plant dictionaries and gardening books, visited local nurseries, and ordered catalogs, including the delightfully chatty one Will Tillotson published for his appropriately named California business Roses of Yesterday and Today. Knowing how the gardens of English village

David at age four in the Cottage Garden

Center bed of Cottage Garden, September 2015

cottagers had inspired Sackville-West, I began to call the little patch
outside my kitchen door with its picket fence and preexisting tool
shed the Cottage Garden.

It sounds absurd to compare my naively conceived Wainscott effort
to one of the great landscape masterpieces of the English aristocracy's
golden twilight. But after laying out the Cottage Garden with artistic
and horticultural help of my friend Lynden Miller, I ordered several
of Tillotson's old heritage roses: the 1750 Damask 'Celciana'; the 1834
Alba 'Felicite Parmentier'; 'Konigen von Danemark' (Queen of Den-
mark), an Alba introduced in 1826; the China rose 'Old Blush' from
1752; 'Madame Isaac Pereire,' an 1880 Bourbon rose; another Bourbon, the exquisite and tender 'Souvenir de la Malmaison' from 1843;
and the Gallica 'Rosa Mundi' versicolor, dating from Elizabethan
times. For height and contrast with the white paint of the picket fence
I chose the eighteenth-century 'Rosa Rugosa Rubra,' and to overtop
the arbor I built as the entry to the Cottage Garden I chose the mid-
twentieth-century climbing rose 'White Dawn.'

I then bought a copy of an English stone urn to serve as an ornamental centerpiece for the square boxwood-hedged center bed. To
announce spring I planted blue grape hyacinths and crocuses next to

the kitchen steps. Then, after reading Russell Page's classic book *The Education of a Gardener,* I dug another planting bed in the back of the house, where I copied his idea for mixing black and white tulips and under-planting them with blue forget-me-nots.

Mastering a bit of botanical Latin and learning some horticultural ABCs were satisfying, but it was still the ambience and painterly beauty of the surrounding landscape that mattered most to me. Here is how I expressed it in my journal:

MAY 27, 1978

Memorial Day weekend bringing as it almost always does the full ripeness of spring and coming of summer. In the fields the new potato plants are up, still discrete files amid the reddish-brown loam. Some of their vines will intermingle as they blossom with pale lavender flowers and the new fields will be a verdant haze accentuated by the luminous sea air. Fragrance of grass and lilacs promises roses as we move toward June, the gardener's month.

Park Gardener

Becoming a serious gardener and assuming my role as director of the Central Park Task Force proved synergetic. The following journal entry gives an idea of the fun I was having gardening in the park alongside a group of summer interns:

JULY 28, 1978

"Watch out for the poison ivy!"

"Any in here?"

"Hey, here comes Kenny! We knew you wouldn't miss pay-day, Kenny." Laughter.

"Man, it was raining."

"Yeah, not hard enough to stop working."

These are the voices of teenagers in a group of twenty recruited from all five boroughs of New York City. We call them summer interns, and it is my job to find useful tasks for them that will further what I am optimistically calling the restoration of Central Park. Today we are weeding the rhododendron beds on the slope beside the eastern margin of the Reservoir. Winnie and I are working in tandem under the instruction of Marie Ruby, the young horticulturist I have hired as their supervisor, whose pretty face is illumined with enthusiasm for this, her first job. We pull out Japanese knotweed by the roots but leave whatever creeping vines there are and only clip maple and other unwanted "weed tree" seedlings to the ground so that their roots will remain to anchor the soil and prevent further erosion of the slope. We are squatting with our pruning shears beneath a hawthorn tree, the parent of a tiny forest of six-inch-high hawthorn seedlings.

Yank. I pull out a piece of knotweed. This is the most invasive volunteer plant in Central Park. It springs up unbidden everywhere, inserting itself into rock crevices and spreading across large swaths of the ground in the Ramble and around the Loch in the park's northern end. It is practically impossible to eradicate as it puts out rhizomes that snake underground, so, even if you pull up one shoot, there are more ready to spring up lushly here,

Betsy weeding in Central Park, 1975

Central Park Task Force intern pruning, 1975

there, and everywhere as the energy of the piece of knotwood you have just removed is transferred back into the lateral suckers and adventitious roots put forth at intervals along these underground stems.

"A bee, a bee!" someone yells. Everybody in the group is bee-conscious this week because a few days ago one of the interns received four stings when she inadvertently plunged her hand into a beehive beneath a tangled skein of hedge bindweed that encumbered one of the rhododendrons. Marie and two other interns got a sting apiece as angry bees swarmed out of the hive. "Fortunately," Marie says, "none of us was allergic, but I worry about some of the kids who have never been stung before. They don't know whether they are allergic or not."

"Did you get rid of the hive?" I ask Marie. Pointing to the rhododendrons, she replies, "Actually there are two hives in there. I'd love to get the bindweed removed from those bushes. It looks kind of funny to see them smothered like this when the rest of the place has been weeded and cleaned up. But then I thought of the role of the bees in the park, their importance in pollinating all the other plants, so I decided it was best to leave them alone." The students appear to concur in the vote for ecology over possible pain. "It wasn't too bad," says Emily, referring to her sting.

The interns are given a break from the routine of work three afternoons a week when they are turned over to Jeff Dullea, an environmental education specialist from the New York Botanical Garden. This summer some members of the group are doing a user study to determine the environmental impact people have on the park. The others are collecting and pressing plant specimens for their Central Park plant herbariums. While handling them, the kids display a healthy respect for nature's booby traps. "If there's any poison sumac in this park," announces Kenny, "I'm not putting it in my herbarium!"

With the knowledge they have gained from this exercise in plant identification, the students can readily distinguish between shoots and weeds in the rhododendron beds. Emily: "It's a sassafrass. Don't cut it." Ann: "Emily, it's got to go." Crack. Emily, grabbing the cut end and inhaling: "Ummmm, I love the smell!"

Parallel Universe

Although I no longer had time to spend a happy summer morning weeding with a group of teenagers, the connection between my work in Central Park and the continuing building of the garden on Long Island increased as the Conservancy took up the banner under which the Task Force had formerly marched. All of the landscape improvements in the park did not have to be done within the context of capital projects. Removing the invasive Japanese knotweed and planting understory trees and shrubs were an ongoing part of the Conservancy's park restoration agenda. Clearing tangles of undergrowth and dead brush and transforming formerly unkempt woodland acres into attractive park scenery were now routine work. In the process of planning these horticultural improvements, I became familiar with some of the nurseries within a hundred-mile radius of New York City from which we purchased shrubs and trees.

So far I had gardened only on the front acre of my property, but now I saw how in the unkempt second-growth woods beyond the back lawn I could have my own miniature Ramble. I would take my cue from the Greensward plan and, using mostly native plant material, would create a naturalistic impression in the Olmstedian manner. Thus, on my drives out to Wainscott for the weekend I would sometimes stop at Baier Lustgarten's nursery in Middle Island and buy hemlocks and rhododendrons for the edge of my woods. Stuffing as many of these plants into the back of my battered brown secondhand Oldsmobile station wagon as possible, upon arriving I would lug them in a wheelbarrow to my miniature Ramble-in-the-making. When they were too heavy or too large for me to manage alone, I would hire a man to help dig holes in the places where I wished to put them.

As the small hemlock trees gained height and the rhododendrons coalesced into dark green clumps, my hitherto-unvisited Wainscott back acre now had a landscape screen that gave the impression that a woodland lay beyond. I still had to take into account the fact that the real Ramble in Central Park was thirty acres in area with numerous winding paths carrying one into its Romantic recesses. Nevertheless, I felt that, with some outside labor and advice, I could conjure up its character on a small scale if I pushed my project further toward the property line in back.

So far this chapter has been written in the first-person singular because my former husband Ed, who had always been good at sports, was more interested in playing tennis than in gardening. Things changed in 1984 after I married Ted. When I pointed out to him how many spindly locust trees were crowding each other in the area behind my woodland screen, he went to work with a chain saw, stacking the trunks and limbs of the cut trees in a large pile to one side of the sunny opening he had created. Unlike in my time of troubles in the Central Park Ramble, in this instance there was no one around to protest. We covered the now-bare ground with grass seed, and, taking a hint from the Greensward plan, in which Olmsted and Vaux had conferred place names such as Dene, Meer, Loch, and other poetical titles on various areas of Central Park, we christened this part of the garden the Glen after our neighbors' daughter called it that when she asked if she and her fiancé could get married there. To connect the back lawn with this sunlit patch of grass, I created a path of river-washed stepping-stones surrounded by moss and ferns.

Advice on the design of the entire property came from my landscape architect friend Bruce Kelly, whose collaboration on the restoration for Central Park had been instrumental in the development of

my own Olmstedian design perspective. "You can't just have the backyard and the woodland meet in a straight line," he said in his Southern
drawl as we walked around the property together. "In fact, the whole
lawn needs to be curvilinear," he added. I got out a couple of garden
hoses, and we laid them in a gently sinuous manner around the edges
of the grass. After studying the effect and rearranging the hoses a bit, I
followed their lines with stakes and string—the kind of eyeballing-in-
situ garden design I enjoy. With this on-the-ground blueprint established, I planted various reliable groundcovers—pachysandra, vinca
minor, and lamium—to give visual definition between the lawn and
its borders. Then it occurred to me that if I carried my curvilinear

Path leading to the Glen, 1992

Beneath the woodland arbor, May 7, 2010

lines in a couple of big swoops into the backyard of our next-door neighbors, the united lawns would become something of an Olmstedian meadow in appearance. "You must be out of your mind," said Ted when I told him that I was going over to discuss my idea with them. Fortunately, they agreed, and I happily went about adding a big bed of daylilies that looped around the edge of our lawn and into theirs. I then did some further next-door landscaping, planting more of the same native rhododendrons at the far edge of their backyard as I was planting in ours.

To attain the kind of structural rusticity that would add some informal architectural interest, I was able to hire David Robinson, the rustic carpentry craftsman who had formerly supervised the Conservancy's restoration crew before establishing his own business building garden furniture and gazebos. Out of the pile of cut locust tree trunks and branches we had stacked at the far end of the Glen, he constructed an arbor. As yet, the arbor only led one into an almost impenetrable thicket of catbrier. I could see, however, that here the land sloped down slightly, creating a shallow hollow that would be

Pond under construction, 1989

a perfect site for a pond. To make one would require a building permit from East Hampton Township, and we would also have to hire
a heavy-equipment operator to dig the ground to a specified depth.
Bruce came on the scene once more, this time in a formal capacity as
our paid landscape architect for drawing up a plan for the pond and its
surrounding area.

To build the pond, we hired our neighbor Alan Montoya, a local
landscape contractor who owned the necessary machinery to dig the
basin and install the clay liner that was needed to retain water. Next,
with Bruce and me looking on and giving directions, Alan moved the
boulders we had picked out at a nearby stone yard with his front-end
loader until we had them located just so.

A preexisting stand of native pitch pines ringed the pond. Here,
as elsewhere in the woodland garden, we maintained a plant palette
limited to the vegetation of the American Northeast and mid-Atlantic
region. Hemlocks gave height and evergreen seclusion, and our understory included clethra, witch hazel, and rosebay rhododendron. For the
ground plane I ordered trillium, trout lily, wood geranium, bleeding

Trillium and moss in the woodland garden

Rustic bridge over the edge of the woodland garden pond

heart, jack-in-the-pulpit, lady slipper, and Virginia bluebell seedlings, along with several kinds of ferns from a native-plant nursery.

To gain a real impression of a natural forest floor, I looked for moss. Since it is not sold in nurseries, I had to harvest it from wherever I found patches growing in my lawn or those of other people, who typically think of moss as an unwanted intruder in the grass. Tamping it into pockets of soil here and there, I hoped that in time it would imitate the moss growing in Japanese gardens and spread to become a single cushiony emerald surface throughout my shady woodland.

Wainscott Pond with irises, 1990

Beyond the arbor, I encircled the pond with a pine-needle-blanketed path. I then asked David Robinson to build a rustic bridge over one end in order to link the front half of our Wainscott woodland with the newly created section extending to our back property line. My walks in the garden now allowed me to see the pond as a sky-mirror with reflected vegetation, become startled by the splash of a frog as it jumps from the bank, or listen to the music made by a small trickle of water issuing from the semblance of a spring-emitting grotto—in reality the recesses of a tumble of overhanging rocks with a concealed hose attached to a recirculating pump beneath the pond's surface.

As in the Central Park Ramble, this naturalistic scene is entirely an artifice. The same irrigation system that feeds water to the pond also supplies a network of subsurface pipes going to sprinkler heads that can be turned on in dry weather to ensure that the ferns and other plants remain lush and the moss green.

A garden is, of course, never finished, and mine continues to be revised in form and revisited with new impressions. I can, however, roughly date the year of its completion as 1988, when I wrote this poem:

BUILDING THE POND

No, it wasn't a Japanese water garden
But we did plant the rocks
With monk-like devotion
Eyeing them individually and
In composition, nestling in
A fern bank here and there a mossy shadow
We even painted in some fish
To give a silky iridescence
Amid the undulating hair of water plants
Pointing "over there" to the man with the front
  end loader
I thought of the magnificent indifference
Of the force that made the rocks in the first place
The bake and heave of ancient sea beds
That gave them their first prominence
How frost crack and torrents
Of the timeless before
Tore and tumbled them
And old tides bumped and rolled them
Until they were gathered
In the frozen glacier's hold
A random cargo to be deposited
A few millennia later
And now with careful calculation
Made to seem as uncalculating
As nature's intrinsic art.

It is clear from this poem that the story of the building of Central Park as a great Romantic tour de force in which geology plays a primary role had stimulated my imagination to the point where the garden I had begun fourteen years earlier as an English love affair could now be thought of as Central Park East. When I stop and think about it, my Cottage Garden had become, with Lynden Miller's suggestions, a compact version of the Conservatory Garden, while my woodland garden had not surprisingly taken on the aspect of the Ramble.

Chapter Twelve

GOING ABROAD

Central Park represents but one moment in the continuum of landscape design history. Olmsted's travels as a journalist in the South on the eve of the Civil War, as well as his visits to England and France, were made with a discriminating eye focused on both natural and designed landscapes. My eye was similarly educated by travel, for after the Conservancy's success story had begun to spread, I started to receive invitations to speak in foreign cities as well as ones in the United States where, in an effort to improve their urban parks, citizens were attempting to follow the model of the Central Park Conservancy by establishing public-private partnerships.

In light of the fact that my talks were of the show-and-tell variety, necessitating a body of illustrative images, it was fortunate that I had realized shortly after our initial restoration projects were under way that photographic documentation of the Conservancy's progress in restoring the park would be a good idea. For this reason, in 1984 I had hired Sara Cedar Miller[*] to be the Conservancy's staff photog-

---

[*] A recently retired Conservancy employee and a Central Park historian in her own right, Sara has published *Central Park, An American Masterpiece: A Comprehensive History of the Nation's First Urban Park* (Abrams, 2003), *Seeing Central Park: An Official Guide to the World's*

rapher. These were the days before digital photography and Power-Point, and as we continued to amass a collection of before-and-after slides, Sara would help me organize them in twin Kodak carousel trays for my now-frequent dual-projector presentations. Then we would rehearse until the narrative thread of my talk was effectively synchronized with the images that told the Conservancy's story of rebuilding Central Park. Thus equipped, I visited cities in other parts of the world where I was able to both convey and extend my own education in the design, restoration, and management of historic landscapes.

Earlier, however, during the years when my children were young and I was busy managing the Central Park Task Force summer intern program, I did not have many opportunities to travel abroad. Back then my favorite getaway destination besides Wainscott was Penob-scot Bay in Maine, where instead of gardening and biking through the Long Island potato fields, I went hiking in fern-carpeted spruce forests and skinny-dipping in Long Pond.

Acadian Idylls

I loved these Maine vacations with Lisa and David, when he was old enough to accompany us. We would stay on Isle au Haut in my friend Anne Davidson's rustic cabin overlooking Moore's Harbor, a con-verted barn dating from the days when sheep still grazed on the island. From here we could walk down a slope covered with low-bush blue-berries to go in search of mussels along the rocky coastline.

Living on Isle au Haut for a week or two in resourceful con-tentment without electricity, phone service, and transportation other than our own feet was an educational and spiritually nourishing con-trast to my comfortable city apartment and the busy streets of New York. Trying to grasp the meaning of this new-to-me part of the

---

Greatest Urban Park (Abrams, 2009), and *Strawberry Fields: Central Park's Memorial to John Lennon* (Abrams, 2011), all of which are illustrated with both historic photographs and ones she took during the thirty-three years she was in the park on a daily basis.

world on my first trip, I wrote in my journal while waiting for the mailboat that would take us from Stonington on Deer Isle to Isle au Haut:

FRIDAY, JULY 30, 1978

Driving to Deer Isle from the airport in Bangor you can see how, lurking just behind the extraordinary summer beauty of fern brakes and lush roadside wildflowers, is the stark, bleak, and above all, *long* winter. I think of those seafaring explorers of hundreds of years ago, gulled by gracious summer, then wretchedly marooned and half-starving in the pitiless cold of their encampments and rude forts beside ice-bound harbors. The primly prosaic, boxlike wooden houses, with their almost-but-never-quite gaudy pastel colors, that we see en route hint at an attempt to counter winter's monochrome austerity as do the brief bright gardens of annual flowers that make the most of the short summer.

In Stonington we discover we have missed the last mailboat, which is probably lucky because of the uncertainties of making our way to Anne's house in the darkness once we are on the island. Also we need to decompress in stages from our convenient urban ways.

After settling in for the night in Mrs. Chatto's boarding house, Lisa and I go out and dine on fried clams at the Fisherman's Friend. Then after supper we take a tour of the town. A wedding is in progress, and a group of teen-agers is decorating the bridal car with a "Just Married" message written with shaving cream. The newly-weds, who also appear to be teen-agers, soon drive away with a din of tin cans jangling from the rear bumper.

The next morning, after our arrival on Isle au Haut, we settled ourselves in our vacation nest with its bunk beds, old-fashioned wood stove, kerosene lamps, and cistern to collect rainwater. Here is how I took stock of our situation:

Still weighted with the heaviness of sleep. (Why I wonder is sleep heavy or, for that matter, sound?) Mine was a curious sleep. Awakened at 1:30 by an insufficiency of blankets and ravenous from a supper of only bread and apple butter, I lit the kerosene lamp in the kitchen and turned on the gas stove, discovered a can of corned beef hash on the shelf, fried it, poached an egg, made cocoa, and assuaged my hunger. Now we have just eaten our light breakfast of blueberries, yoghurt, and coffee. Already, Lisa says, "I've fallen in love with this island." I have too.

But at first there was a moment of doubt. Decompression takes time. Yesterday we were too busy with the mechanics of travel to register our initial feelings. The mailboat deposited us on the landing in a light rain, and we had to leave our hopelessly heavy paraphernalia—groceries, books, clothes—on the dock as we went to look for a ride. In the little string of lobstermen's houses clustered near the dock we managed to find the house of Anne's friends Virginia and Skeet MacDonald. He is a lobsterman, and she works as the town's sole part-time volunteer librarian. Like the handful of other Isle au Haut lobstermen and their wives, the MacDonalds spend the winter in Stonington and then reopen their house on the island when the ice in the bay thaws and Skeet can trawl for lobsters again.

We introduced ourselves to Virginia, who gave us a ride to Moore's Harbor in Skeet's ancient Plymouth. Looking at a heap of abandoned old cars beside the road, I realized that almost all the motor vehicles on the island are antiques, since once transported from the mainland, they never go back, which is why those beyond repair can be seen rusting away here and there in a fern brake.

Alone in the house, Lisa and I look at each other. "It's awfully quiet," I say. "There just isn't much noise." The gull cries over Moore's Harbor sounded positively mournful. "A whole week, Ma," says Lisa. "At least I'll get plenty of reading done." She has brought *War and Peace,* which she is planning to start after she finishes *Mansfield Park*. I thought to myself, "That should do something to make the days pass!"

We debate going to the Town Hall for the Saturday night dance. It is an appealing idea, a good way to achieve quick immersion into the local culture, but we're too tired and so opt for reading instead. For supper Lisa scrambled eggs sprinkled with chives—actually onion grass she had pulled up outside—and made biscuits. Since we were tired and our only light was that of the kerosene lantern on the kitchen table, we went to bed early.

MONDAY, AUGUST 2

As I blew out the lamp last night I saw stars shining in the sky, auguring a good day, which this certainly has been. An unblemished, most perfect summer day. We breakfasted on coffee and Lisa's leftover biscuits as we began to plan our outing. A trip to town was essential since we were in need of groceries. Also, our butane gas-powered refrigerator was not functioning, and this had to be reported to the part-time caretaker, another Isle au Haut lobsterman.

But the day was too beautiful to squander merely on errands, so we studied our trail map for picturesque roundabout routes to town. First, however, we had to perform our main chore: carrying pure drinking water from the brook. I think I will always remember the feel of its icy coldness and the sound it makes as it spills over the rocks embraced by fern-covered, moss-padded banks. I took a picture of Lisa filling the bucket, and on the way home I photographed a field of fescue grass with dew still shimmering on light lavender seed heads.

We discussed trail options as we packed a light lunch. Finally, however, we just went down to the harbor and poked around, taking pictures of tidal pools and bits of coastal vegetation that struck our fancy. The children of a neighbor ran down to the rocky shore, and Lisa joined them in a hunt for crabs. It was just a game, for the crabs are too small for eating. They deposited the ones they found in a tidal pool and watched them swim around or clamber out onto the rocks—sideways, of course. We sunned ourselves on a large rock, grateful for its warmth and the beauty of the day.

At last, having shared a can of sardines, Lisa and I decided to head for town. We followed the brook to the trailhead where we began walking over springy moss footpads. We stopped to study and photograph these at close range, stroking the moss, which felt like the wiry coat of some great green dog.

On a rocky wind-torn ridge we observed for the first time some pines—stunted ones and twisted—rising above the sea of spruce that blankets the hillside all the way down to the bay. Back in the woods, we noticed that this ubiquity of spruce is varied by birches and, here and there, a few maples. I have discerned variety in the spruces too; among the seedlings some appear glaucous, others bright green.

In town we met Anne's friends, the Sawyers, at the island's single store alongside the dock, and they offered us a ride in their antiquated green truck to Turner Cove on Long Pond. We hopped aboard after having first bought groceries, mailed our postcards, and availed ourselves of the Town Hall bathroom, the flush toilet being a comparative luxury after our treks to the outhouse behind Anne's kitchen.

Lisa and I hadn't brought bathing suits, so I sequestered myself in an inlet away from the others and bathed naked. The water felt delicious, especially since this was my first bath since leaving New York. Lisa, more modest than me, only removed her jeans and then swam over to join the others.

Foreign Lands

It is easy to see why I made a tradition of these Isle au Haut vacations. Such Thoreau-like idylls when I was a young mother reveling in nature with my children have provided some of the most valuable stock in my portfolio of travel memories. My trips to Isle au Haut continued for a couple of years following my marriage to Ted in 1984, but by this time Lisa had graduated from Yale and David's summers were being spent at camp elsewhere in Maine. For this reason our holiday plans took us more frequently to England and Europe. It would be hard to characterize these holidays as working vacations, but some parts of them were in fact that, since we never missed an opportunity to visit a public park or other landscape partly for the sake of comparison with Central Park.

The memorable trip to Sissinghurst that had ignited my passion for gardening had included a wide circuit of other garden stops. Among those I had previously visited were Henry Hoare's Stourhead, Capability Brown's Blenheim, and Humphry Repton's Sezincote. Now that I was immersed in the restoration of Olmsted and Vaux's mid-nineteenth-century landscape masterpiece, I wanted to see these again, along with several of the other great eighteenth-century estate gardens that represented a revolutionary departure in style from the geometrical gardens of seventeenth-century France. As if this were a necessary reason to cross the Channel, I was keen to see firsthand André Le Nôtre's Versailles and Vaux-le-Vicomte. Then, of course, there were the great sixteenth-century villa gardens of Italy, which naturally led me to want to understand how the ruins of ancient Rome had fertilized the imagination of Renaissance garden designers.

Germany offers fine examples of the Baroque and Rococo styles as applied not only to architecture and the decorative arts but also to landscape design. The Netherlands, too, has many gardens that compress within that country's small geographical compass stylistic precepts and garden features derived from Versailles. Thus, there were never any trips to the Bahamas, since our desire was to visit as many cities, parks, and gardens in Europe as we could.

Built according to entirely different aesthetic principles, there are the gardens of Japan. As Yoko Ono had said when I proposed that the restoration of Strawberry Fields serve as the flagship project in the realization of the Conservancy's management and restoration plan, "Olmsted is not so different from Japanese garden designers." No one would mistake Strawberry Fields for a Japanese garden such as Saihō-ji, with its groundcover of moss and underlying Zen aesthetic, but you might stop to notice sometime how Bruce Kelly's use of the park's native bedrock outcrops and his artful planting of magnolias, dogwoods, and hollies evoke Olmsted in a manner that has an underlying affinity with the gardens of Japan.

It is evident how much these journeys to other countries helped me place Central Park within the continuum of the history of landscape design. However, since good daily maintenance is as important a factor in judging the quality of a public landscape as is its plan, no matter how brilliant that may be, visiting the great parks of the world provided me with the opportunity to observe, compare, and judge the ways in which park maintenance in other places was being performed.

I was thrilled when in 1986 I was invited to speak at a three-day conference in Osaka on public-space greening. This was my first trip to Japan and therefore my first opportunity to see Japanese gardens. Ted joined me, and in the four days preceding the conference I was able to go with him to Tokyo and Kyoto. Rereading the journal I kept at the time, I find that many of my observations fall in the category of maintenance shoptalk.

MAY 6, 1986, TOKYO

After breakfast we decided to visit Hibiya Park where Ted called my attention to the meticulously pruned shrubs and newly planted and staked trees with trunks wrapped in straw, which were paradoxically surrounded by tall weeds. There was not a scrap of litter anywhere, and yet here was all this messy rank vegetation. Maintenance in Japan must be task-specific and maybe weeding will be assigned to a special cadre of workers later on. But this is just a guess. It still seems peculiar to see the juxtaposition of exquisite maintenance and attention to beauty as an isolated phenomenon, a concentration on the particular rather than the whole. Still the early morning park is soft and lovely in the drizzle. Everywhere azaleas are in bloom and often used as hedges, even in the median strips of roadways. Dog walkers (the morning people of parks everywhere) are out and about along with a few strollers. Like Central Park the place has that restful, slow-to-get-moving Sunday pace.

Rereading my next entry, I can see where I got my inspiration to plant moss in my woodland garden on Long Island.

WEDNESDAY, MAY 8, 1986, KYOTO

We start out from our pleasant ryokan for Saihō-ji, the Rinzai Buddhist temple garden, which is familiarly known as Koke-dera, or Moss Garden. Upon arriving, we prepare to start down a gravel path encircling a pond surrounded by a cushiony car-pet of moss. But there is a gate, and we are not allowed to enter until we first accomplish a WRITING LESSON! This is done in the main hall of the temple, kneeling at a small desk where we are instructed in wood block rubbing, after which we dip our brushes in ink and then trace the faintly outlined characters of the sutra we have been given at the admission gate. This goes on for a very long time, or so it seems to our excruciatingly bent legs. Finally, our task about half complete, we get a nod meaning

Saihō-ji, path from temple

that we are to sign our sutra and present it to the presiding priest as we kneel before the statue of the Amida Buddha and pray that we may be granted long, prosperous, and happy lives. Then we are allowed into the garden, which is on this perfect May day following the rain a luxuriant spectacle. It is actually two gardens, an upper one and a lower one, which were designed by Muso Soseki, a famous Japanese master gardener some 600 years ago.

How do they maintain moss—one hundred and twenty varieties of it? They sweep it—lovingly. It cannot get littered with leaves. The lake which lies at the bottom of the lower garden is *kokoro*-shaped, meaning that it is formed like the Japanese character for "spirit" or "heart." We amble around it and then begin our climb to the upper garden, which Muso created in *karesansui* style, meaning that it is a carefully composed dry garden of meticulously raked gravel and stone. I am particularly impressed with the path work and the beautiful way steps are set into the hillside. This is not unlike the way in which Central Park stonecutters incised bedrock outcrops to create stairs.

Moss maintenance

Saihō-ji dry garden

In addition to viewing foreign landscapes with a park administrator's eye, I became focused upon them as art-historical records of
changing cultural values over time. By now I had begun to seriously
contemplate a return to my beginnings as a writer about historic
landscapes. I therefore continued to plan almost all our vacation itineraries around the self-education I had undertaken, enabling me to
contextualize Olmsted and Vaux's work within the broad spectrum of
landscape design history. But this was only a secondary outcome of a
project that had become far-ranging and ambitious: the publication in
2001 of my book *Landscape Design: A Cultural and Architectural History.*

Where to begin? If you wish to write a book about garden history, there is no better place to start your on-the-ground
research than in Italy. Visiting Rome with Ted not just once but several times provided the cornerstone of my landscape traveler's education. Taking side trips to Frascati, Tivoli, and Bagnaia to wander
through the great sixteenth-century Italian villa gardens in these

towns as well as those in Rome itself—Villa Medici, Villa Borghese, Villa Pamphili, Villa Madama—gave me an understanding of the ways in which Renaissance popes and princes of the Church asserted their power in garden itineraries based on allegorical humanism. Thus I learned how to look at landscapes as cultural metaphors, windows on period and place.

But you don't have to be a landscape history scholar to appreciate the sensory pleasures of an Italian Renaissance villa garden. Here is my account of a day spent at Villa D'Este in Tivoli:

JULY 15, 1989

On Saturday we furthered my garden history education with a trip to Tivoli. Tourist-packed as it is, Villa d'Este was a great delight. Here is the Renaissance garden par excellence! The exuberant melody of water is everywhere. Rivulets coursing over

Villa D'Este, overview, July 2012

Alley of the Hundred Fountains, Villa D'Este, July 2012

carved stone, the ferny cool of moist grottoes, fountains gushing, spouting, spilling, trickling—everywhere there is sparkling water and sky-catching water mirrors. How infinitely cool and refreshing is this ingenious oasis in the sunbaked landscape! Then, too, one must mention the stately cypresses and the smell of oleander and box, the flights of carved stairs, and the architecturally framed statuary. We strolled, and I photographed for over an hour as a group of nuns (mostly Asian) shared with us the thrilling beauty.

French Tutorial

In addition to traveling in Italy, which gave me the chance to imbibe the beauty of the Roman Campagna and the Tuscan countryside as well as the cultural riches of Venice, Florence, Siena, Naples, Sicily, and places in between, my trips to France enabled me to focus a professional eye on the public landscapes of Paris. This was an opportune time for observing them, because the 1980s were a period in which the Socialist Party president, François Mitterrand, and Paris's mayor, Jacques Chirac, a Gaullist member of France's political right wing, had undertaken, somewhat competitively, to add a series of contemporary parks to the Parisian environs. I was naturally pleased when in the spring of 1989 the French-American Foundation sponsored an exchange trip to France in which I was invited to participate. This would make it possible for me to talk directly with contemporary French urban planners and landscape designers and to see firsthand some of Paris's new parks. I would, of course, not pass up the opportunity on this trip and others to visit the Tuileries and the Jardin du Luxembourg, legacies of ancient royalty, as well as the mid-nineteenth-century parks that were part of Haussmann's makeover of the city. Here is my record of the appearance of Paris's new and old parks at that time, one in which I assumed the role of landscape design critic.

FRANCE, APRIL 17–24, 1989

Brasserie lunch and then a visit to Parc de la Villette. Had not expected to like it so much. Found it very liberating to think of creating a twentieth-century park on this scale and of the opportunities architect Bernard Tschumi had to work on a relatively blank page. How will it be used? Will it work, socially speaking, as well as the tranquil, old, traditional parks? From the city planning perspective, I like the idea of period layering in parks as well as in architecture.

Our next stop was Parc des Buttes-Chaumont, a hundred-and-twenty-year leap backward in time from Parc de la Villette and a very interesting comparison with Central Park, with which it is exactly contemporaneous. Built in an abandoned quarry, the dramatic possibilities of the site were romantically heightened by Adolphe Alphand, Haussmann's chief engineer and urban designer. Like Central Park, Buttes-Chaumont is experientially orchestrated as a series of picturesque scenes. With its cascade-penetrated grotto and lake with an island in the middle rising as a sheer mass of real and artificial rocks surmounted by a circular

Buttes-Chaumont, Temple of Love

temple, it is more theatrical in intention than Central Park, but the now-mature trees were very poetic in the soft dampness of the day.

A last stop for this tireless tourist was a new park in an Algerian/Chinese/African neighborhood, Belleville. Designed as a place where kids can come for unsupervised play, it somehow fails to have much coherence as a design. Interesting nevertheless and another example of the scale on which Paris is building new parks.

The uncertainty that I had expressed about the success of Parc de la Villette in my April journal entry was dispelled by my return visit to Paris with Ted in the fall:

A Sunday in Parc de la Villette, 1989

Museum of Science and Technology, Parc de la Villette, 1989

On Sunday we visited Parc de la Villette. When I first saw it back in April on an overcast weekday, I couldn't ascertain whether it was simply a contemporary architect's exercise in the currently fashionable deconstructivist style or, as in the case of Central Park, a true people's park. Now, however, I was able to observe on a warm, golden Sunday afternoon that the new park, which was filled with people of all ages, many engaged in games of Frisbee, croquet, and soccer, had indeed become a popular leisure-time destination for Parisians. Tschumi's grid of cubic red-enameled follies, the bamboo belt, the catwalk paralleling the canal, the gleaming geodesic globe—a shimmer of silver beside the bold, new Museum of Science and Technology—the handsome cast-iron frame of the old abattoir, which has been salvaged and now serves as an exposition hall: all this was laid out, I thought, as a strikingly original new approach to park design.

Continuing my critique of the new Parisian parks, two days later I wrote the following:

Today we visited Les Halles, site of the historic market referred to by Zola as the "Belly of Paris," which since the twelfth century had occupied the same site in the heart of the city. Its demolition in 1971 to make way for a new hub of the RER (Réseau Express Régional), Paris's system of Metro-connected commuter train lines, was much lamented at the time. That the underground station was combined with a large glittering American-style shopping mall called Le Forum des Halles has given further offense to the defenders of Old Paris. To mitigate popular dismay, a design competition was held for a park to be constructed adjacent to it, and I have been eager to see the result.

After getting off the Metro, we came up a series of escalators to the boutique-filled mall. Having reached the principal level of the park, we were glad to walk out into the open. The park, however, was disappointing. The contemporary treillages of green-painted iron slats are probably intended to evoke the treillage work at Versailles, and the overall design is diffuse, a compilation of disparate parts with no real axial integration or other means of holding the park together visually. Nor do the surrounding buildings, many of which are crisply postmodern in contrast to the warm brown flank of St. Eustache on the northern edge of the park, define the landscape in any meaningful way. There is no sense of there being a center, and therefore the space just leaks away at the edges. With its cutesy kiddie playground and other Disneyesque features, it lacks the coherence and frank modernity of Parc de la Villette.

Symptomatic of the planning weakness of the Les Halles park is its desultory character (at least at the time of my two visits, both on weekdays), the main patrons being alcoholics and pedestrians taking a short cut to non-park destinations. Even the sound of water, which is normally a soothing masker of urban traffic roar, takes on the timbre of a motor highway. The place is clearly not delightful to the senses and thus repels instead of invites one to linger.

Indeed, we did not linger, crossing over to the left bank to stroll through the Luxembourg Gardens. Here *is* sensory delight, with people, many of them students from the nearby Sorbonne, sitting on benches alone reading or in little, conversational twos or threes or fours. Yes, there are occasional winos, but they are simply sad and not grouped with one another like the vaguely menacing panhandlers at Les Halles. The character of the place is so firmly and powerfully established by the sense of an overall design comprised of a central axis, the artful manipulation of grades, and the chestnut *bosquets* with their sweet-smelling leaves now littering the ground that encroachments such as the enclosures for tennis and children's play are hardly objectionable.

Next we visited the Bois de Vincennes on the eastern edge of Paris. Originally a royal hunting park, it served as Haussmann's complement to the Bois de Bologne on the western perimeter.

Like Buttes-Chaumont, it was designed in the Romantic style by Alphand. Since in the mid-nineteenth-century Parisian parks and Central Park were in various stages of construction at the same time, they offered Olmsted, as they do for me now, an interesting stylistic comparison. I found the Bois de Vincennes a rather formulaic *jardin anglais* and decided that the curvilinear paths and picturesque features that characterize this and other nineteenth-century parks of Paris act as a kind of Romantic stage set that lacks our Olmsted's spatial generosity and essential naturalism.*

The proprietary possessive pronoun "our" in the last sentence is evidence of the degree to which I identified with Olmsted. But we lived, of course, in disparate eras, and the Central Park I was "saving" with such passionate commitment bore a basic but considerably altered resemblance to the rus in urbe of Olmsted's day.

German Lessons

At this point we need to remind ourselves that each layer of Central Park's historic landscape is a reflection of New York City at a particular point in time—both physical and social. The same is true for other cities, as I saw when I was invited to participate in a parks conference in Berlin. Here is how I described my visit to the Tiergarten, that city's analog to Central Park:

---

* On December 28, 1859, after his return, Olmsted gave the following report to the board of commissioners of Central Park: "At Paris I met with Mr. Phelen, formerly a Commissioner of Central Park, and yet retaining undiminished interest in the work. By him I was introduced to M. Alphand, head of the government department of Roads and Buildings, under which the suburban improvements of Paris are carried on, who kindly supplied me with such information as I required, and directed an Engineer to attend me in my visit to the Bois de Bologne. I remained a fortnight in Paris, examining as carefully as practicable in that time, all its pleasure-grounds and promenades, also visiting the parks of Versailles, of St. Cloud, and the wood of Vincennes, the improvement of which is now being prosecuted under the general direction of M. Alphand."

After reaching the Tiergarten, I chose the nearest quadrant of the park for my ramble, entering one of the straight allées, a remnant of the original Baroque plan, which the nineteenth-century landscape gardener Peter Lenné allowed to remain when, between 1833 and 1840, he romanticized—Anglicized—the old, royal hunting park that Frederick the Great had transformed into a *lustgarten,* or pleasure garden. At the time Lenné began work, the Tiergarten was further altered to become a *volkspark,* or people's park, a means of stirring German patriotic sentiment. Subsequently, during the reign of Emperor William II, it gained the *Siegesallee* (Victory Avenue), and under William III, the *Prachtboulevard* (Magnificence Boulevard), both grandiose statements of Prussian pride. Ornamented with monuments to royalty and German genius, these were intended to serve as didactic expressions of national glory and cultural greatness. Thus, today one finds memorials to royalty alongside statues of Goethe, Wagner, and other prominent literary figures as well as the *Komponistendenkmal,* a grand memorial honoring Germany's trinity of great composers: Beethoven, Haydn, and Mozart. With the addition of a zoo in 1844 shortly after Lenné's work was accomplished, it became known by its present name, Tiergarten, or animal park.

Lenné's redesign consisted of retaining its formal elements while providing numerous paths winding around open lawns and through wooded areas crossed by streams flowing into lakes with small islands. The park's combination of straight promenades and curving pathways actually works quite well and is an intelligent planning synthesis accommodating large numbers of promenaders, while providing surprise and seclusion for pedestrians meandering along the byways. Large, pleasant meadows lie on either side of the gravel walk, some posted with signs forbidding active sports. It is a beautiful, warm afternoon and the green meadows are filled with sunbathers: young adults in various degrees of nudity, women usually with bikini bottoms only and men without a stitch. Soon I found myself in a rose garden,

Sunbathers and Frisbee players, Tiergarten

ose Garden in the Tiergarten

and eventually I had the not unpleasant feeling of being slightly lost in this tranquil paradise. On the paths I encountered several Moslem families, the women with long skirts and heads draped with hijabs, cooking on grills and fathers playing with children. I found a secluded playground tucked among the trees on an edge of the park; then wandering back alongside a watercourse, I came upon the statue of the young Queen Louise. The monument and its surrounding landscape have been recently restored by Klaus von Krosigk, the Berlin landscape architect and professor who is our conference leader. I took notice of the especially fine iron fencing, historic benches, and crisply edged gravel paths. Opposite the monument to the Prussian queen, there is a statue of King Frederick William III, which is surrounded by a bed of flowers.

With Central Park never far from my mind, I thought of the monuments on Literary Walk at the southern end of the Mall— Columbus, Shakespeare, Robert Burns, and Walter Scott—and those elsewhere in Central Park—William Jennings Bryan, Humboldt, Alexander Hamilton, Daniel Webster, and Hans Christian Andersen, to name but some.* Not surprisingly, with no monarch and no "Iron Chancellor" Bismarck to promote a patriotic nationalist agenda in the interests of establishing European hegemony, our republican nation, and especially New York City with its large immigrant population, chose a more cosmopolitan class of heroes to honor, and only three of the ones mentioned above were Americans.

---

* It is worth noting that Olmsted fought unsuccessfully to keep the park's naturalistic landscape uncluttered by such encroachments. Today, in spite of numerous applications to add more memorials in Central Park, the Parks Department has been able to adhere to an enough-is-enough policy. At the same time, the Conservancy's bronze restoration program has restored and systematically maintained all of the park's existing twenty-nine sculptures and monuments. Interestingly, the most revered memorial is not a monument as such, but rather the black-and-white-tile mosaic with its single word "Imagine" paying tribute to John Lennon.

Home Grounds

I am not sure how my regular travels in Central Park with a most unusual companion began, but they became as significant to me as the travels abroad I have described above. His name was Lambert Pohner, and among the birders and park naturalists whom I have known over the years, I count him as my special guru, for his was the kind of instruction that provided not only knowledge but also spiritual insight into the miracles of nature that Central Park offers. In his sixties at the time we met, he lived with his mother, a former garment worker, in one of the few tenement buildings that had not been torn down after the removal of the Third Avenue elevated subway line spurred redevelopment of this part of New York's Upper East Side. His interest in natural history was wide-ranging and not limited to simply identifying the birds or trees of the park. As an example, his wedding present to Ted and me was an album of his own hand-drawn pictures of all the species of butterflies to be found in Central Park. After he had completed this census of *Lepidoptera,* he went on to the difficult task of discriminating between the different varieties of wild grasses he discovered on his daily forays into the Ramble and North End.

As will become apparent in the following journal entry, I was always rewarded with a miracle of nature whenever Lambert offered to take me on a mini-vacation with him in Central Park.

JANUARY 3, 1980

A cold crystalline morning with the wind from the west. As Lambert and I set out walking, the frozen ground felt like rough pavement beneath my feet. He noticed that my going-to-work-later-in-the-day brown pumps were hardly the right shoes for our excursion, but I was warm in my down coat and ready for the surprise he has promised me. We stopped when we reached the northern section of the path encircling the Reservoir, and he solemnly handed me an envelope with my name on it. Inside, I found the following piece of note paper:

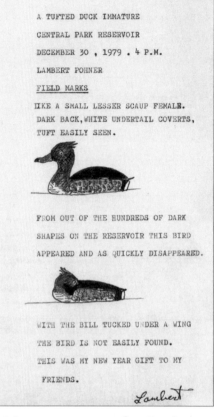

A TUFTED DUCK IMMATURE

CENTRAL PARK RESERVOIR

DECEMBER 30 , 1979 . 4 P.M.

LAMBERT POHNER

FIELD MARKS

LIKE A SMALL LESSER SCAUP FEMALE.
DARK BACK,WHITE UNDERTAIL COVERTS,
TUFT EASILY SEEN.

FROM OUT OF THE HUNDREDS OF DARK
SHAPES ON THE RESERVOIR THIS BIRD
APPEARED AND AS QUICKLY DISAPPEARED.

WITH THE BILL TUCKED UNDER A WING
THE BIRD IS NOT EASILY FOUND.
THIS WAS MY NEW YEAR GIFT TO MY
FRIENDS.

A January 3, 1980, note from Lambert Pohner

As we scanned the water looking for this relatively inconspicuous bird amid a flock of Scaup, I asked him who first discovered the presence of the Tufted Duck and telegraphed the news through the Central Park ornithological grapevine. He said proudly, "I did. This bird was Central Park's Christmas present to me. It was like a miracle. I caught a glimpse of its tuft, and at first I thought I might be having an ego trip. Hallucinating. But I knew there was no reason to think that—just walking in the park is my ego trip. So I looked some more. It appeared and then disappeared again. But it was there in the flock. A miracle."

The Tufted Duck is a Eurasian bird, and its rarity in this range is the source of Lambert's and the other regular birdwatchers' excitement. Lambert says this is the first time that he knows of that one has been sighted in Central Park, adding, "There was one a few years back in a flock of Scaup around Hellgate in the East River. The species belongs to the same family as the Scaup, so when a Tufted Duck strays into the North American flyway after leaving its breeding ground in Iceland, it will eventually settle into a flock of these ducks. A bird flying several thousand feet up in the air can see great distances, and a duck searching for food may spy a chain of landfalls that carry it progressively farther and farther astray from its normal migratory route. It will under such circumstances cohabit with its most proximate species." He further explained that the Tufted Duck, like the Scaup, is a diving bird. The flock would continue to enjoy the moveable feast of the nutrient-laden currents around Hellgate, but because of the freezing weather, along with a number of Canvas-back Ducks and Goldeneye Ducks, it had chosen the Reservoir as its temporary inland refuge.

The Tufted Duck was somewhere in the midst of the Scaup, but neither of us was able to spot it. Then suddenly Lambert began jumping up and down, beaming. "There, there!" he pointed. To my unpracticed birding eye it was completely indistinguishable from the other ducks. "Where, where?" I asked. Helpfully, he instructed me to fix the Chrysler building with my binoculars and then come directly down on the flock. I did. "Now," he said, "look in the front line. It's right before us." Sure enough, there was a small duck with a flyaway topknot. We observed it for a few minutes, as I thought to myself, "Where else in the world could you rake your binoculars down from such an extraordinary Art Deco pinnacle to focus on an off-course migratory bird?"

I told Lambert as we moved on that, although the bird had been a great treat, the park on such a beautiful winter day and the walk itself were happiness enough for me. He agreed but maintained that nevertheless the day had somehow been blessed by the bird. "It is a fairy princess," he added, meaning the unexpected delight, the minor but precious miracle of this feathered foreigner visiting Central Park.

Lambert's reverence and passion for nature are inspirational to me and others who know him. My own spiritual impulses are awakened whenever I am with him. His greatness lies not so much in his expertise as a naturalist as in the childlike anticipation with which he goes forth to discover nature's wonders each day. I think of him too as something of a philosopher. As we walked south past the Great Lawn he told me how he had recently warned a fellow Central Park regular, who had just received a job after a long stretch of unemployment, not to get lost in the World of Reality.

Lambert's own lifestyle suits him perfectly: he spends three days a week at a part-time job in the World of Reality selling soft drinks at a concession on Staten Island in order to sustain himself and prepare for his more arduous pursuits in the World of

Beauty. "I put on my pedometer and do ten miles or more a day in the World of Beauty," he said, "and then I tell my friends that I need to rest up. In the World of Reality I probably only clock a mile in a day on my pedometer." During our stop at the Swedish Cottage Marionette Theater where we drank hot coffee with the puppeteers, he concluded, "The way you know you belong in the World of Beauty is because your feet are cold and you refuse to take notice." Thinking of my own, I replied, "That's really because they are numb."

Lambert accompanied me as I headed back through the Ramble to my office in the Arsenal. Looking down, we saw poking out of the hard, sere ground and decayed leaves tufts of field garlic. "Just think," he said, "spring is only some sixty days away!"

I kept and still have as a good-luck charm the pressed four-leaf clover that Lambert gave to me in 1982, at the end of the controversy over the tree cutting I had authorized in the Ramble. During all the furor he had staunchly defended me when the other birdwatchers, who were also his friends, continued to fulminate. His self-portrait in a toga holding a pressed four-leaf clover like a scepter symbolizes for me the gentle soul of this peacemaker.

Self-portrait of Lambert holding a pressed four-leaf clover

Chapter Thirteen

DARKER SIDE

I f my walks with Lambert were always on the brighter side of
my life in Central Park, there was a darker reality as well. The
scourge of AIDS in the 1980s spelled the loss of several gay friends,
including my Central Park colleagues Bruce Kelly,[*] who died in
1993 at age forty-four, and Phil Winslow, who succumbed four
years earlier at the age of forty-eight. In addition to their important
contributions to the development of the Conservancy's management and restoration plan between 1982 and 1985, each was responsible for specific restoration projects. Phil left his mark on the park
in the renewal of the landscapes around the Cherry Hill Fountain,
Bethesda Terrace, and the Mall, while Bruce's legacy includes the
design of the Pat Hoffman Friedman Playground south of the Metropolitan Museum, Strawberry Fields, and the James Michael Levin
Playground at Seventy-Sixth Street and Fifth Avenue, along with

[*] As mentioned above, Bruce was my first professional colleague in Central Park, and our
association dated back to the days of the Central Park Task Force. During the many walks
we took together in those pre-Conservancy days, his observations were instrumental in
shaping my vision of how the park might be restored.

the restoration of the Shakespeare Garden behind the Marionette Theater.*

As the AIDS epidemic continued to rage, politics and government were, as usual, the principal subject matter of the daily news. Society columns and magazines devoted to celebrity and style extolled the ongoing Central Park renaissance, making its restoration a chic cause and an invitation to join the Conservancy board a sign of social status.

Although security in Central Park had greatly improved, the forested North End continued to be forbidding. Then, on April 19, 1989, terror struck. I was away at the time at the French-American parks conference mentioned earlier and only learned about what had happened upon my return five days later. Here is how I registered my shock at the time:

MONDAY, MAY 8, 1989

On Monday the 24th of April, Ted met me at Kennedy Airport on my return from France. In the car going home he told me what had happened in the park the night of the 19th at the 102nd cutoff between the East and West Drives overlooking the Ravine where just now the white birch trunks look their loveliest against the backdrop of soft green willow leaves. There at 1:30 a.m. a young woman had been found naked, gagged, tied up, and covered in mud and blood. Still comatose, she is not expected to

---

* The Shakespeare Garden is not an original park landscape but rather a rock garden built in 1912, which was relocated to its present site near West Seventy-Ninth Street in 1934, at which time it was officially named in honor of the Bard and planted with floral species mentioned in his plays and poems, along with a mulberry tree reputed to be a scion of one growing in his birthplace, Avon. Like the rest of the park in the 1970s, it had become a vandalized ruin, and in the 1980s the Central Park Conservancy solicited funds to create a new garden on the site. When Mary Griggs Burke, noted collector of Japanese art and early supporter of the Central Park Conservancy, stepped forward with a gift to initiate the project, I hired Bruce, who had by then formed a partnership with landscape architect David Varnell, as its restoration designer. Subsequently, in 1987, the May and Samuel Rudin Foundation made a gift to underwrite its completion and provide a maintenance endowment to fund a member of our growing cadre of zone gardeners.

live. The police have rounded up and detained some members of a posse of around thirty young black men allegedly out on a "wilding" spree that night, and five are now in custody and being questioned.* The public outrage is intense, and the newspapers are filled with articles reporting on her condition and speculating on the identity and motives of the suspects. Not since the much-publicized Kitty Genovese attack in Kew Gardens, Queens, thirty years ago has the city regarded a crime such as this as a reflection of its moral ill health. It is horrible to think of this bright Wellesley graduate–turned–investment banker (her name is currently being withheld at the request of the family)† with her fine, strong body, good mind, and exhilarating sense of being an athlete as a victim of random violence.

I immediately realized that many of my working days in the coming weeks would be focused on park safety. The installation of various kinds of hardware (emergency phones, additional lights, television cameras, et cetera) was proposed. Searching for the best means of ensuring ongoing park security, I asked political veteran Herb Sturz, a lawyer whose expertise was criminal justice, to chair a Conservancy blue-ribbon panel on long-term strategies. Further addressing the heightened concern about future safety in the North End following the rape of the Central Park jogger, board member Ira Millstein assembled the Conservancy's own internal security committee and then spearheaded one of its recommendations: the renovation of the North Meadow Recreation Center as a youth athletic facility.

At this time Ed Koch's term as mayor was coming to an end, and I was naturally concerned about the effect the imminent change in the

---

* Only in 2014 was it finally determined that the five alleged African American assailants were not guilty of the crime, at which time they were released from prison and collectively awarded a $41 million settlement.

† Not expected to live, Trisha Meili, the Central Park jogger, made a heroic recovery. In 1989 she returned to her job with Salomon Brothers, and in 1995 she ran the New York City Marathon with Ted as her Achilles Track Club companion runner should she need assistance. I had tears of joy in my eyes as I watched her complete the twenty-six-mile course and cross the finish line with a running time clocked at four and a half hours. In 1996 Ted and I had further cause to celebrate when we attended her wedding.

governance of the city and the administration of the Parks Department would bring. Reflecting my own uncertainty about the consequences and at the same time my surprising rise to the status of minor celebrity, I wrote the following:

This past Thursday we celebrated the completion of the Shakespeare Garden's restoration by the Rudin family. Mayor Koch was there, looking somewhat beleaguered. In his recent public appearances he has exhibited much less ebullience than in former days, but here he was, "my" mayor, and it is hard to imagine how life in this most-difficult-to-govern city could be improved by any of the current candidates. Choosing among them, however, is what voters will have to do in November, as the mood for change—never mind change to what—is strong.

The garden itself is so very pretty. I am proud of Bruce for his excellent design and so pleased that the Olmstedian landscape-restoration vision he has helped me nurture these past ten years is slowly materializing. Already people love this new garden in the park, and the *House & Garden* editors have rushed in to photograph it.

Speaking of magazines, I spent Wednesday morning in a boat in the middle of the Lake being photographed for an article in *Town & Country.* I never knew how much artful staging (and what expense!) goes into taking a single shot like this. At 7:00 a.m., Garcia, the make-up artist, appeared at my door, and for an hour he blow-dried my hair and made up my face. Knowing that my mother would have told me that the little Jaeger pants suit in the closet wasn't really up to *T&C* high-style standards, I put on a costume I had bought at Bergdorf's for this occasion: navy blue silk pants and a pretty, scarf-tied, strapless bodice and wide-shouldered jacket in white silk with a nautical design of ropes and anchors.

It is all well and good to flip the pages of this slick magazine for the stylish rich, bemused by so much false façading, but when it comes my turn, I'm apparently ready to queen it up with the best of them. So there we were dockside beside the Loeb Boathouse: the photographer and her oarsman getting into one rowboat; our Conservancy publicist together with the *T&C* health and beauty editor and her assistant, who was holding light baffles, flash equipment, and food for the ducks in order to make them swim into the picture, stepping into another; and in a third the versatile Garcia (now metamorphosed into an oarsman), helping me board. No longer a mere rowboat, it should have been called a barge, so embowered was it with ferns, calla lilies, and delphiniums.

We stopped in the middle of the tranquil Lake near Bow Bridge, and Garcia, who was crouched in the bottom of the rowboat cum barge with his head tucked under some Boston fern fronds so as to remain out of the picture, continued to fuss with the flowers and other props, including my straw hat—a regular millinery ice-cream sundae complete with artificial maraschino cherry on top. I played my part, smiling on cue, and—obedient to the instructions of the photographer calling out from her boat and the "stagehands" from theirs—I happily fell into the whole wonderful folly of it, slightly chagrined by my own vanity yet pleased with anticipating the pride that the publication of the picture will bring to my mother when a copy of the magazine arrives in her mailbox in San Antonio.

Changing Roles

While I welcomed this kind of reputation-boosting publicity for the Conservancy, my real satisfaction and pride came from the strides we were making with the implementation of our park-wide management and restoration plan. The Conservancy's role both within the Parks Department and with the public at large was changing as it became an established New York City institution. The same kind of work that Bruce and Phil had successfully demonstrated at Strawberry Fields and Cherry Hill was now being systematically carried forward by the Conservancy's in-house design team. Landscape architects Marianne

Cramer and Timothy Marshall (later succeeded by Douglas Blonsky, recently retired president and CEO of the Conservancy) were coprincipals in what was in effect a landscape architectural firm numbering at any given time around twelve employees. Chief among them were Laura Starr, now with a practice of her own, and Christopher Nolan, who is the Conservancy's chief operating officer today. Clearly the Conservancy had staying power, and although I was still thoroughly immersed in my job, I began to aspire to new challenges.

For me the park had been from the beginning a window on the larger world of the art of landscape design. For this reason, in addition to absorbing the lessons I gained from visiting other parks during my travels in the United States and abroad, writing and teaching became related side careers even as I continued my leadership of the Conservancy. At the same time, the confidence I had gained from building the Conservancy into a stable, ongoing organization gave me reason to consider pursuing a challenging related opportunity when it presented itself. My final entry in the journal recording the events of the previous twelve months closes, therefore, with this entry:

DECEMBER 29, 1989

The year ends with one professional satisfaction and one (perhaps, but perhaps not) professional disappointment. I have not written in this journal for several weeks because I was researching and writing lectures for the park-history course I plan to teach at the Cooper-Hewitt Museum in the new year. With Sara Cedar Miller's help, I put together three slide talks, and this exercise has allowed me to flex my intellectual muscles while also providing the base for similar work in the future—more teaching or maybe a book. I enjoyed my performances at the Cooper-Hewitt, the nervousness that put me on my toes, and the confidence that came from recognizing my ability as a public speaker.

Then there was my unsuccessful campaign to become the next parks commissioner now that Dinkins has been elected mayor. Encouraged by Ted, Lewis Bernard, and Gordon Davis, I realized that I was indeed the best-trained and most able person for the job and the one who would give the greatest effort to trying to apply the Conservancy's high management standards to the other parks in the city. I realized too that I had reached a plateau in my work in Central Park and that a difficult new job would nourish my professional growth. I wrote a carefully crafted letter to Gordon to assist him in promoting my candidacy, and with his approval and the advice of Ted and Lewis, my "campaign managers," I was off and running. But discreetly, because Henry was heart and soul after keeping the job himself, even though it was highly improbable that the new mayor would ask him to stay on. It was, in fact, improbable that Dinkins would appoint anyone other than Betsy Gotbaum, his chief fund-raiser, since she had openly declared that she wanted the job as her reward for helping the new mayor get elected.

A committee was set up to screen candidates. I was interviewed and my name submitted to the mayor-elect along with those of the other interviewees: Henry, Prospect Park administrator Tupper Thomas, Parks Council executive director Linda Davidoff, and environmental advocate Tom Fox. Although Betsy Gotbaum's name was not on the list, it was foreordained that, with the new mayor's debt to Labor and her spousal connection to Victor Gotbaum (between 1965 and 1987 he was the president of District Council 37, the city's largest municipal union), she would be appointed parks commissioner. And this indeed is what happened. Henry declared that this was less of a put-down of him than if I had been chosen, which I suppose was an unintended compliment, meaning that, in terms of public recognition and power, we now enjoy a sort of parity.

Fortunately, I was soon able to divest myself of the notions of "my administration" and the leadership plans I had begun formulating. It was in fact a relief to be free of the anxieties I had had regarding the administrative and political challenges the park commissionership would have posed for me, and I realized that I was lucky to be able to go on doing a job for which I was by nature better suited. I was glad, too, that by not becoming parks commissioner I could continue to teach part-time and to accept the increasing number of invitations that regularly came my way to speak in other cities to citizen groups that wanted to learn about the workings of public-private park partnerships in the hope that they could emulate the Conservancy's successful modus operandi.

In the final analysis, the experience of being a candidate for political office marked a psychological milestone for me inasmuch as it bolstered my sense of my professional worth within the world at large.

Chapter Fourteen

GROWING PAINS

As an organization grows in size, prestige, and financial resources, it inevitably assumes a new character that is reflected in its governance structure. I might consider the Central Park Conservancy to be "my" organization, and indeed it had been such at its inception and throughout the first ten years of its existence. I had recruited the first chairman of the board, William Beinecke, and he had helped shape the membership of the first group of directors and put in place the audit, nominating, and executive committees. As a philanthropist experienced in the world of not-for-profit cultural institutions, he saw his role as one of establishing the structure whereby the Conservancy board could exercise its fiduciary responsibilities, elect officers and new members, and approve the actions of its chief executive officer, which in this case was me. Investment banker Lewis Bernard, the Conservancy's first vice chairman, had helped Gordon and me launch the Conservancy even before Beinecke became its chairman, and he was the board member to whom I felt most accountable as well as the one to whom I invariably went for advice. We had weekly phone conversations, and he frequently invited me and members of the executive committee of the board for lunch in the Morgan Stanley dining room, where we discussed how to deal with organizational issues and further the agenda of the Conservancy within the constraints of our budget and our relationship with the city.

Teamwork

In 1985, when Bill decided to step down, Lewis helped me recruit James Evans, the about-to-retire CEO of Union Pacific Railroad, as our second chairman. As a trustee of the Rockefeller Brothers Fund and the founding chairman and life trustee of the National Recreation and Park Association, Jim was a friend of Laurance Rockefeller, a prominent force in the field of nature conservation. With such connections he was able to further build the Conservancy's profile and fund-raising ability.

Courteous and amiable, Jim was the right man to help lead our young organization into a new era. I felt that, under his chairmanship and with the contemporaneous publication of the management and restoration plan, we were ready to launch our first capital campaign. The Conservancy thereupon hired as its first development director Myra Biblowit, a professional fund-raiser who was then senior vice president of the Mount Sinai–NYU Health System. Together Myra

James Evans

and I made calls on prospective donors and built a development staff to organize philanthropic, foundation, corporate, individual, and direct-mail support. Systematic organization and management of a donor database was something still in the future, for ours was a closely collaborative and intuitive style of fund-raising. "Sweetie," she would say to me, "you've got to ask for more. The rising tide raises all the boats." Thus emboldened, I overcame my shyness about making face-to-face appeals for money, and with Myra's coaching and the connections of Jim and other trustees, we were able to meet a three-year $50 million capital campaign goal.

Coaching Sessions

In 1991, at the same time that Myra left the Conservancy to become vice president and executive director of the capital campaign for the American Museum of Natural History, Jim retired as chairman of the Conservancy. Trustee Ira Millstein, a senior partner in the law firm of Weil, Gotshal & Manges, was elected as his successor.

"What do you mean, you're doing all this without a contract from the city!" he expostulated. I admitted that the Conservancy's partnership with the city was indeed based on nothing more than my

Ira Millstein

ability to maintain good relations with whoever was parks commissioner. In addition to setting to work to remedy the Conservancy's ambiguous legal status, Ira made no bones about the fact that he found my management skills deficient. Lewis, who had watched me come this far, also felt that I needed coaching in order to be a more effective president as the Conservancy entered the next stage of its maturity.

Always the eager student, I actually enjoyed the management tutorials they arranged for me and my staff. One was run by a consulting company that used a program called "I Speak Your Language," which is designed to analyze the character traits and communication styles that employees bring to the job. Based on test results, we were able to see which of four categories we belonged to and, presumably with a more insightful and open attitude regarding our respective differences, increase our collegiality as team members. To give examples: "Thinkers" operate on facts and are analytical, deliberative, rational, and objective if sometimes rigid, indecisive, and unemotional. "Feelers" are loyal, persuasive, and empathetic but may also be subjective and sentimental. "Sensers" are pragmatic, results-oriented, technically skilled, and well-organized if sometimes too judgmental or impulsive. In comparison with these, "Intuitors" are future-oriented, conceptual, innovative, imaginative, idealistic, and creative, yet sometimes unrealistic and impractical.

Having been typed in the last category, I began to understand better how the dynamic of personality differences was being played out within the Conservancy now that it had advanced beyond its mom-and-pop phase. What an awakening! Was it really true that predictability and expectation were more congenial than innovation to most of my employees? Were routine and order rather than inspiration and entrepreneurship what they were actually more comfortable with?

As I pondered these truths, we divided into groups and the consultant guided us in the performance of an exercise called "Desert Rescue." While discussing with my teammates how to collectively work our way out of the supposed crisis in which we found ourselves, I realized that were I to be in a real-life dangerous situation, my leader of choice would be "Senser" Doug Blonsky. This brought home the understanding that there are clearly other ways to lead than with single-minded energetic enthusiasm, an assessment confirmed by Doug's strategic thinking and sanguine equilibrium in his later role as president of the Central Park Conservancy.

A nice metaphor to help curb my moving ahead at too fast a pace with what I considered to be wonderful initiatives was provided by Ted Ryan, another of the organizational management consultants the board had hired to tutor me. "When you sit down at a staff meeting and say, 'I have an idea,' you think you are sending a beautiful balloon into the air, but what the staff sees are a lot of bricks falling into their wheelbarrows."

There may have been too many bricks dropping from the sky, but to my credit I have always considered the building of the Conservancy as a group endeavor. For this reason I feel a moment of grateful pride when one of my former staff members tells me, "You hired me and then just let me perform my job without interfering." Well, the truth is that I am not a micromanager by nature, and my staff's creativity and competence provided the yeast in our rising loaf of success. Here is how I put it at the time:

SATURDAY, FEBRUARY 24, 1990

On Friday the 9th, I presided over an all-day staff retreat at Wave Hill. I like feeling my powers of leadership and the comradeship of my Central Park associates. Their spirit and belief in this enterprise, which was once merely my dream but is now the substance of their careers, is a constant source of satisfaction for me. More and more I am transforming our governance into something collegial and collective as I incorporate the sensible advice and good opinions of a staff that, like me, continues to grow in its abilities. An important lesson in good leadership: Don't cede your authority to your employees but seek their advice on all issues. Listen to their ideas, which are often better than yours. Develop a democracy of decision-making. In the end, absorb all blame and share all praise.

It would be five years before I was ready to resign from what I considered to be "the best job in the world"—or at least the best job for me that I could ever have imagined, in spite of its frustrations, past and future. During that time there was still much to learn about how to achieve a harmonious and effective relationship between city government and a private-sector civic organization.

Chapter Fifteen

TWO BETSYS

As I have said, my disappointment at not being appointed parks commissioner was short-lived. I actually felt energized about entering a new phase of my old career as I set about adapting the Conservancy's agenda to that of Betsy Gotbaum. Many Parks Department colleagues soon began to refer to "the two Betsys" because of our common first name. With "the other Betsy"—which is how we were respectively differentiated—I found, as I had before with Henry, that it was difficult to be subservient to the commissioner's ultimate authority, and I was not always as deferential to her as I should have been. Nevertheless, I admired Betsy and was glad to be working with the first female commissioner in the Parks Department's history.

Although I was in my tenth year as Central Park administrator, I felt that there was still more to accomplish to put the Conservancy on a sound footing and realize some

Betsy Gotbaum

important remaining objectives of the management and restoration plan. My old enthusiasm for my job was still strong, in spite of my having temporarily envisioned a new role for myself as the next parks commissioner. Indeed, I was honestly glad that I had been passed over, for now I would be able to continue to do what I liked most: oversee the design of the Conservancy's park restoration projects, develop more educational programs, and build the Conservancy's maintenance workforce into one in which there was accountability for the performance of every functional task and the condition of every single acre of Central Park's 840-acre landscape.

Power Plays

The change in mayoral administrations brought a new set of park politics to the fore, as it presented an opportunity for the Conservancy's opponents to rise again and publicly complain. As an example, soon after Betsy took office, she was presented with a public letter from the New York City Americans for Democratic Action, damning the Conservancy and exhorting the mayor and parks commissioner "to appoint as Central Park administrator a person independent of any private or quasi-private/public organization." Other detractors had now begun to call the Conservancy "elitist," and indeed on the society front, the organization appeared to be so. That the rich had adopted the park's revival as a popular cause, however, was to my way of thinking a good thing. Here is a glimpse of my appreciation for the social circuit's manner of raising money:

SATURDAY, JANUARY 27, 1990

My calendar for the past two weeks shows the busy pace of my present life. On the 16th there was a very glamorous Conservancy benefit at the Plaza organized by Fernanda Niven. The gossip columnists in attendance touted it, and I quite enjoyed seeing an old dream of mine materialize: Jack Haley Jr.'s production of a film collage made up of clips of some of the great old movies shot in Central Park (or on a Hollywood back-lot set simulating the park). There were Fred Astaire and Ginger Rogers on roller skates, Fred Astaire and Cyd Charisse dancing, the "Aquarius" number from *Hair,* and other wonderful clips showing the perennial popularity of the park as an American icon and stellar box-office attraction. Delightful even though Henry appeared to be miffed because I welcomed the new commissioner and forgot to mention him.

A few days later I hosted what I dubbed a "Parks Power Breakfast" in the Oak Room of the Plaza Hotel in an effort to bond with Betsy and further her acquaintance with Tupper Thomas, Linda Davidoff, Ellen Chesler, Susan MacDonald, and Myra Biblowit—female colleagues, of whom two (Tupper and Linda) were also-rans in the commissioner-appointment interview process. Betsy was quite capable of setting her own agenda for the Parks Department without the help of what I liked to think of as her kitchen cabinet; nevertheless, it was a pleasant gathering of old and new friends and we proceeded to make a date for another "Power Breakfast" a month later. Here is a record of that occasion:

SUNDAY, FEBRUARY 25, 1990

On Thursday morning the "Parks Power Breakfast Club"— Ellen Chesler, Linda Davidoff, Tupper Thomas, Myra Biblowit, and me—met again with Betsy Gotbaum at the Plaza. We offered ideas for her new administration and discussed organizational cooperation between the Parks Department and the Conservancy on summer youth programs and other matters.

But what do you suppose constituted the real power moment for this group of successful professional women? The appearance of the new owner of the Plaza Hotel and bachelor-to-be Donald Trump! From where I sat, I was able to watch him at his corner table with my right eye and at the same time admire with my left through the large window of the Edwardian Room our resplendent re-gilding of St. Gaudens's equestrian statue of

General Sherman. The general's entry into Atlanta could have hardly caused a greater sensation than the Donald's arrival in our midst following his abandonment of Ivana and the press accounts this past week of model Marla Maples spending her days in a Southampton hideaway. There is gossip of Ivana's tearful birthday party (on Valentine's Day!) with her well-wishing Trump in-laws, and of course the settlement stakes (the disputed minimum being $25 million), the estate in Greenwich, and custody of the children.

Is the power of money the ultimate aphrodisiac? There wasn't too much doubt when all heads swiveled as Trump entered, nor did we protest when later he stopped at our table, paused for introductions all around, and then removed the bill, telling the maître d' that we were his guests.

Like Henry, Betsy did not share my commitment to long-range landscape planning or see it as a means of articulating a vision for her administration. A small but telling example of the same kind of city-versus-Conservancy jockeying for primacy I experienced with Henry is illustrated by the fact that when I showed Betsy the sleeve patch with the Conservancy logo that I had had designed for the Conservancy's field employees, she forbade its use, allowing that only the Parks Department maple leaf logo should appear on workers' uniforms. Having T-shirts remain the only permissible dress identification for our employees, even as the city workforce in Central Park was declining and ours was growing, rankled. It brought home the realization that until we had a formal contractual relationship with the city that provided legal sanction for what the Conservancy had now become, the principal funder of the management of Central Park, its growing workforce would remain partially incognito and the divided role between the public and private sector's stewardship of the park would continue to be ambiguous.

With regard to the other city parks, Betsy was herself an excellent fund-raiser and had soon set up within the Parks Department her own not-for-profit organization, the City Parks Foundation, as a means of soliciting donors for tax-deductible contributions to a shopping list of projects and programs. Pragmatic by nature, she was not inclined toward long-term comprehensive landscape restoration and focused instead on a series of quick fixes. In Central Park she promptly claimed my old battle sites, giving the existing Tennis House a face-lift and a new operator while at the same time taking charge of the Summerstage concert series the Conservancy had initiated in the Bandshell in anticipation of the program's transfer to a portable rental stage on the defunct Rumsey Playground.

Betsy's four years in office coincided with David Dinkins's term as mayor. In 1993 Rudolph Giuliani was elected his successor. Liberal Party power broker Ray Harding's delivery of votes to Giuliani was rewarded with the new mayor's agreement to accept Harding's recommendations for various political appointments. Thanks to his connection to the Liberal Party and Ray Harding, Henry was able to make clear his readiness to take advantage of this opportunity to be reinstalled in his former job. It also didn't hurt that at the time Guiliani was campaigning for office, Henry had been able to place his ablest former Parks Department aide, Richard Schwartz, within the mayor's circle of advisers on government agency matters. In such fashion, his availability for another term of public service was recognized and rewarded.

Now, it was as if Henry had never left office, and he began to speak of the Dinkins era in which Betsy Gotbaum had served as commissioner as the interregnum. But as we moved forward once more in our odd-couple fashion, I realized that, in addition to having improved my management abilities, I now knew how to take advantage of the fact that equal to the power of politics is the power of money.

Chapter Sixteen

MONEY MATTERS

M oney attracts popularity, and as total Conservancy contributions had nearly reached the $100 million mark, some of that
popularity rubbed off on me. Although I had no illusions that the
honors I received with increasing frequency came solely because I was
dedicated to the preservation of Frederick Law Olmsted's great work
of landscape art, it was obviously a source of pride to me that I was the
Conservancy's standard-bearer.

Family Affair

As the following journal entry makes clear, accepting awards and hearing myself lauded as the chief protagonist in the Conservancy's success
story inevitably gave me a little glow of pride.

APRIL 4, 1990

My spring lecture circuit continues after the very pleasant congratulatory pause occasioned by the Parks Council's Monday

night dinner in my honor.* Its establishment of the Elizabeth Barlow Rogers Fund is a gratifying recognition of the Conservancy's success and my perseverance in steering a steady course through difficult times. I look on this group of friends as my first civic family after I moved to New York City in 1964 and think of the organization as my school for volunteer service in the public sector.

It was a sweet congratulatory moment, but I am realistic enough not to be smug and think that I am being honored solely for my accomplishments. Like the bestowal of other honors and accolades, this occasion is about money—not necessarily the money the Parks Council hopes to raise through the special fund bearing my name and the sale of benefit tickets—but rather as a tribute to the money that the Conservancy has raised to date. The realization of my dream of its evolution into a New York City institution respected and accepted by former opponents as well as friends is, when I look back, something beyond my wildest imaginings.

The Plaza ballroom was filled with tables adorned with centerpieces of tall tulips and flowering crab-apple branches. There was soft candlelight and a wonderful dance orchestra.

Martin Segal and Karen Karp, the benefit chairpersons, introduced Brooke Astor, my first park benefactor when there was as yet no Conservancy, only the Central Park Task Force. The presenter of my award, she is still beautiful at eighty-plus and was gracious in her praise of me. On this occasion I did not attempt to respond extempore but instead read the remarks I had prepared in order that I would not forget to thank one or another important friend who has helped me along the way. At the end I issued a roll call of my senior staff members, asking them to share the credit with me, for truly it is they who are in large measure responsible for my success. I have the greatest affection for them individually and collectively; they are my Central Park family.

---

* The Parks Council constituted a merger of the Parks Association with the Council for Parks and Playgrounds. Today the organization is called New Yorkers for Parks.

Rereading these words, I see how often I write that word "family." "My civic family," "my park family"—these overlapping circles of friends, colleagues, and donors do not substitute for my immediate family as far as the kind of love that fills the heart with unbounded joy and occasional grief is concerned; nevertheless, I cherish my bond with them as well as the one I have with the great city that has been my adopted home for half a century.

Dollars Speak

With a solid financial base and general donor satisfaction with the completion of each new project, the Conservancy had achieved what every not-for-profit organization must have in order to succeed: stability and a reputation for reliability. Another boon of equal importance was the city's altered role regarding the public and private sectors' respective roles vis-à-vis parks. No longer was the concept of private-sector support of parks resisted by city officials, and opposition within the Parks Department to the Conservancy's right to assume control over the design and implementation of capital projects within Central Park had been dispelled at last. It is important to emphasize, however, that on several fronts this did not constitute an abrogation of the city's ultimate authority. The public interest remained protected by the fact that Central Park is an official New York City landmark, and all projects within it are subjected by law to public hearings before both the New York City Landmarks Commission and the Public Design Commission. As we saw in our discussion of the aborted Tennis House project, they also undergo review by adjacent community planning boards.

None of these public review processes is a mere formality, and as we have seen, public officials and citizen opponents can cause a proposed project to be scotched. As is also evident by now, my frustration during Henry's tenure as parks commissioner was acute when political calculation and personal prejudice affected his response to privately funded projects presented for his approval. Such was the case when the Conservancy originally submitted its plans in 1987 for restoring the Great Lawn and the strip of grass alongside the remnant of the Old Reservoir called Belvedere Lake. Henry, with his penchant for naming, had already rechristened Belvedere Lake Turtle Pond, and now he gave a portion of its shoreline a special designation, "Dragonfly Preserve." This was his sly reference to the fracas that had occurred at the project's Landmarks Commission hearing caused by a group of entomologists, who claimed that the Conservancy's plan to remove the invasive *Phragmites* reeds proliferating around the perimeter of the pond would destroy a prime dragonfly breeding ground. By grasping this ostensible ecological handle, Henry was in effect vetoing the entire restoration of the Great Lawn, of which Turtle Pond at its southern edge was a part. The Conservancy's plan for reconfiguring and enlarging the pond and increasing the size of the area adjacent to the Delacorte Theater where people relax and picnic was thus left on hold and did not go forward during the four years Betsy Gotbaum was parks commissioner. The seemingly permanent paralysis of this project, however, was about to change.

As mentioned earlier, my husband Ted ran thirty-three consecutive New York City Marathons, and I was always somewhere near the finish line to greet him as he completed the last two-mile lap. But because of the congestion created by spectators also eager to see the end of the race, an area where relatives and friends can reunite with their particular runners afterward is set aside some distance away. Today this occurs outside the park on Central Park West, but in earlier times the Great Lawn was the designated family reunion area. Thus, on marathon day in 1993, after cheering Ted on as he entered the park at Fifth Avenue and Ninety-Second Street, I walked over and sat down under the letter *R* on the bare hardpan to wait for him to rejoin me. While I was waiting I tried to think of how to get the restoration of this important section of the park back on track. I realized that, should Henry continue to keep the project on hold by claiming an insufficiency of funds in the Parks Department's capital budget, the only way to solve the dilemma was with a private gift large enough to make refusal of permission untenable. Musing further, I thought, why not at the same time push forward with the restoration of the derelict areas along the west side of the park adjacent to the Great Lawn?

I knew whom to ask for help: Richard Gilder. Dick was a founding trustee of the Conservancy and a philanthropist who thought and acted as a private investor, which is what he is in the world of business.

He had already seen a sound return on his previous park benefactions in the form of visible and sustainable results. When I called on him a few days later, his response to my request for funds to restore the Great Lawn and the park's west side perimeter was immediate: "How much will it cost?" With unhesitating guesswork, I replied off the top of my head, "Around fifty million dollars." "Okay," he said, "I will pledge one-third of that amount contingent upon the Conservancy and the city each providing a third."

Gilder's magnanimity sparked the launch of our second comprehensive capital campaign, the goals of which focused on, but were not limited to, the Great Lawn and areas along the western perimeter of the park.* By way of example, on the East Side, at the Fifth Avenue and Sixty-Seventh Street park entrance, the north-south pathway in the Dene was christened Wallach Walk in honor of the donors, Miriam and Ira Wallach, whose gift had been originally directed to the ill-fated proposal to build a new Tennis House, and not far from where it would have stood, Robert Moses's Ninety-Fifth Street Recreation Center was renovated and programmed with youth activities.

Continuing to concentrate on work in the North End, we now had sufficient funds to undertake one of the Conservancy's earliest priorities, the dredging of the Harlem Meer and removal of the adjacent burned-out, heavily vandalized boathouse that had been built by Moses in 1947. The construction of the Charles A. Dana Discovery Center for environmental education on the site went hand in hand with replacing Moses's hard-edged reengineering of the Meer's shoreline with a naturalistic one that allowed access to the water's edge. To ensure that the siting of the Dana Center would follow Olmsted and Vaux's principle of making the park's architectural features an integral part of its landscape, I instigated a collaboration between in-house landscape architect Laura Starr and outside architect Samuel White of Buttrick White & Burtis. The result of Laura's suggestion to extend the footprint of Sam's Vaux-inspired building partially over the water pleased me so much that, following the opening of the new Dana

---

* The designated series of capital projects was estimated to cost $51 million, and the $20 million that was added to cover the Conservancy's annual operating costs over the four-year period of the campaign brought the goal to a total of $71 million.

Charles A. Dana Center

Great Lawn following restoration

Center, when the Reverend Calvin Butts of the Abyssinian Baptist Church made a charismatic appeal at the fund-raising breakfast we had organized to solicit support of the environmental education and community events programs we planned to offer there, I found myself pledging a gift of a thousand dollars.

Certain projects have been for me symbolic milestones. The resodding of the Sheep Meadow in 1981 had amounted to the throwing down of a green flag signifying the dawn of a new era in the life of Central Park; the opening in October 1997 of the restored Great Lawn, where dusty hardpan had been transformed into a lush carpet of grass, represented the coming-of-age of the Central Park Conservancy as a major civic institution; and the renaissance of the North End with the replacement of the burned-out boathouse—we had purposefully left it in its ruined state as a visible statement of our commitment to its future phoenix-like resurrection—epitomized our success in gaining popular acceptance of the concept of the park as an integral landscape spanning the distance of fifty-one city blocks from Midtown to Harlem.

At the same time that the Conservancy's landscape architects were kept busy at their drawing boards creating blueprints for these and other park restoration projects, we ensured that maintenance needs were given equal priority with capital construction and that the two went forward in conjunction. For the improvement and upkeep of other landscapes in the North End in addition to the area immediately adjacent to the Harlem Meer, we hired a full-time woodland manager. This made it possible to recruit and supervise a group of volunteers engaged in the removal of the rampant Japanese knotweed blanketing the slopes of the Ravine and choking out more desirable native plants along the banks of the nearby Loch. As an additional benefit, this increased level of landscape maintenance served as a form of crime prevention in the North End.

Moving On

Clearly, it was fund-raising success plus my self-prescribed "three Ps"—patience, passion, and persistence—that had helped the Central Park Conservancy grow into a securely established public-private partnership. In furthering this enterprise, I had been sustained by talented staff members and helpful outside advisers as well as by my unwavering allegiance to a vision of restoring the park in the spirit of Olmsted and Vaux's Greensward plan. Like these progenitors, I maintained that the park's principal purpose is to serve as a gathering place for people of all ages, classes, and ethnicities, and I could now rejoice that the ongoing fulfillment of the Conservancy's original mission statement "to make Central Park clean, safe, and beautiful" had converted it back into the democratic landscape they had intended it to be. I had accepted and overcome my presumed deficiencies as an organizational manager. Now, as I continued to travel and write about other great landscapes throughout the world, I knew that I wanted to return to my first career as an author.

The stages of institutional growth that Ted had explained to me ten years earlier involved leadership transfer at the appropriate time. I now felt that the Conservancy had passed from the entrepreneurial stage to one requiring a president with greater aptitude and appetite for the necessary day-to-day tasks of administration than I had. For this reason, December 31, 1995, marked my last day as a New York City public servant and founding president of the Central Park Conservancy.

The first person to whom I told my intention to retire was Lewis Bernard, the Conservancy's longtime vice president and, next to Ted, my most valuable counselor as I grew in my job and the Conservancy developed into an organization with staying power. Concurrent with my decision to step down, Ted and I bought an apartment on Eighty-First Street and Central Park West in the same apartment building where Lewis and his wife Jill live. Their anonymous gift to the Conservancy in commemoration of my years of service in restoring and improving the management of Central Park is marked by a bronze plaque at the foot of the steep bedrock outcropping that rises at the edge of the park across from our mutual front door. Called Summit Rock since it is the park's highest elevation, its surrounding landscape on the park's western perimeter is one of a series of restoration projects that the Conservancy had recently completed as part of the capital campaign initiated by Richard Gilder's $50 million gift. Because Manhattan schist is the park's geological fundament and its bedrock outcrops its most prominent topographical features, I found this to be a monumental tribute in every sense.

Leafing through the final journal I kept during my term in office, I see that I had already written my Central Park valedictory six years earlier.

FRIDAY, MARCH 20, 1989

A person is (can be) bigger than his or her present job, but this is a hard thing for those of us who love our work and derive a large psychic income from it to imagine. And a job, too, can be bigger than the person who performs it. It is therefore important to compute one's contribution on a different scorecard than that of individual satisfaction. I would like to feel this way about what I still consider to be the best job in the world in spite of its trials and tribulations and to believe that when the time comes for me to return to my original career as a writer on landscape subjects that it will be by choice and not with regret. There are particular challenges, however, when one is as much the author of one's work as I am at the moment, for resignation from my dual role as Central Park administrator and president of the Central Park Conservancy must come with the knowledge that organizational perpetuity and an increasingly beautiful and well-cared-for park is all that truly matters.

New Horizons

After leaving office, I obviously hoped that the basic Olmstedian restoration aesthetic and management principles I had instituted would be perpetuated. However, I knew that, even though the board had given me the honorific title of lifetime trustee, once the farewell party with encomiums was over, it would be inappropriate for me to attempt to influence the board's governance and the organization's operations after they had been placed in the hands of a successor. This, of course, did not mean that the park would ever be other than the true home of my heart, nor did it mean that, however ready I was to write a new chapter of my life, I would consider my twenty-year professional association with it as merely a line on my résumé. Neither did resigning from my job as Central Park administrator and president of the Central Park Conservancy mean that I had lost my passion for good civic design.

Next Steps

With the formation of the Cityscape Institute in 1996, I embarked on a new, much less successful chapter of my career. Assisted by Lane Addonizio, a recent Harvard graduate with a major in urban planning, I set up an office under the auspices of the Fund for the City of New York. Its mission was to develop prototype streetlights and litter receptacles along with a new street signage template, in order to replace the city's highway-style cobra-head fixtures, battered wire-mesh street-corner trash containers, and ill-designed public-space graphics. With funds raised from a consortium of investors put together by Dick Gilder, I hired architect Hugh Hardy to design what we called an integrated "family of fixtures."

To have undertaken such a mission during Rudolph Giuliani's mayoralty, rather than later, in Michael Bloomberg's administration, proved unfortunate. The commissioner of the Department of Transportation and the agency's engineers, as well as the Department of Sanitation officials with whom we met, were indifferent at best when presented with the various elements of our streetscape redesign. When I obtained a grant that allowed me to take two deputies in the mayor's office to Paris to see the new street furniture that had been installed there, they sent representatives who thought of the trip merely as a junket and never responded to my phone calls after our return.

Although I did not yet have a publisher for my book, during this period I continued my self-education in the history of landscape design. Finally, with a contract with Harry N. Abrams, I was able to bring to completion a comprehensive survey totaling 340,000 words. When published in 2001, it proved to be a stepping-stone to a new chapter of my career.

This occurred when Susan Soros, founder and director of the Bard Graduate Center, asked me if I would develop garden-related courses as part of her decorative arts curriculum. I took her request one step further and gained her approval to initiate a degree-granting program called Garden History and Landscape Studies.

I had always enjoyed teaching and was pleased when I was able to enroll our first class of students. However, as I might have expected given my temperament as a self-starter and after having been my own boss for so long, I chafed under the policy constraints of academia during the four years of the program's existence. Although it was with regret that I left the Bard Graduate Center following the spring semester of 2005, I have maintained a warm relationship with most of my former students, two of whom ended up working for the Central Park Conservancy, as did my invaluable colleague Lane, who is now the Conservancy's associate vice president for planning. Moreover, the Bard experience provided me the opportunity to have ongoing contact with scholars in the growing field of landscape history, some of whom became board members of the Foundation for Landscape Studies after its incorporation in 2005. With their advice, support, and volunteerism, this not-for-profit organization is able to publish the journal *Site/Lines* and in other ways fulfill its mission "to promote an active understanding of the meaning of place in human life."

Chapter Seventeen

GOLDEN AGE

By the time I left office at the end of 1995, the Conservancy had put slightly more than $100 million of private money into the park. Today that total has grown to $1 billion. During this time, the annual visitor count has risen to more than 42 million. Under the terms of its contract with the city and as a result of its tangible and financial success, the Conservancy has become a major New York City charitable organization. Today it enjoys a degree of prestige similar to that of the New York Botanical Garden, the American Museum of Natural History, the Wildlife Conservation Society (formerly known as the Bronx Zoo), and the New York Public Library—all of which, incidentally, are situated within parks.

Fulfilling Dreams

As much as or more than the trees and shrubs in a homeowner's garden, the park needs continual horticultural care. Some of the original restorations accomplished during my tenure, including the Dairy and the landscape surrounding it (originally named the Children's District); the Belvedere and its stonework terrace and loggias; and several cast-iron bridges and stone arches, are now, a generation later, receiving major structural repairs. Many of the projects on the Conservancy's wish list since the publication of its management and restoration plan in 1985, including the $18 million dredging of the twenty-acre Lake and relandscaping of its surrounding shoreline slopes, have been accomplished due to the largesse of a new generation of donors. Fundraising for the Conservancy's budget covering more than two-thirds of the park's $67 million annual operating costs, continued support for mandatory repairs, and sustained building of its $212 million endowment are essential to the park's prosperity.

Fortunately, as the park's appearance has continued to improve each year, so has its donor base. Success breeds success, and with the ongoing completion of the items put forth in the 1985 management and restoration plan, multimillion-dollar contributions have become common. These gifts account for such things as the Ramble's revival as a special rustic enclave within the park, a project that had been stymied since 1982 because of the birdwatchers' fury when the young Conservancy attempted to open up some of Olmsted's original view lines; the re-creation of the bosky retreat known as the Hallett Sanctuary, which occupies the peninsula that juts into the Pond at the park's southern edge at Fifty-Ninth Street—an area that was always in plain sight but off-limits behind a chain-link fence erected in the Moses days; and in the northern reaches of the park, the realignment of the large dislodged rocks and boulders that serve as streambed ledges over which three waterfalls spill as the Loch takes its course through the Ravine.

Several recent gifts have been directed toward the Conservancy's campaign to renovate all of the park's twenty-two playgrounds. In addition to installing play equipment that does not appear obtrusive within the scenic context of the park, the Conservancy's team of landscape architects is visually uniting the redesigned playgrounds with the surrounding landscape by replacing Robert Moses's cagelike iron palings with low fences made of inconspicuous wire mesh. Another significant improvement is the replacement of the ugly candy-colored polyurethane manufacturers' equipment previously installed in response to liability insurance concerns with custom-designed play features that are both safe and attractive.

Fortune's Wheel

That Central Park now enjoys a golden age is undeniable. But the perpetuity of golden ages cannot be taken for granted. Indeed, if you were to plot on a graph the fortunes of the park over the years of its existence, you would see a series of hills and valleys. There is an ascending curve during its Greensward years as the scenic landscape conceived by Olmsted and Vaux matured. By the end of the nineteenth century a declining line represents a lapse in this ideal, as active forms of recreation were imposed on the park's original naturalistic design. More drastically, the numerous extraneous, often eccentric, proposals at this time would have appropriated most of its open spaces for purposes that would have obliterated all traces of the Greensward plan. Indeed, during these years the continued existence of the park as a park was in question. But, as we have seen, from 1934 until the early 1960s, a dramatic change in its fortunes took place. Certainly Robert Moses never conceived of restoring Olmsted's vision of Central Park as a scenic *rus in urbe*, but his authoritarian reign as parks commissioner brought it back to its intended recreational mission, albeit one that incurred numerous encroachments that transformed many multiuse scenic acres into sites for single-purpose facilities for sports, games, and children's play. Then, in the 1960s, following Moses's retirement, the lapse in park rules, regulations, management policies, and maintenance standards presaged the nosedive in which the fortunes of Central Park reached their nadir. The story of the Conservancy's reversal of a decline that has been recounted in previous chapters charts a new pinnacle in the imaginary graph we have been plotting. But what about the future?

Although the Central Park Conservancy has been blessed with a shower of gold, money alone cannot ensure that the park will enjoy the current high level of stewardship that has made it a role model for parks worldwide. That the park is the cynosure it is today is due in no small measure to something that goes beyond successful fundraising: the twin skills of good leadership and sound management. Doug Blonsky, who is now retiring from his dual position as Central

Park administrator and president of the Conservancy, has served as a wildly admired role model in this regard, thereby setting a high bar for his successor.

Doug's excellence as a park manager has never been in question from the time I hired him in 1985 to supervise the recently formed crew responsible for carpentry and masonry repairs and the reconstruction of vanished rustic bridges, gazebos, and arbors. It was also at this time that the systematic rebuilding of Central Park outlined in the Conservancy's newly published comprehensive plan began in earnest. With the Parks Department's acquiescence, the Conservancy became entitled to bid out construction projects and select contractors of its own choosing. After my promotion of Doug to the job of construction manager, there were no more bureaucratic delays and capital projects were completed on time and on budget. With degrees in both plant science and landscape architecture, he was able to add to his construction supervision responsibilities the leadership of the Conservancy's entire planning and design team, and in this role integrate into the design process the specification of horticultural practices and maintenance protocols necessary for post-construction sustainability.

In his subsequent position of Central Park administrator beginning in 1998, Doug was able to professionalize and expand the tree, turf, masonry, rustic carpentry, planting, bronze conservation, and graffiti-removal crews I had established earlier. Most important, as funds became available, he was able to extend the system I had initiated of zone gardeners accountable for the maintenance of specifically defined areas beginning with Strawberry Fields to forty-nine sections covering all 843 acres of Central Park.

In putting this operational system on a sound footing there was yet a necessary hurdle to overcome. As we have seen, forging a satisfying working relationship between city government and the Conservancy had been accomplished only gradually, and the actual authority of the Conservancy had remained ambiguous as long as day-to-day jobs were being performed by a dual rather than a single workforce. Thus, in his role as Conservancy chairman, Ira Millstein and his law firm initiated a series of discussions with Henry and the New York City Corporation Counsel to clarify the respective roles of the city and the Conservancy with regard to Central Park. In 1997, after two years of negotiation, a management contract was signed, formalizing the arrangement that had heretofore depended on diplomacy and the respective assets of a declining city budget and the Conservancy's sustained fund-raising ability. In this fashion the dual field workforce in Central Park became unified within a structure whereby both the Conservancy's employees and those remaining on the city's payroll until retirement reported to Doug and his staff.

This does not mean, as some people at the time charged, the "privatization" of Central Park. As stated in several places elsewhere in this book, it is a given that the park is public property and policy authority with regard to it is rightfully the province of city government. But by heading a unified management system as well as by establishing a sound working relationship with Adrian Benepe, Henry's successor as commissioner, Doug revitalized the politics of public-private partnership to a significant degree.

Today the Conservancy has become a paradigm for the creation of other public-private partnerships and the improved management of various city parks in New York City and elsewhere. Its Institute for Urban Park Management provides a series of seminars both in a classroom setting and as online webinars. The curriculum covers everything from the management of zone gardeners and volunteers, to the essentials of turf and tree care, to methods of park programming, to establishing and enforcing park rules and regulations. In addition, its Center for Urban Park Discovery offers an educational program aimed at visitors, families, adults, students, and teachers.

When I asked Doug recently to comment on the ways in which strategic park management works both in Central Park and as a model for parks elsewhere, he replied, "It is really based on constant oversight of every section of the park as well as the digital technology that facilitates the collection of a multiplicity of park-wide data. Here is an example: the zone gardener will walk his or her site daily and report such things as a broken bench or tree limb to the section supervisor, who in turn will relay this information to our maintenance headquarters at the Seventy-Ninth Street Yard where it will be logged into a database. This provides a way to determine what level of attention is required, prioritize the tasks that need to be done, and develop a schedule for dispatching the appropriate staff or outside contractor."

He quickly added, "We couldn't get nearly as much accomplished—in fact the park wouldn't look half as good as it does now—without our three hundred and fifty regular volunteers. Altogether, more than three thousand volunteers perform various maintenance tasks throughout the year. They log in online, and the Conservancy can therefore track the number of hours they work, which in 2015 added up to more than sixty thousand." As Doug recited these statistics, I thought to myself, "Oh my, how far things have come since the days of the Central Park Task Force when I was organizing school groups, summer interns, and a few green thumbs to pull weeds and perform some other horticultural good deeds in random locations—now the volunteers are a regular army!"

Reading a recent *New York* magazine article titled "Will They Ever Finish Central Park?" the theme of which is the park as a great work-in-progress, and thinking back to my own 1976 article in the same magazine, "32 Ways Your Time and Money Can Rescue Central Park," I am both amazed and gratified. That I had the notion back then of public-private partnership as a new operational concept for a municipal park and had four years later applied the term "conservancy" to denote the type of organization that engages in such an effort is naturally a source of personal pride.* To have nurtured into being and participated in the rise of the first and foremost conservancy, from its origins as a small task force composed of volunteers and high school summer interns into a paradigm of excellence in park administration, seems astonishing.

It was a matter of good fortune that in a period when cultural prejudice still prevented most women from becoming serious players within the spheres of law, business, and government, I should have embarked on a career in an area in which attitude toward gender was absent as an

---

* According to a report published in 2015 by the Trust for Public Land, there are forty-one citizen-supported park organizations, of which twenty-seven bear the name "Conservancy." See: https://www.tpl.org/sites/default/files/files_upload/ccpe-Parks-Conservancy-Report.pdf.

obstacle. I find it flattering to still be invited to other cities to tell the Conservancy success story. Although it can't really be boiled down into a simplistic how-to formula, when asked how it can be emulated elsewhere, I frequently tick off the following imperatives: (1) a vision, (2) a management and restoration plan, (3) a good relationship with government officials and community organizations, (4) a strong board with the capacity to provide financial support, (5) advisory committees to help chart the course of future organizational development, and (6) the proverbial three Ps: patience, passion, and persistence. I will sometimes summarize as follows: "There has to be a Pollyannaish leader who is something of a 'zealous nut' in the first place, you must never take no for an answer, and you must accommodate, or simply endure, the opposition of your opponents." There is much more to say when it comes to the professionalization of organizational administration, but since I am no longer the official voice of the Central Park Conservancy, these words belong to someone other than me.

Field Trip

At 7:00 on a recent morning I stopped by the Seventh-Ninth Street Yard to meet with Doug; Russell Fredericks, chief of operations; Marie Hernandez, director of horticulture; and Caroline Greenleaf, director of community relations. One of the most satisfying things I took away from the time we spent together poring over a Central Park map on which the boundaries of each zone are clearly delineated was not only the efficiency with which things are done nowadays, but also the fact that the Olmstedian aesthetic governing the entire enterprise that had motivated me from the beginning remains alive. Since I am in the park almost every morning, I see the progression of "fine touches" being added to the restoration projects that have already been accomplished. But it was rewarding to have Doug point to areas where several of these long-awaited small restorations were at the time being undertaken by field crews. For instance, in woodland areas there are a number of new wood-chip paths that look like hiking trails. These unobtrusive additions to the regular circulation system are sometimes a means of legitimizing the old compacted dirt trails known as desire lines; at other times they offer an invitation to discover nature's manifold secrets within formerly inaccessible areas of the park.

Remembering the old 1982 brouhaha in the Ramble when the protest for opening up "views and vistas" raged and how Henry had once embraced a large London plane and told a group of reporters covering an Arbor Day celebration, "I won't let her cut you down as long as I am around to protect you," I was happy when Doug called my attention to places on the map where removing a certain tree or getting rid of a patch of invasive undergrowth had created a broad view or scenic prospect. Russell, Marie, and Caroline elaborated on the ways in which the Conservancy tree crew, zone gardeners, and volunteers were accomplishing this goal. "You know," Doug added, "no one likes to see a huge old tree toppled to the ground, but Hurricane Sandy and some of the other recent storms actually produced a favorable result as far as opening up some of the park's original view lines." On hearing this I remembered the days between 1982 and 1985 when "The Park Is One" had been a mantra for the landscape architects who were in the process of preparing the management and restoration plan. It was the same design approach that had guided Frederick Law Olmsted and Calvert Vaux when they created the out-of-sight sunken transverse roads and interwove meadows, woods, and water into a single flowing landscape with long vistas in which one scenic element melded with another.

Doug said that he needed to site a bench that the rustic carpentry crew had just finished building and invited me to drive up to the North End with him. Although I always try to remember that I am no longer boss, I couldn't restrain myself from falling into my old role and saying, "Wouldn't it be better to move the bench down the slope just a few feet and turn it a little bit more to the right in order to improve the view?" He nodded and directed the crew to oblige me. I complimented them on the artistry with which they had fashioned the sinuous branches of a recently fallen locust tree into this beautiful piece of park furniture, and my heart swelled with happiness and pride as we all shook hands.

Remembering as we drove south on the West Drive past the Great Lawn where I had once sat on the dusty hardpan under the sign marked

Betsy and Doug on a newly constructed rustic bench in Central Park

with the letter *R* waiting for Ted to join me after running across the marathon finishing line, I said how impressed I had been lately with how well such park-impacting events are managed nowadays. "We've got the marathon down to a science," Doug replied. "With the Roadrunners and all the other groups that organize mass activities in the park, it's a matter of getting them to put their trucks, portable toilets, and other equipment in the footprint we have designated. We used to kill ourselves doing all the cleanup until we realized that this was really their responsibility and we should only take a supervisory role. Now we work with them to make sure things run smoothly within the guidelines we have set up. It's in their best interest to comply, since if the people they hire are the ones cleaning up the park, it's expensive for them if they don't do it efficiently."

After we said goodbye, I thought about what may prove to be the most memorable mass event in the history of Central Park. This was *The Gates,* the project that Cristo and Jeanne-Claude first discussed with Gordon Davis and me in 1981, when Gordon had just begun to reform a moribund, dysfunctional city agency that was at the time notorious as a patronage parking lot for political paybacks and virtually paralyzed by its disorganized, mismanaged bureaucracy. Back then, as we sat at the conference table outside the commissioner's office, I had only to look out the window to see broken benches, eroded slopes, and the cracked asphalt paths they planned to overarch with saffron-colored fabric.

In turning down Cristo and Jeanne-Claude's permit application, we had maintained that the park itself, degraded as it was, was a great work of art and that even a temporary installation superimposed on it would perpetuate the notion that its landscape was nothing more than a blank canvas that outside event sponsors could appropriate for non-park purposes. The story behind how what had then appeared to be an exploitation of the park as New York City's most conspicuous public art venue could twenty years later be considered a celebratory declaration of the Conservancy's success in saving Central Park from ruin is one that deserves a chapter of its own.

Chapter Eighteen

SAFFRON CELEBRATION

In an essay titled "Frederick Law Olmsted and the Dialectical Landscape" written in 1973, Robert Smithson, widely considered to be the progenitor of land art, maintained that Central Park, dangerous and near-destroyed as it was then, was a great earthwork involving the excavation of swamps to create lakes and the movement of millions of cubic yards of topsoil to form rolling meadows and lawns. He saw how effectively Olmsted and Vaux had used the glacier-polished outcrops of Manhattan schist as elements in their design. "The magnitude of geological change is still with us, just as it was millions of years ago," he wrote. "Olmsted, a great artist who contended with such magnitudes, sets an example which throws a whole new light on the nature of American art."

Smithson's words were not intended to endorse park preservation; rather, they implied recognition of a prototype for the manipulation of the landforms of nature on a massive scale to innovate a new type of conceptual art. Christo and Jeanne-Claude's proposal to install *The Gates* along every pathway throughout the 830-acre park contained an element of the same bravado found in Smithson's frequent use of the word "dialectical" as a means of setting up tension and opposition, a polarizing stance in which the breakaway independent artist, divorced from the gallery dealer, is a heroic figure engaged in Herculean endeavors in spite of, or because of, their difficulty, cost, and initial public and governmental opposition.*

However, one difference between their work and that of Smithson and other land artists such as James Turrell and Michael Heizer is the fact that, although similar in size and ambition, Christo and Jeanne-Claude's oeuvre consists of temporary installations in conspicuous locations rather than lifetime projects in remote landscapes. The tangible existence of *The Gates* over time rests not in their actual realization but rather in the hundreds of drawings sold in galleries to finance their fabrication and erection as well as in the photographs and videotapes documenting this process.

Back Then

Christo and Jeanne-Claude were anything but unknown in 1981 when they met with Gordon and me in the Parks Department's conference room to discuss their original proposal to exhibit *The Gates* in Central Park. Their growing reputation as art world celebrities derived from unique projects such as *Valley Curtain* (1970), a 45,000-square-foot fabric hung on four steel cables fastened with iron bars fixed in concrete on opposite slopes of a valley in the Rocky Mountains near Rifle, Colorado; *Running Fence* (1973), another span of cloth strung on cables, this one traversing a five-and-a-half-mile stretch of landscape in Marin and Sonoma Counties, California; and *Wrapped Walkways* (1977), covering the paths of Loose Park in Kansas City, Missouri. Erecting *The Gates* in the world's most famous park provided the logical next opportunity to demonstrate the couple's tenacity in not taking no for an answer when their projects were first conceptualized.

---

* The documentary filmmaker Albert Maysles has covered almost all of Christo's projects from inception to completion. His footage relating to *The Gates* captures the first meeting with Davis and Parks Department officials in the Arsenal. Like his other Christo documentaries—*Floating Islands* in the Bay of Biscayne (1983), *Christo in Paris* on the wrapping of the Pont Neuf (1985), and *Wrapped Reichstag* in Berlin (1995)—it tells the story of the couple's persistence and final triumph after years of opposition.

Over the twenty-five years since the parks commissioner and the nascent Conservancy had turned down the proposed *The Gates* on the grounds that Central Park itself was, as Smithson had proclaimed, America's greatest work of land art, Christo and Jeanne-Claude had demonstrated their expertise in overcoming bureaucratic obstacles to the realization of their projects. On January 22, 2003, after the Central Park Conservancy's support was won following much arduous debate by its board of trustees and several meetings between the artists and Doug to establish the project's ground rules, Mayor Michael Bloomberg, who had already backed the project when he was a Conservancy trustee, signed the permit that would allow *The Gates* to be installed two years later.

Design Development

The mayoral and Conservancy approvals meant that *The Gates* project plans previously developed by Christo and Jeanne-Claude's engineer, Vince Davenport, could now go forward more or less as orignally planned. The most important difference between 2005 and 1981, when the permit had been denied, was the set of strict conditions required by the Parks Department and the Conservancy for the erection of the supporting structures that would allow the draping of banner-like squares of orange fabric over the park's pathways.

The original proposal called for fifteen thousand stanchions to be set directly in the ground and later filled with what was promised to be "clean dirt." The early drawings also show gates lining every single park path, irrespective of overhanging tree branches or their location in areas serving as wildlife sanctuaries, notably the Ramble and the North Woods. To ensure that the conditions set forth by Parks Commissioner Adrian Benepe and the Conservancy could be enforced, Doug flew to Seattle to meet with Davenport and his wife, Jonita, who serves as his partner in working out the specifications and logistics of Christo's projects. According to Doug, "As soon as I met Vince I knew we could do business." Davenport apparently felt the same way about him. "We couldn't have done the project without Doug and the Conservancy. We were blessed with that partnership," he said when I interviewed him.

The necessity of placing the posts on steel footings set on the asphalt edge of the paths rather than in the ground was quickly agreed upon. Vince, Doug, Christo, Jeanne-Claude, and Adam Kaufman, the director of Central Park operations at that time, walked the park's entire pathway system. Wildlife-rich woodlands were declared off-limits, and wherever there was a stretch of path where a gate potentially would interfere with an overhanging tree branch, an interruption of their regular flow was mandated. Thus, the originally proposed number of 15,000 gates lining fifty miles of pathway was reduced to 7,503 lining twenty-three miles. Blueprints were prepared showing the position of every gatepost. According to Doug, "Walking the park with Vince and then my going out to see his operation in Seattle developed the relationship. We synthesized our goals and developed a strong bond. It became a true collaboration, a challenge, something we knew we could do together."

"Challenge" is a word that Vince Davenport likes. He had been working with Christo and Jeanne-Claude since 1989, when he helped engineer *The Umbrellas,* which rimmed portions of the Pacific coastline in both California and Japan. The son of a general contractor who "could do anything," he enjoys exploring options and finding solutions to novel problems. As an example, it took him three months to design one of the invisible components of *The Gates.* This was the eight-inch-square steel leveling plate cupping a central pivot ball that would allow the assembled gates to be tilted slightly one way or the other in order to make the posts perfectly plumb as they were being securely screwed into their bases. In this way they would be uniformly upright, whatever degree of incline the hilly park paths took.

Christo and Jeanne-Claude studied several mock-ups that Vince erected on his own property in order to decide upon such things as fabric texture, color, dimensions, the fullness of the pleats to give the right amount of billowing in the breeze, and even their exact hem width. In March 2003 Vince and Jonita rented a Manhattan apartment and took up a two-year residency a few blocks from Central Park. Vince then searched the city's outer boroughs for a warehouse large enough to accommodate the assembly and fabrication of all the materials—steel bases, vinyl posts, nylon fabric, aluminum sleeves—and ended up renting a 25,000-square-foot space in Maspeth, Queens. Meanwhile, Jonita managed the project's website and a database containing the names of two thousand people who had applied online for jobs as helpers. The requests to sign up came from near and far. A number of applicants had worked on previous Christo projects. Some were themselves artists, while others with regular jobs had decided this was an exciting way to spend their vacation time.

Manufacturing Miracle

At the same time that Jonita Davenport was screening and hiring the workforce, Vince set about contacting manufacturers and suppliers, trying to find ones in as close proximity to New York City as possible in order to minimize trucking costs, an important consideration in this case because ten million pounds of material had to be delivered. He found a steel company outside Philadelphia that could make the footings, each of which weighed between 613 and 837 pounds, depending on size. The company agreed to paint them a dark gray color to match the park's asphalt paths. A firm in Poughkeepsie, New York, was able to produce sixty miles of orange-colored vinyl, which was extruded from five-by-five-inch-square horizontal molds in eighteen-foot sections, for the stanchions and crossbars that would be assembled into gates.

One million square feet sounds like a lot of nylon fabric, but this was too small an order for U.S. mills; Vince therefore contracted with the same mill in Germany that had manufactured the fabric for Christo and Jeanne-Claude's previous three projects. Workers in his temporary factory then cut the vinyl into sixteen-foot posts and crossbars of twenty-five varying lengths, ranging from five feet and six inches to eighteen feet, according to the path width particular sets of gates would span. They also produced the aluminum sleeves he had designed to fasten the posts and crossbars together when they were assembled as gates in the park. A further design refinement called for the incision of a one-half-inch keyhole slot running the length of each crossbar, from which the rolled fabric inserted in its hollow interior could be unfurled. The fabric was cocooned in a cardboard cylinder so that it would billow without wrinkles on the day *The Gates* was officially opened.

Military Maneuvers

The next stage in realizing the project required a military organizational structure and meticulous management system. Together Doug and Vince hammered out the schedule and logistics governing the delivery and distribution of three hundred truckloads of materials to the park prior to the first week in February 2005, when *The Gates* installers would begin assembly. Of equal importance was the advance planning necessary to train and deploy the seven-hundred-person workforce. This meant developing a chain of command. The bottom rank consisted of installers, monitors (friendly "ambassadors" who interacted with the public after the gates were installed), and disassembly workers to take down the gates at the end of the sixteen-day exhibition. Each worker would be paid $6.25 an hour and would be required to work a minimum of one week. They were divided into seventy-three eight-person teams overseen by twenty-one zone supervisors reporting to seven area leaders. Twenty-eight professional leaders, most of whom already were known to the Conservancy because they had previously managed events or film shoots in the park, acted as lieutenant generals.

In the fall of 2004, with drawings showing every gate precisely placed and numbered, Vince and two helpers stenciled small green leaves and dots to mark where each set of gates would be placed on the asphalt paths. "I realized that arrows would arouse public concern, so I decided on the green maple leaf, which also has a point and is the logo of the Parks Department," he told me. "A leaf pointing in one direction indicated the beginning of a set of gates and another pointing in the opposite direction its end. The dots stenciled at twelve-foot intervals between the two markers showed the exact position of each gate." The length of a run was determined mostly by the Conservancy-mandated gate-free intervals where paths were overhung with tree branches.

Christo and Jeanne-Claude, 2005

The steel bases—a total of five thousand tons in weight—were delivered in December and stockpiled in the North End. During the first week in January, they were collected and distributed to various sections where they were picked up by forklifts and positioned with the proper spacing and alignment in accordance with the stencil marks on the paths. Bundles of stacked orange vinyl posts and crossbars were delivered to designation points along the park's circuit drive.

On February 7, the installers who were to erect the 7,503 gates assembled at the Central Park Boathouse. Christo and Jeanne-Claude were there, as they were on every subsequent day throughout the duration of *The Gates,* to encourage the workers. Vans were ready to take each of the teams of eight and the area supervisors to their assigned sections of the park. Team captains, who previously had received a weeklong training course, carried sets of plans showing the location and specifications for the slightly more than one hundred gates each team would install by the end of the week.

I found it fascinating to watch the speed and dexterity with which the installers assembled the parts of each gate as if these were pieces of a giant erector set, positioning the posts on the leveling plates that had been fastened to the steel bases, fitting in place the aluminum sleeves holding the posts and crossbars together, raising and leveling the just-constructed gate, and then tightening the bolts that held it in place. By opening day, February 12, in spite of a previous fifteen-inch snow-

storm that had held up the execution of some of the carefully calcu-
lated logistics, the *Gates* exhibition was ready to be officially "opened"
by Mayor Bloomberg. Workers were at their stations throughout
Central Park. After the mayor, Christo, and Jeanne-Claude raised
long poles with hooks on the end and snagged loops attached to the
rolled-up fabric, releasing the Velcro that held it in place beneath the
crossbar, the workers did the same, and the park's paths were quickly
overarched with billowing orange banners. By the next day, the hooks
on the ends of the poles had been covered with tennis balls, and the
teams of monitors that had replaced the installers were acting as stagehands, bumping back as necessary a piece of fabric that a breeze might
have flipped over its crossbar. Their main function, however, was
to serve as exhibition docents, answering questions and dispensing
small squares of fabric to people seeking a souvenir. Their presence
also ensured public order and prevention of sub-rosa theft. Vandalism
of this sort would have been impossible in any case, because of the
throngs of gates-gazers walking everywhere throughout the park by
day and also because of the sixty-person force of security guards and
police patrolling the park by night.

On February 28, the official closing day of the exhibition, disassembly crews began taking down the gates with the same organized
efficiency with which the first teams of workers had installed them, a
process that lasted until March 15. During this time it was possible for
park visitors to have a progressively truncated better-late-than-never
viewing of *The Gates*. The steel bases, aluminum sleeves, vinyl posts,
and fabric were put in separate dumpsters stationed along the park
drives. All the material was now ready to be removed from the park—
the steel going to a recycling plant in Jersey City, the aluminum to
one in Brooklyn, the vinyl and fabric to another in Pennsylvania. The
show was over.

Art Review

When I asked Jeanne-Claude what the enormous popular success of
The Gates signified to her and Christo, she replied, "We did not do
this as a gift to New York City. We did not do this for the park. We

Monitor as stagehand during The Gates *exhibition*

are artists. We did this for ourselves!" Nevertheless, both detractors and admirers had reservations about whether to call *The Gates* an art-work or an event. Perhaps the most frequent complaint by the former was the color: a bright orange with a strong resemblance to the plastic material used to cordon off construction sites for safety reasons. The latter declared that *The Gates* had been a great thing for New York City. It had boosted citizen morale and been an economic and pub-lic relations shot in the arm. Some people referred to the project as a great good event in comparison with the horrific event of 9/11, as if in some way the lingering notoriety of that catastrophe could be amelio-rated by the buoyant mood engendered by *The Gates*. After all, smil-ing and well-behaved crowds—3.7 million people in all—had moved happily along twenty-three miles of park pathway, seeing areas of the park into which they had never ventured before. The North End drew most of the praise, and I heard several longtime New Yorkers admit with chagrin that they had never before seen that part of the park.

For myself, I liked the curious dialogue, albeit unintended on the

The Gates *following a snowfall*

part of Christo and Jeanne-Claude, between the Olmstedian park and
the one that they had temporarily transformed in such a striking way.
With camera in hand like almost everybody else, I shot image after
image of rippling orange fabric in juxtaposition with the park's rustic
arbors, cast-iron bridges, and carved stone arches or as foreground or
backdrop for prominent architectural features, such as the Belvedere. I
visited almost every corner of the park and often was drawn to the top
of rock outcrops to get overhead views. The scene was always changing as the park experienced different kinds of weather. I also liked
watching how people dressed for the experience, many wearing some
bit of orange apparel, such as a scarf or jacket.

During the days in which I enjoyed the park from this novel perspective, I reflected on the fact that Christo's concept for *The Gates*
was born in the establishment-rejecting, countercultural 1970s, when
Robert Smithson and other like-minded artists had adopted a radical
anti-art-world stance. These artists, including Christo, stood at the

threshold of reinvention of the original terms of modern art, which at the beginning of the twentieth century had also been revolutionary in its break with established conventions of pictorial composition and figurative representation. But Pablo Picasso and Henri Matisse, and later Jackson Pollock and Robert Motherwell, never dreamed of abandoning the studio, gallery, or museum or of giving up the use of traditional artists' materials—pen, chisel, brush, ink, paint, paper, canvas, clay, wood, stone, bronze. Now museums and galleries routinely exhibit video art, performance art, and installations composed of found objects. Land art has become part of the Western canon. The fact that *The Gates* was an ephemeral, unique, and unrepeatable exhibition made it magnetic, drawing international attention and lasting acclaim as a major artwork of the twenty-first century.

The sixteen-day mass event could perhaps be thought of as a nostalgia-inspiring throwback to the period of its genesis more than twenty-five years earlier. Yet there were differences. The era of cultural unrest that had swept the country during the civil rights movement and the Vietnam War was over. Mass events in the park in the sixties and early seventies were hardly polite. Unlike the lawn-trampling crowds that attended the happenings of that period, further destroying the park's already severely bruised landscape, those who came to see *The Gates* in 2005 seldom strayed from the paths. Nor were the mass events of the 1970s even by a small fraction as well orchestrated and managed as this one.

By the third week in March, not long after *The Gates* had been dismantled and was just an extraordinary memory—an erased inscription on the park's ever-evolving palimpsest—another event was set in motion. This time it was a universally welcomed annual one: the coming of spring. One could see the saffron stigmas in the center of the opening crocuses, and on an upper window pediment, just below the sheltering cornice of an apartment building on Fifth Avenue and Seventy-Fourth Street—after a contentious squabble precipitated by the removal and then, under intense public pressure, reinstallation of the supports for their twiggy nest—a famous pair of red-tailed hawks was again in residence. A telescope trained on the nest presented the spectacle of the male bird's dusky orange-tinged tail feathers as he soared to a landing with food for his mate.

Over and over I heard people say, "I was glad to see them come and glad to see them go." Often they added, "It's good to have the park back." On March 27, Easter Sunday, Central Park was as thronged with visitors as it had been on every day when *The Gates* was on view. I was one of them, and I, too, was glad to have the park "back"—as if it had ever gone away.

ACKNOWLEDGMENTS

Every writer knows the importance of a preliminary manuscript reader as a mentor and guide. In this I was very fortunate to have Amanda Urban as my agent. She made invaluable suggestions that helped me improve my first two drafts before she showed the third one to my Knopf editor, Ann Close. After that it was Ann's encouragement plus some surgical advice that helped me improve the book's narrative flow as well as the tone of certain passages.

As work progressed I was lucky in having friends with ready expertise close at hand. A primary debt of gratitude goes to historian Sara Cedar Miller, the Central Park Conservancy's recently retired associate vice president of park information and the park's official photographer for thirty-three years. Her knowledge and assistance both as a manuscript reader and in furnishing me with forgotten names and dates greatly reduced my chances for error. Numerous illustrations in these pages are from photographs Sara has taken almost from the inception of Central Park Conservancy's restoration to the present. As such, they represent a major holding within its photographic archive. Sara's own books about Central Park and this large collection of images will be as valuable a resource for future park historians as they have been for me.

Corresponding thanks go to Lane Addonizio, the Conservancy's associate vice president for planning, for scrupulously assisting me in matters of factual accuracy and for generously providing me with digital copies of several images from her collection of stereopticon photographs and historic postcards of Central Park. Marie Warsh, the Conservancy's director of preservation planning, discovered and scanned for me the Central Park Task Force's archival photographs from the 1970s, and for this I am also grateful.

Among those whom the reader has met within these pages is my husband Ted Rogers. He not only lived through fourteen of the twenty years I was involved with Central Park on a daily basis but also was there for me during the past three years as *Saving Central Park* was coming to fruition.

Above all, I cannot give sufficient thanks to those to whom this book is dedicated: the men and women who built and rebuilt Central Park. Without them, there would be no story to tell.

BIBLIOGRAPHY

Central Park, General

Barlow, Elizabeth. "Central Park's Renaissance: 33 New Ways You Can Help." *New York* magazine, June 6, 1983.

————. "32 Ways Your Time or Money Can Rescue Central Park." *New York* magazine, June 14, 1976.

Barlow, Elizabeth, Vernon Gray, Roger Pasquier, and Lewis Sharp. *The Central Park Book*. New York: Central Park Task Force, 1977.

Board of Aldermen. *Report of the Special Committee of Parks, Relating to Layout of a New Park in the Upper Part of the City*. Document No. 83, January 2, 1852. New York: Municipal Printing Press, 1853.

Cranz, Galen. *The Politics of Park Design: A History of Urban Parks in America*. Cambridge, Mass.: MIT Press, 1982.

Heckscher, Morrison H. *Creating Central Park*. New York: Metropolitan Museum of Art, 2008.

Kelly, Bruce, for Central Park Task Force and New York City Department of Parks and Recreation. *The Ramble in Central Park: An Historic Landscape Report and Master Plan*. 1980.

Miller, Sara Cedar. *Central Park: An American Masterpiece: A Comprehensive History of the Nation's First Urban Park*. New York: Harry N. Abrams, 2002.

Parsons, Mabel, ed. *Memories of Samuel Parsons, Landscape Architect of the Department of Public Parks*. New York: G. P. Putnam's Sons, 1926.

Parsons, Samuel, Jr. *The Art of Landscape Architecture*. New York: G. P. Putnam's Sons, 1915.

————. *Landscape Gardening*. New York: G. P. Putnam's Sons, 1891.

Report of the Select Committee of the Senate, to which was referred the Assembly Bill in Relation to the Establishment of a Central Park in the City of New York. New York: C. Van Benthuysen, 1853.

Rogers, Elizabeth Barlow. *Rebuilding Central Park: A Management and Restoration Plan*. Cambridge, Mass.: MIT Press, 1987.

Rosenzweig, Roy, and Elizabeth Blackmar. *The Park and the People: A History of Central Park*. Ithaca, N.Y.: Cornell University Press, 1992.

Schuyler, David. *The New Urban Landscape: The Redefinition of City Form in Nineteenth-Century America*. Baltimore: Johns Hopkins University Press, 1986.

Strong, George Templeton. *The Diary of George Templeton Strong*. Ed. Alan Nevins. 4 vols. New York: Macmillan, 1952.

Central Park Guidebooks

Cook, Clarence. *A Description of the New York Central Park*. New York: F. J. Huntington, 1869; reprint, New York: B. Blom, 1979.

Forrester, Francis. *Little Peachblossom, or Rambles in Central Park*. New York: Nelson & Phillips, 1873.

Miller, Sara Cedar. *Seeing Central Park: An Official Guide to the World's Greatest Park*. New York: Harry N. Abrams, 2009.

Perkins, F. B., with photographs by W. H. Guild Jr. *The Central Park*. New York: Carleton, 1864.

Reed, Henry Hope, and Sophia Duckworth. *Central Park: A History and a Guide*. New York: C. N. Potter, 1967.

Aesthetics of the Picturesque

Gilpin, William. *Observations on the River Wye*. London: R. Blamire in the Strand, 1782.

——. *Remarks on Forest Scenery, and other Woodland Views, relative chiefly to Picturesque Beauty: Illustrated by the Scenes of New Forest in Hampshire*. London: T. Cadell and W. Davies, 1808.

Knight, Richard Payne. *An Analytical Inquiry into the Principles of Taste*. London: T. Payne & J. White, 1805.

Olmsted, Frederick Law. *A Journey in the Back Country*. New York: Mason, 1860.

——. *A Journey in the Seaboard Slave States, with Remarks on Their Economy*. New York: Dix & Edwards, 1856.

——. *A Journey Through Texas; or a Saddle-Trip on the Southwestern Frontier*. New York: Dix & Edwards, 1857.

——. *Walks and Talks of an American Farmer in England*. New York: G. P. Putnam, 1852.

Price, Uvedale. *An Essay on the Picturesque, as Compared with the Sublime and the*

Beautiful. 1794; reprint, Cambridge, U.K.: Cambridge University Press, 2014.

Frederick Law Olmsted and Calvert Vaux

Barlow, Elizabeth. *Frederick Law Olmsted's New York.* New York: Praeger/ Whitney Museum, 1972.

Beveridge, Charles E., and David Schuyler, eds. *The Papers of Frederick Law Olmsted: Vol. III. Creating Central Park, 1857–1861.* Baltimore: Johns Hopkins University Press, 1983.

Beveridge, Charles E., Carolyn F. Hoffman, and Kenneth Hawkins, eds. *The Papers of Frederick Law Olmsted: Vol. VII. Parks, Politics, and Patronage, 1874–1882.* Baltimore: Johns Hopkins University Press, 2007.

Fein, Albert. *Frederick Law Olmsted and the American Environmental Tradition.* New York: Georges Braziller, 1972.

Kelly, Bruce, Gail Travis Guillet, and Mary Ellen W. Hern. *The Art of the Olmsted Landscape.* Vol. 1. New York: New York City Landmarks Preservation Commission and The Arts Publisher, 1981.

Kowsky, Francis R. *Country, Park & City: The Architecture and Life of Calvert Vaux.* New York: Oxford University Press, 2003.

Martin, Justin. *Genius of Place: The Life of Frederick Law Olmsted.* Philadelphia: Da Capo Press, 2011.

Olmsted, Frederick Law, Jr., and Theodora Kimball, eds. *Frederick Law Olmsted—Landscape Architect.* New York: The Knickerbocker Press, 1922.

Roper, Laura Wood. *F.L.O.: A Biography of Frederick Law Olmsted.* Baltimore: Johns Hopkins University Press, 1973.

Rybczynski, Witold. *A Clearing in the Distance: Frederick Law Olmsted and America in the 19th Century.* New York: Touchstone, 1999.

Schuyler, David, and Jane Turner Censer, eds. *The Papers of Frederick Law Olmsted: Vol. VI. The Years of Olmsted, Vaux, and Co., 1865–1874.* Baltimore: Johns Hopkins University Press, 1992.

Simpson, Jeffery. *The Art of the Olmsted Landscape: His Works in New York.* Vol. 2. New York: New York City Landmarks Preservation Commission and The Arts Publisher, 1981.

FREDERICK LAW OLMSTED PAPERS

http://www.nps.gov/frla/upload/LC-guideupdated-2.pdf.
http://www.nps.gov/frla/upload/LC-FLO-Sr-papers-finding-aid.pdf.
National Association of Olmsted Parks and National Park Service, The Olmsted Research Guide Online (ORGO), http://ww3.rediscov.com/olmsted/.

Robert Moses

"Art Group Fights Ramble Building." *New York Times,* November 29, 1955.

Ballon, Hilary, and Kenneth T. Jackson, eds. *Robert Moses and the Modern City: The Transformation of New York.* New York: W. W. Norton, 2007.

Caro, Robert A. *The Power Broker: Robert Moses and the Fall of New York.* New York: Alfred A. Knopf, 1974.

"Compromise for the Ramble Is Pressed on Park Tour: Ramble Is Visited by Borough Head." *New York Times,* November 27, 1955.

Crowell, Paul. "Naturalists Win Battle of Ramble: Private Fund Withdraws Its $250,000 Offer for Park Recreation Project." *New York Times,* December 1, 1955.

Illson, Murray. "Bird-Lovers Balk at Moses Project: Resent Fencing Ramble in Central Park for Old Folks' Recreation." *New York Times,* October 2, 1955.

Morris, Newbold. *30 Years of Progress: 1934–1964.* http://www.nycgovparks .org/sub_about/parks_history/library/pdf/thirty_years_of_progress.pdf.

Moses, Robert. Memorandum on 1935 Budget Request for the Department of Parks.

————. Park Department Report to August 1934.

"Moses Yields to Mothers; Drops Tavern Parking Lot." *New York Times,* July 18, 1956.

New York City Department of Parks Press Releases 1934–1970: https://www .nycgovparks.org/news/reports/archive#pr.

Robert Moses Papers 1912–1980. New York Public Library Rare Books and Manuscripts Division, Central Park–related correspondence 1934–1961: http://www.nypl.org/sites/default/files/archivalcollections/pdf/moses .pdf.

Schumacht, Murray. "Parking Lot Foes Routed by Moses." *New York Times,* April 25, 1956.

Talese, Gay. "Tiffany's Sues to Bar Park Cafe Lest Portent of 1928 Come True." *New York Times,* July 8, 1960.

Thomas Hoving

Blumenthal, Ralph. "Remembering Hoving's Service as Parks Commissioner." *New York Times,* December 11, 2009.

"Old Central Park Will Rock 'N' Roll." *New York Times,* March 28, 1866.

Weinraub, Bernard. "Hoving's Artistic Happening Draws Hundreds to Park; Pop Painting by Amateurs Covers 105-Yard Canvas." *New York Times,* May 16, 1966.

———. "Out of the Cloisters—A Happening Called Hoving." *New York Times Magazine,* July 10, 1966.

Whitehouse, Franklin. "Concerts and Dancing to Discotheque Combos Planned for Summer." *New York Times,* March 28, 1966.

August Heckscher

Heckscher, August. *Alive in the City: A Memoir of an Ex-Commissioner.* New York: Scribner's, 1974.

Pace, Eric. "August Heckscher, 83, Dies; Advocate for Parks and Arts." *New York Times,* April 7, 1997.

"Vigil in Park Planned for Landing on Moon." *New York Times,* June 23, 1969.

Elizabeth Barlow Rogers

Carmody, Deirdre. "City Unveils Blueprint for Renovating Central Park." *New York Times,* April 28, 1985.

———. "Renewal of Central Park Stirring Broader Debate." *New York Times,* June 24, 1982.

Clines, Francis X. "From Forest to Garden: A Vision for Central Park." *New York Times,* April 18, 1979.

Dunlap, David W. "Revamping Great Lawn Is Weighed." *New York Times,* January 28, 1987.

Dunlap, David W., and Susan Heller Anderson. "New York Day by Day; Shelter in the Park." *New York Times,* May 21, 1985.

Goldberger, Paul. "New Victorian-Style Kiosk Fits Victorian Style of Central Park." *New York Times,* August 9, 1979.

Gross, Michael. "Bergdorf's Party Toasts Pulitzer Fountain." *New York Times,* September 19, 1986.

Hawes, Elizabeth. "Whose Park Is It Anyway?" *New York Times,* September 5, 1982.

Langer, Harry L. "Save the Band Shell and Keep Central Park for All New Yorkers." Letter to the Editor, *New York Times,* June 11, 1992.

Martin, Douglas. "Restoring the Children's Zoo, Seriously: Fairy Tales Are Out, Unless Fairies Really Exist and Have Tails." *New York Times,* September 28, 1995.

———. "Who Should Pay for Parks? Voices from the Field." *New York Times,* January 23, 1995.

Nemy, Enid. "In the Park with Elizabeth Barlow Rogers; Trying to Make Money Grow on 26,000 Trees." *New York Times,* September 30, 1993.

"New Central Park Overseer." *New York Times,* February 28, 1979.

New York City Parks Department Central Park Official Reports and Central Park Conservancy Annual Reports

Central Park Commissioners Annual Reports, 1857–1869, together with Parks Department Annual Reports and Minutes, 1870–1934. http://www.nyc govparks.org/news/reports/archive.
http://www.nycgovparks.org/sub_about/parks_history/annualreports.html.
Central Park Conservancy Annual Reports: www.centralparknyc.org/about/ annual-reports.html.

INDEX

Page number in *italics* refer to illustrations.

Alice in Wonderland statue, 110–11, *111*

Ancient Playground, 37, 111

Andersen, Hans Christian, 110, 228

Angel of the Waters fountain (Stebbins), *68,* 69–70, 177
  Central Park Conservancy logo, 75–6

Arthur Ross Pinetum, 103

Astor, Brooke, 39–40, 42, 47, 76, 254

Auchincloss, Adele, 38–40

Ballplayers House, *88,* 120, 183

Barbra Streisand concert, 136

Barlow, David, 30, 37, *37,* 155, *192,* 208, 213

Barlow, Edward, 31–4, 49, 198

Barlow, Lisa, 32, 33–4, 35, *37,* 187, 208, 209–13

Beame, Abraham, 14, 38, 83–4

Beaux Arts style, 90, 103–4

Beinecke, William S., 47–9, *48,* 241–2

Belvedere, *10,* 47, 62, 69, *102,* 120, 265

Belvedere Lake, 115, 255–6

Benepe, Adrian, 43, 269, 277

Bernard, Lewis, 48, 238–9, 241–2, 244, 260

Bethesda Fountain, 8, 68–70, *68,* 177
  Conservancy logo, 75–6, *77*
  restoration, 76–8

Bethesda Terrace, 9, *11,* 69–70, *70,* 78–80, 123, 176–8, *177*

Biblowit, Myra, 242–3, 249

Birkenhead Park (England), 56

Blockhouse Number 1, 67–9, *67*

Blonsky, Douglas, 238, *273*
  Conservancy leadership, 244–5, 267–74
  The Gates installation, 277–80

Bloomberg, Michael, 42–3, 262, 277, 282

Bloomer, Kent, 128–9, *129*

Bow Bridge, 237

Bowling Green, 18*n*

Brace, Charles Loring, 96

Bryant, William Cullen, 17–19, *18*

Cascade, 63, *63*

Casino, 100–3, *100,* 114, 169, 174, 176

Central Park, An American Masterpiece (Miller), 207–8*n*

Central Park Board of
Commissioners, 22, 25, 58–9,
84–5
Central Park Book, The, 45
Central Park Community Fund,
48–9
Central Park Conservancy, xi–xii,
259–61
accomplishments, 265–74
annual budget, 266
benefactors, 39, 47, 50, 75–9, 158,
254
Bethesda angel logo, 75–6, *76*
board of directors, 47–9, 241–6
Center for Urban Park Discovery,
269
design and construction division,
131–2, 237–8
endowment, 266
environmental education
programs, 47, 122, 257–9
founding, xiv–xvii, 14, 47–53,
140
fund-raising, 156–61, 242–3,
248–50, 254–9
The Gates installation, 275–86
Institute for Urban Park
Management, 43, 269
Landscape Design Team, *127*
leadership development, 244–6
leadership staff, 136, 140, 155–6,
238, 260–1, 267–8
management and restoration plan,
43, 47, 80, 116–17, 119–22, 156,
160, 247–8, 268
mission statement, xvii
official authority, 268
official relationship with the city,
140–1, 163–4, 243–4, 250, 255,
268–9
opposition to, 14–15, 161, 248, 269
publicity, 207–8, 236–8, 240

volunteers, 270
Women's Committee, 52, 157–60,
157
See also public-private
partnerships
Central Park gondola, 76–9, *79*
Central Park jogger, 234–6
Central Park Task Force
educational outreach, 45–6
funding, 38–9, 42–5, 254
volunteers, 44
youth employment program,
39–40, *41, 196*
Central Park Visitor Center, 47
Central Park Zoo, 43, 98, 110
Charles A. Dana Discovery Center,
257–9, *258*
Cherry Hill, 89*n,* 97*n,* 133–4, 233
Chess and Checkers House, 108–9,
108
Christo and Jeanne-Claude, 274–86,
281
The Gates proposal, 136–9, *137,*
276–7
implementation of *The Gates,*
277–86, *283, 284*
land art projects, 276, 278, 279
Christopher Columbus statue, 90, 91,
228
City Parks Foundation, 176, 250–1
Clark, Jean, 157–8, *157*
Clarke, Gilmore D., 95, 103
Claude glass, *54, 55,* 164
Clurman, Richard M., 13
Columbus Circle, 90
Concert Ground, 167–82, *168, 170,*
174, 175
Conservatory Garden, 50, 52, 103–5,
104, 105, 158–9
Cramer, Marianne, 120, 237–8
Croton Aqueduct, 18–21, 59, 70
Croton Reservoir, 63

Dairy, 47, 109, 265

Dana, Norma, 157–8, *157*

Dancing Bear statue, 110

Dancing Goat statue, 110

Daniel Webster statue, 91, 228

Davis, Gordon, xiv–xvi, *xv*, 3, 25, 46, 125, 130, 238–9, 274

  mass public events policies, 136–9, 169

  resignation, 149, 151

  restoration debates, 146–8

Delacorte Theater, 115

Dinkins, David, 152, 183–5, 238–9, 251

Downing, Andrew Jackson, 18–19, *18, 53*

East Green, 46

East Meadow, *88*

Elton John concert, 137–8

Embury, Aymar, II, 95, 98, 107

environmental education programs, 47, 122, 257–9

Evans, James, 242–3, *242*

Fitch, James Marston, 38–9

Forests and Wetlands of New York City, The (Rogers), 36, 191

Frances Hodgson Burnett Fountain, 104–5, *105*

"Frederick Law Olmsted and the Dialectical Landscape" (Smithson), 275–6

Frederick Law Olmsted Awards Luncheon, 52, 157–60

Frederick Law Olmsted Papers Project, 36*n*

Frederick Law Olmsted's New York (Rogers), 37, 39, 138*n*, 191

Fredericks, Russell, 271, 272

French gardens and parks, 213, 219–25

Friedman (Pat Hoffman) Playground, 112, 233

The Gates installation, 136–9, *137,* 274–86, *283, 284*

Geldzahler, Henry, 136–7, *137*

German gardens and parks, 225–8

Gilder, Richard, 48–9, 256–7, 262

Gilpin, William, 23, 54–6, *55*

Giuliani, Rudolph, 152, 251, 262

Gotbaum, Betsy, 176, 239, 247–51, *247, 256*

Grand Army Plaza, 90, 160–1

Great Hill, 103

Great Lawn, 19–20*n*, 59, *102*, 103, *258*

  erosion, *12,* 46

  mass public events, 137–8

  polo arena proposal, 7–8

  restoration and maintenance, 127–8, *127,* 255–9

Green, Andrew Haswell, 84, 86

Greensward plan, 58–70, 120, 142, 164–72, 267

Group of Bears statue, 112

Hall, A. Oakey, 84

Hallett Sanctuary, 266

Hamilton, Alexander, 228

Hans Christian Andersen statue, 110, 228

Hardy, Hugh, 262

Harlem Meer, *12,* 63, *65,* 87*n*

  Boathouse, 9, *11,* 257

Hartford, Huntington, 5, 115–16

Hawes, Elizabeth, 145–8

Heckscher, August, 8–9

Heckscher Ballfields, *12, 13, 88*

Heckscher Playground, 99, 110

Hoving, Thomas, 3–9, *4,* 116

Hunt, Richard Morris, 90

"Imagine" mosaic, 134–5, *135*, 228*n*
Indian Hunter statue, 91, *165*, 166
Institute for Urban Park Management, 43, 269
Irving, Washington, 22
Isle au Haut (Maine), 208–13
Italian gardens and parks, 217–19

Jacobs, Jane, 32–3
James, Henry, 180
James Michael Levin Playground, 110, 233
James Taylor concert, 126, 137
Japanese gardens and parks, 213–17
Jones Wood, 17–22
Journey in the Back Country in the Winter, A (Olmsted), 25, 37
Journey in the Seaboard Slave States, A (Olmsted), 25, 37
Journey Through Texas, A (Olmsted), 25, 36

Kelly, Bruce, 38–40, *39*, 47, 120, 198–201, 233–4
    Ramble, 142–4
    Shakespeare Garden, 234*n*, 236
    Strawberry Fields, 134–5
Kerbs Model Yacht Boathouse, 109–10
Kinderberg, 47
Kingsland, Ambrose C., 19
Knopka, Andy, 132
Koch, Edward I., xiv–xv, *xv*, 42, 133, 139–40, 152–3, 235–6

La Guardia, Fiorello, 98
Lake, 62–3, 69, 71, 106, 176–7, 236–7
    Central Park gondola, 76–9, *79*
    Loeb Boathouse, 9, 109–10, 129–30
    Point, *10*, 142–4, *144*

Landscape Design: A Cultural and Architectural History (Rogers), 217, 262
Lasker Rink and Pool, 63, 65–6, *65*, 113*n*
Lehman, Herbert H., 112
Lennon, John, 134–5, *135*, 228*n*
Levin (James Michael) Playground, 110, 233
Lindsay, John Vliet, 3, 6, 13–14, 83–4, 146
Literary Walk, 166, *168*, 172, 228
Loch, 63–6, *64*, *65*, 113*n*, 195, 266
Long Pond, 208, 212

Maine Monument, 90
Mall
    Concert Ground, 167–82, *168*, *170*, *174*, *175*
    concerts and large public events, 89, 136–8, 169
    design, 69, *69*
    Indian Hunter statue, 90, 165, 166
    Literary Walk, 166, 168, 172, 228
    Naumburg Bandshell, 125, 167–72, *170*, 174, 176, 178–82, 251
    restoration, 75, 233
Manhattan schist, 21, 71–2, 260–1, 275
Manship, Paul, 111, 112
Marble Arch, 105, 172
Marionette Theater, 232, 234
Marshall, Timothy, 238
McGowan's Pass, 66–7
McLaughlin, Charles, 36
Miller, Lynden, 50, 52, 159*n*, 193, 205
Miller, Sara Cedar, 207–8, 238
Millstein, Ira, 235, 243–4, *243*, 268–9
Mineral Springs Pavilion, 109–10, *109*, 120

Montayne's Rivulet, 63
Moses, Lucy, 39, 75–9, *78,* 158
Moses, Robert, xii, xiv, 9, 93–117,
    93, 121, 267
  autocratic style, 96, 100, 112
  highway system, 36
  Hoving's response to, 4–6
  New York World's Fairs, 116, 153
  opposition to, 112–17
  public relations skills, 97–8, 105
  vision for Central Park, 94–107,
    167
Mould, Jacob Wrey, *70, 71*
Moynihan, Daniel Patrick, 15
Mumford, Lewis, 33, 106–7
Music Pavilion, 120, 171, 173–4

National Association of Olmsted
    Parks, xvii
Naumburg Bandshell, 125, 167–72,
    170, 174, 176, 178–82, 251
New York City Landmarks
    Commission, 116, 169–71, 178,
    255–6
New York City Marathon, 50, 256,
    272–4
New York City Parks Department,
    xiv–xvi
  annual reports, 95n
  Arsenal headquarters, 4n, 66n
  under Benepe, 269, 277
  Boss Tweed era, 84–5
  City Parks Foundation, 176, 250–1
  contractual relationship with the
    Conservancy, 268–9
  under Davis, xiv–xvi, 3, 25, 46,
    125, 130, 136–9, 146–9, 169, 274
  under Gotbaum, 176, 239, 256
  under Moses, 93–117, 267
  under Stern, 151–5, 161, 163–71,
    179, 183–6, 239, 251, 255–6
New York Shakespeare Festival, 115

Ninety-Fifth Street Recreation
    Center, 257
Nolan, Christopher, 238
North End, 41, 46, 66–7, 257
  Central Park jogger, 234–6
  Conservatory Garden, 159n
  restoration, 257–9, 272–4
North Meadow, 46
North Meadow Recreation Center,
    110, 235

Old Reservoir, 74, 103, 255
Olmsted, Frederick Law, xii, xiv,
    xvii, *23*
  background, 22–4
  Central Park job, 25, 53–4, 57n,
    58, 71, 85–6
  on Central Park's purpose, 81–2
  collaborations with Vaux, 37, 53,
    56–7, 86
  publication of papers, 36
  publishing career, 24–5, 57
  travels, 25, 36–7, 205, 225n
  written works, 25, 36–7, 56, 57,
    141
Ono, Yoko, 134–5, 213

Papp, Joseph, 115
Parisian parks and gardens, 219–25
Parks Association, 35–6, 101, 112,
    254n
Parks Department. *See* New York
    City Parks Department
Parsons, Samuel B., 86–7
Pat Hoffman Friedman Playground,
    112, 233
Picturesque style, 54–7, 59–60, 90,
    154
  Central Park restoration, 164–71
  movement through space
    aesthetics, 165–7, 171–8
Pilát, Ignaz Anton, 71

Pilgrim Hill, 37
playgrounds, xiv, 37, 87–8, 94–7, 99, *99*, 111–12, 233, 266
Pohner, Lambert, 229–32, *230, 232*
Pond, 71, 266
Price, Uvedale, 23, 54
Public Design Commission, 255
public-private partnerships, xiv, 14–15, 42–3, 154, 160, 240, 270
    contractual relationships, 140–1, 163–4, 243–4, 250, 255, 268–9
    union labor response, 14, 25
Pulitzer Fountain, 160
Purnell, Marguerite, 157–8, *157*

Queen Anne Gothic style, 90

Ramble, 37, 44, 69, 74, *145, 177,* 195, 266
    restoration, 44, *44*
    rustic design, 62–3, *62*
    safety, 37*n,* 41
    tree-removal debate, 112–13, 142–9, 232
Ravine, 63, 259
Rebuilding Central Park: A Management and Restoration Plan (Central Park Conservancy), 122*n,* 156, 160, 167–9, *171*
Reed, Henry Hope, 5, 7
"Report Relative to Laying Out a New Park . . ." of 1852, 21
Revolutionary War, 66–7
Rheingold Central Park Music Festival, 7, 8
Robinson, David, 200, 203
Rock Against Racism concert, 125–6, 169
Rockefeller, Laurance, 242
Rogers, Elizabeth Barlow, ix–xvii, *78, 157, 183, 195, 273*
    background, 27–34

    campaign for Parks Commissioner, 238–40
    Cityscape Institute, 262
    departure from the Conservancy, 260–2
    early NYC park work, 35–52
    honors and awards, 253–5, 260–1
    Long Island house and garden, 187–205, *188, 192, 193, 199, 200, 201, 202, 203*
    teaching, 263
    travels, 207–28, 262
    written works, 36, 37, 39, 138*n,* 191, 217, 262
    See also Central Park Conservancy
Rogers, Ted, 49–53, 155–6, 198, 200, 260
Ruby, Marie, 40, 47, 195, 196
Rumsey Playground, 101–3, 110, 112, 174–6
Ryan, Ted, 245

Savas, Steve, 48–9
Seeing Central Park: An Official Guide to the World's Greatest Urban Park (Miller), 207–8*n*
Segal, Martin, 254
Seventh Regiment statue, 89*n,* 90
Shakespeare Garden, 234*n,* 236
Sheep Meadow, 8, 101, *101*
    erosion, 9, *12,* 13, 46
    mass public events, 8–9, 46, 125–7, 137
    restoration and maintenance, 126–7, 132–3, 138, 259
Silver, Mitchell, 43
Simón Bolívar statue, 89*n*
Sissinghurst Castle Garden (England), 191–2, 213
Smith, Alfred, 98
Soros, George, 48
Soros, Susan Weber, 263

sports facilities, xiv, *12,* 87–8, 91, 94,
    97–107, 116–17, 127–8, 182–6
Starr, Laura, 239, 257
Stebbins, Emma, 69–70, 177
Stein, Andrew, 128
Stennett, Erana, 141
Stern, Henry, 4, 134, *152, 183,* 239
    appointments as parks
        commissioner, 151–5, 251
    Central Park restoration priorities,
        164–71
    relationship with the
        Conservancy, 161, 163–4, 179,
        183–6, 255–6
Strawberry Fields, 134–5, *135,* 213,
    233
*Strawberry Fields: Central Park's
    Memorial to John Lennon* (Miller),
    207–8n
Strong, George Templeton, 72–4,
    179
Sturz, Herbert, 235
Sulzberger, Iphigene, 39–40, 76, 101,
    158
Summerstage program, 174–6, 251
Summit Rock, 260–1

Tavern on the Green, 101, 113–15
Tennis House, 110, 183, 251, 255, 257
"32 Ways Your Time and Money
    Can Rescue Central Park"
    (Rogers), 43, 270
Thomas, Tupper, 239, 249
Tice, Pam, 136
Tiergarten, Berlin, 225–8, *227*
Tintern Abbey, *54, 55*
Torrey, John, 20
Trump, Donald, 130–1, 249–50

Tunnard, Christopher, 33
Turtle Pond, 72, 115, 255–6
Tweed, William Magear (Boss), 83–4

Untermyer Fountain, 104n

Vaux, Calvert, xii, xiv, 36, 53–60, *53,*
    71, 85–6
Viele, Egbert, 22, *22,* 57
Vista Rock, 62, 72

Wagner, Phyllis, 157–8, *157*
Walker, James J., 100
*Walks and Talks of an American Farmer
    in England* (Olmsted), 24, 56
Wallace, Lila, 158
Wallach, Ira and Miriam, 182–4, 257
Wallach Walk, 257
Ward, John Quincy Adams, 90, *165,*
    166
Waring, George, 71
Weinstein, Geraldine, 40, *40,* 47, 142
Weisel, Edwin, Jr., 38–40
White, E. B., 180–1
White, Samuel, 257
Whitman, Walt, 179–80
Wien, Lawrence, 79
William Shakespeare statue, 91, 228
William Tecumseh Sherman statue, 90,
    160, 249–50
Winslow, Philip, 120, 233–4
Wisteria Pergola, 169, 171, 173–4, *173,*
    182
Wollman Rink, 7, 8, 105–7, 130–1
Works Progress Administration
    (WPA), 4, 94, 110

Zimmerman, Elyn, 178

ILLUSTRATION CREDITS

A NOTE ABOUT THE AUTHOR

Elizabeth Barlow Rogers is the president of the Foundation for Landscape Studies and the author of nine previous books, most recently *Green Metropolis*. She has long been involved in historic landscape preservation and was the first person to hold the title of Central Park administrator, a position created in 1979. In 1980, she was instrumental in founding the Central Park Conservancy, a public-private partnership supporting the restoration and management of the park. She served in both positions until 1996. A native of San Antonio, Texas, she has made New York her home since 1964.

A NOTE ON THE TYPE

The text of this book was set in Bembo, a facsimile of a typeface cut by Francesco Griffo for Aldus Manutius, the celebrated Venetian printer, in 1495. The face was named for Pietro Cardinal Bembo, the author of the small treatise entitled *De Aetna* in which it first appeared. Through the research of Stanley Morison, it is now generally acknowledged that all old-style type designs up to the time of William Caslon can be traced to the Bembo cut.

Composed by North Market Street Graphics, Lancaster, Pennsylvania

Printed and bound by Tien Wah Press, Malaysia

Designed by Iris Weinstein